The Woman's Day® Help Book

The Woman's Day® Help Book

The Complete How-to for the Busy Housekeeper

by Geraldine Rhoads and Edna Paradis

Designed and Illustrated by Liney Li

VIKING

DISCLAIMER

Some brand names are mentioned in this book to help the reader identify
products in the market. It has not been possible to list all trade names or
"store brands." No endorsement of companies or their products is intended in these mentions; nor is criticism implied by the omission of
products with similar functions.

If you use any of the homemade recipes for cleaners, we strongly suggest
that you store them in child-proof, labeled containers, to be sure that they
are not mistaken for products that may be safely ingested.

VIKING

Published by the Penguin Group
Viking Penguin Inc., 40 West 23rd Street,
New York, New York 10010, U.S.A.
Penguin Books Ltd, 27 Wrights Lane,
London W8 5TZ, England
Penguin Books Australia Ltd, Ringwood,
Victoria, Australia
Penguin Books Canada Ltd, 2801 John Street,
Markham, Ontario, Canada L3R 1B4
Penguin Books (N.Z.) Ltd, 182–190 Wairau Road,
Auckland 10, New Zealand

Penguin Books Ltd, Registered Offices:
Harmondsworth, Middlesex, England

First published in 1988 by Viking Penguin Inc.
Published simultaneously in Canada

LIBRARY OF CONGRESS CATALOGING IN PUBLICATION DATA
Rhoads, Geraldine.
The Woman's day help book.
1. Home economics.   2. House cleaning.
I. Paradis, Edna.   II. Woman's day.   III. Title.
TX147.R47   1988   640   87-40322
ISBN 0-670-82049-0

Printed in the United States of America by
R. R. Donnelley & Sons Company, Harrisonburg, Virginia
Set in Gill Sans

CONTENTS

ACKNOWLEDGMENTS

This book grows out of the experience and expertise of countless men and women. It could not exist were it not for all the research to develop new tools and materials for housekeeping, and then assist consumers in their productive use.

We have many thanks to give to research and consumer relations in government and industry sectors.

Chief of the government agencies helping us was the U.S. Department of Agriculture, particularly their offices connected with Extension Services. We also owe special gratitude to the forty-three state extension services we consulted. Their work in behalf of American consumers is extraordinary and their advice to us invaluable.

Among the trade associations that shared their expertise were the Air Conditioning and Refrigeration Institute; American Fur Information Council; American Furniture Manufacturers Association; American Pewter Guild; American Gas Association; Association of Specialists in Cleaning and Restoration; Carpet and Rug Institute; Cotton Incorporated; Electronic Industries Association; Feather and Down Association; Footwear Council; International Fabricare Institute; International Silk Association; Major Appliances Consumer Action Panel; Man-Made Fibers Manufacturers; Marble Institute of America; National Decorating Products Association; National Paint and Coatings Association; Porcelain Enamel Institute; Soap and Detergent Association; Sterling Silversmiths Guild; Tile Council of America; Vinegar Institute; Wool Bureau.

We owe very special thanks to Fred Fortess, Professor Emeritus and

Director of Research Services at the School of Textiles at the Philadelphia College of Textiles & Science, who gave us the benefit of his ongoing experience with consumers, as well as his technical expertise.

Finally, the inspiration for this book comes from the readers of *Woman's Day* and its many editors.

Many readers have shared their successes and their mistakes, in their phone calls and letters to the magazine. We have enjoyed their successes and have been able to profit by their mistakes (as well as our own!).

There is no one chapter that can be singled out as the product of their invaluable advice. Inevitably, the whole book resonates with the magazine's credo that everyone's time is valuable, but we might point out some portions that especially reflect this. The overview of housekeeping today and the holiday-planning ideas are in part drawn from features published in *Woman's Day*, and some of the hints in the book originally appeared in the magazine.

If the readers have stood us in such good stead as mentors, it is because the editors have so persistently developed a friendly dialogue with them, a tradition that started fifty years ago and flourishes today, with the magazine's present editors. We thank them all.

Housekeepers Are Different Today— and So Is Housekeeping

There is an old story about a cook who, after serving the same family for thirty-some years, one day just up and quit. The family loved her, and thought she loved them. They were flabbergasted.

Why was she quitting? Wouldn't she miss the children? Did she want more time off?

Yes, she would miss the children; she agreed that would be the hard part for her. But cooking was just too *daily*.

Cooking is daily, along with the cleanup it entails, but most of the chores on a housekeeping list may be done on any schedule that pleases you. So today most people choose the times they'll devote to such work. These working women (and men) and practically all young householders are also choosing what they will and what they *won't* do at all.

Nobody is keeping house today to live up to a mother's standards, or a sister's, or those of the grand old housekeeping perfectionists.

And you know what? These millions of people, with their changed ways, have attractive homes, as clean and orderly as they want. They *love* their homes. They may even admire them more, since they spend less time doing housework they hate.

The most dramatic changes in such attitudes got underway about ten years ago, when millions of women started back to work, and their sisters at home also decided that their priorities ruled out a race to be a perfect housekeeper—or even a near-perfect one.

So it's about time for this book. We have ten years' worth of new thinking and new products—and even new home hints—to bring to the party.

Housework can make a house you enjoy even more beautiful and enjoyable. But it can get you down. Housework can be a drag. Or a threat. You can feel guilty because you hate it, or reproach yourself that you don't do enough, or feel you are a bit of a klutz and fail to get the gleaming results you should achieve. You haven't lived if you haven't experienced those feelings at one time or another, or don't know people that housework affects this way. Let's admit all this, and see what remedies there are.

Try a moment of truth with yourself.

Are you trying to do too much?

Truly, is it more important to you for your house to be clean? Or to be orderly? Of course you are going to avoid menaces to your health like unwashed dishes and unemptied garbage. That kind of cleanliness is essential. But does the bedroom (or living room or whatever) need going over daily, twice-weekly, weekly—or less frequently than that?

Don't judge by what your mother did or by some old manual on the shelf—or even by what you yourself used to do.

A 1986 survey of *Woman's Day* readers shows 38 percent cleaning their houses less well or less often, and another 43 percent skipping or skimping "sometimes." (That adds up to 81 percent who don't subscribe to old-fashioned compulsiveness about housekeeping.)

Incidentally, that survey includes both women in the work force and women who have opted to stay home. When we polled a special group of working women almost ten years earlier, 98 percent said they *never* picked up the children's room, 69 percent *never* did spring cleaning, 34 percent *never* ironed, 34 percent *never* did daily bedmaking.

On the subject of bedmaking, one woman wrote firmly, "I just shut the door!"

We laughed over her retort. Is there anyone who has not surreptitiously shut the bedroom door for a day and run off to keep a special appointment—or just to get somewhere else on time? We laughed because so few of us had ever admitted to such dereliction.

People who once vacuumed twice a week, and then involved themselves in new jobs, new studies, new clubs that absorbed the time they'd devoted to the second vacuuming decided that nobody ever noticed the difference.

There are many houses replete with every modern labor-saver on the market—and no irons or ironing boards. There all the washables bear labels guaranteeing permanent press. (And the customers in this contingent who love linens presumably rejoiced in the fashions that came out a year or so ago "Guaranteed to Wrinkle.")

Some kitchen floors are getting fewer complete scrubbings and more "spot cleanings."

Every house is different. The rules suggest cleaning windows twice a year. But when I lived in a suburban house, one autumn hosedown took care of that matter, and when I lived in a city apartment, my view was marred by dirt almost every time it rained, and sometimes it seemed to rain almost every day.

Your moment of truth may yield the unwelcome news that in your home you have a trouble spot or two requiring extra care. But chances are you'll find ways to skip and skimp intelligently.

In this book you'll find information on everything there is to be cleaned and cared for—complete information on the fastest and best ways to cope. But that doesn't mean you are compelled to do everything.

You're the greatest expert in the world on your own life and what you want. So decide if there's work you can eliminate.

In your moment of truth also think about *when* you want to tackle chores around the house.

When the housework-haters get going on their pet subject, they use words like *lonely* and *boring*. Is there some law that you have to mop the kitchen when no one's around? Some gregarious souls tell us they deliberately schedule work for evening hours when others are home watching TV. Many others pick the slot when a favorite TV show is on to watch while-they-work. One study of women with jobs outside the home and those devoted to full-time at home showed that a higher percentage of the stay-at-homes did their housework on weekends—when there are other people present both to notice and to provide some company.

So many of the professional housecleaners we interviewed tackle their work with *teams,* that this is an idea that cries out to be copied. If you can, dragoon a spouse or a child to join you in tasks, to make the work lighter and more convivial, too. Schedule the job for a time that suits you both.

Considering the fact that some of us are larks, high-energy types at dawn, while others are owls, ready for action at end of day, there should be a law against telling anyone when to do housework. The timing should be your choice.

Just decide when you think you'd like to do the job, and try it: See how that schedule works and if you like it, stick to it.

Maybe the most important decision is when to undertake a job you particularly dislike.

Experts say that the worst plan is to keep tabling the hated task. When you procrastinate, the job often grows harder and costs you just that much more agony. A better idea is to slot it for a time of day when you're at an energy peak and can dispatch it most quickly. Some other people find they handle this best by undertaking it in an interval just preceding something they really love to do, so they push forward to finish it, and go on to their lovely reward!

Sometimes you will luck into it and find someone who really doesn't mind the job you hate. One woman found that the daughter who wouldn't clean her bedroom gladly swapped that job for mopping kitchen and bathroom floors. It's worth shopping around for someone like her.

The amount of time you'll need for your housekeeping depends a lot on your lifestyle. You make many commitments—to jobs, relatives, your church, your club. You buy a bigger house, or decide life will be simpler with a smaller one. Our book takes such differences for granted.

It also reflects our various attitudes about our possessions—some of them new views.

You might say that there are three breeds of householders: the Traditionalists, the Super-Mobiles, and the in-betweens, the Eclectics.

The Traditionalists aim to hand their possessions down to their great-grandchildren. It would not occur to them to throw out a wobbly chair in need of reupholstering and just buy a new one. They repair and recover. They take meticulous care of furniture and tableware and decorative accessories. Even if we all don't aspire to their way of life, surely awe and admiration is their due.

I met my first Super-Mobile when I was chairing a panel at a furniture exposition. She was a twenty-two-year-old Washingtonian, newly married, in her first apartment. She spoke up after the other women had told us how they bought furniture and what they expected from it, and what she said absolutely riveted the audience. Furniture, to her, is something you buy and enjoy, and then you change it—the way people trade in cars.

A Super-Mobile loves the newest and trusts it will last a decent interval with a modicum of care. When an item is no longer the newest or decides it's ready for retirement and goes on the blink, Super-Mobile routinely replaces it with the new "newest." Super-Mobiles truly make the world go round—a little faster than it otherwise might.

The Eclectics are choosy. They may insist that all their wearables and linens machine-wash and they may brag about the way such efficiencies make their lives superior. But when you get back into their kitchens, you observe that they have kitchen copperware that requires (and gets) a polish every mealtime. A lot of us are Eclectics. We'll lavish care on some of our gear and go with slapdash attention to other stuff.

No two Eclectics share the same priorities, and in that respect they're responsible for the way this book is organized—to answer questions about the treasures Reader A cherishes but to which Reader B wouldn't give house-room (and vice versa).

Your house may reflect a vast difference in taste from that of your neighbor's. Here again, you have choices in decorating (and in housekeeping).

If you go on a house tour these days you will encounter "minimalist" decor, and "chic clutter." The minimalist's living room is spotless, speckless, and almost entirely lacking in ornament. Sleek mirror and glass tables tell you they must be perfectly shined to look presentable—and they're kept looking gorgeous. This is a housekeeping challenge missing from the house distinguished by its clutter. Here a single table can hold half a million dollars' worth of precious ornaments that my grandmother would have dismissed as "dust catchers." One of the most famous exponents of this style is said to embrace the maxim: "Don't disturb the original dust."

Most of our houses don't aspire to quite such dramatic heights of design and the upkeep they demand. But we create our own problems with our decorating and the way we live, and we'll go right on doing so. Marge has Junior's football trophies on her sideboard, and you'd better watch your feet at Jean's because the dog's plastic rubber bone is generally in the middle of the hallway. Always. They have no plans to change.

Enemy Number One for most of us is clutter. All standard cleaning manuals tell you to sweep away clutter before touching anything with your cleaning equipment. But, you know, some of it is valuable clutter, and much of the time it's Somebody Else's clutter, and Somebody Else is someone you love far too much to cross him or her over some bit of junk he or she wants to keep.

So who are we to throw the first stone and make rules about what you should toss out? We have limited ourselves to giving some suggestions about coping with clutter and letting it go at that.

In fact, now that we've reached this point: For whom do you keep house anyway? Other people or yourself?

This is a very serious question because you are the one who must be satisfied with the results. You aren't doing this job just to please someone else, to earn praise or money, and while you may do it out of love, it is not the primary way you earn someone's love.

You are Numero Uno on the list of people to please and impress. Who's next? The family? Company?

Ah, company.

The house looks different when company is coming. What seemed clean now looks as if it could use some attention. What seemed new now strikes us as worn. The house we've been enjoying won't tell outsiders what superb taste and standards we harbor!

What to do?

If your first step in party giving is cleaning your house, congratulations! But congratulations, too, to those who bypass the total housecleaning. One of our favorite hostesses always throws a candlelight holiday dinner. "Candlelight flatters everybody," she says, "and nobody can see how the apartment really looks. I *never* clean before a party . . . that comes afterward."

And the last time we discussed this at *Woman's Day,* we found almost everyone had developed tactics to welcome a guest with a confident smile.

First, just close off rooms guests aren't going to use. Fluff the pillows. Even the window shades. Whisk around removing newspapers and tired flowers. Flip the dust off the table with a tissue. (It's a good idea to take this sort of fast house tour with a mini-vac or at least a tissue in your pocket, but if you don't have one, blow the dust away!)

If guests are going to use the powder room, hide the family towels, check up on toilet paper, tissues, and guest towels, and wash the soap or put out a clean cake. Drawing the shower curtain can conceal any problems with the tub. You can spot-clean anything noticeable (even the floor) with paper towels and spray cleaner. If the toilet bowl needs attention throw in some bowl cleaner and let it stand while you spray the mirror. The sparkling mirror is the touch that says your house is in great shape.

This is not to say that blowing dust around is the recommended cleaning procedure in this book, or to question that there is no celebration so grand as a house "opening" when you have just repainted, reslipcovered, rearranged, and otherwise made over the house to express the wonderful person who is the real You.

But good company is a pleasure too great to be denied simply because the house isn't groomed to house-tour perfection.

Also, it is more important for you to be feeling competent and rested than to preside over a dustless domain.

It was commonplace for women who used to engage in the orgy of work known as fall cleaning (or spring cleaning) to wear themselves out and take to bed.

We assume you don't do that. Almost no one does. Whenever you start feeling spent, do something about it. Everybody should take vacations, including those of us who are the housekeepers in our households. Take an occasional break. Much as a house benefits from vacuuming, letting the cleaner stay silent for a week can't produce total wrack and ruin.

Realistically, housework isn't fun. But it can be satisfying if you schedule yourself and the work to suit your own ends. Yours and only yours.

Your house is different from mine. You and your family and your pets are neater (or messier) than mine. Your idea of "clean" may strike me as "so-so" or as so superseptic that I would never aspire to it.

We have different amounts of money, of energy or muscle, of space or expendable time.

We share the goal of wanting a home we can fully enjoy. Our philosophy, today, is that we cannot be perfect, but we'll do what we can when we can. We won't let housework get us down because we're too smart for that. We'll concentrate on essentials—often the rest can wait or even go undone. Working with this book, we'll use our brains (of those we share plenty) to decide what we're going to do and when and how we're going to do it. There are at least a thousand ways to accomplish the work with less effort: We've put some of them together in these pages so you can most conveniently choose the ones that will work for you.

—GERALDINE RHOADS
New York City
August 1987

How to Make the Most of Your Valuable Time

Get What You Want from This Book

You can skim the book and add hundreds of useful home hints to your repertoire.

OR you may make the book your "encyclopedia"—keeping it on a handy shelf and hunting up the remedy for chocolate stains on your suit, the answer to smells in your refrigerator, cleaning methods for a sleeping bag, etc.

OR you may see it as a primer to tell other people how to do things and post notes from the basic Laundry Mini Manual in the laundry room, the basic Dishwashing know-how in the kitchen, the cleaning mini manuals in your utility closet.

We hope the book will serve you in these ways.

But we promised ourselves to do more—*to give you better results with less work.*

If this is your goal, too, would you mind making just three decisions?

1. "I've decided to prevent and cut down work any way I can."

2. "I'm never going to overschedule myself."

3. "This time I'm going to do things the right way, because it's the fast way. The wrong way is the long way!"

Your Number One decision is easy to put into practice. Just learn the five great cleaning secrets on the following page.

These are the precepts of conservators who take care of famous old homes. They are the moneymaking ground rules, too, for businesses that contract to keep places clean. They work as well in any home.

These fabulous five are the first five steps to taking charge of your house instead of letting it run your life.

The Five Big Housekeeping Secrets

OR HOW TO CLEAN LESS
AND STILL ENJOY A CLEAN HOUSE

THESE FIVE PRINCIPLES ARE THE BIG WORK-SAVERS

1. Keep Dirt **OUT**.

Shut windows against dust. Use doormats inside and out to prevent tracked-in dirt. Use mud rooms or other entryways in bad weather.

2. Keep DIRT **DOWN**.

Attack loose dirt before it becomes embedded, before it spreads around some more.

3. **AWAY** with Dirt.

Use your vacuum cleaner to suck dust up and away for good. Consider the treated duster to gather dust—not spread it around. The miracle of most cleaning liquids or liquid mixtures is that they float loose dirt off a surface, hold it in suspension, then let you flush the soil away. Give them time to perform this magic.

4. **OUT** with Clutter.

It's your worst enemy. See how much you can throw out or put out of sight. Start every cleaning stint by first sweeping clutter aside.

5. **DON'T** spread dirt as you clean.

Dust from the TOP DOWN. Wash from the BOTTOM UP.

Don't Ever Let Housework Get You Down

Housekeeping isn't hard. It's just an accumulation of a lot of little jobs. The poet said, "It takes a heap o' livin' t' make a house a home." Yes, and the heap o' livin' creates heaps o' clutter and dishes and puddles. You begin to ask if there isn't something to cure your domestic burnout.

Actually, the secret to housekeeping is the same secret as that of running a huge corporation: You break the big job down into little ones, each doable with a given amount of time and energy.

You decide never to overschedule yourself.

Many of the people who write to magazines complaining that they never get it together are just trying to do too many things at once.

Have you ever been the type? We have. You feel a high-energy day coming on and launch a kamikaze attack on the house: everything must be cleaned at once! If all goes better than you should expect, you just hit the wall by the end of the day and vow never to clean again! If things go as things usually do, you are interrupted and never get to finish. Or, as you race to wind up your impossible job, the tray of glasses (oops!) slips from your hands and you have yet another chore to do. Overscheduling invites accidents. The answer is taking things task by task, day by day, week by week.

Your first goal is *today's* goal: What are you going to do today, to leave a presentable house behind you when you have practically no time?

Our answer is the Daily Getaway—a cleanup you can manage in fifteen minutes . . . or twenty minutes at most. Take your choice!

Try it. If you follow the system for a while, it will be as automatic and easy for you as revving up your car and driving it to the mall and back. And you'll have done everything necessary to put the house in shape on a strictly daily basis.

Adapt it to your own individual needs. Maybe you should pencil in some other commitments. Dog to feed and walk? Brown bags to prepare? Exercise you combine with a favorite TV program? Add them into your Getaway— just *don't* overschedule. (One day when we were running horribly behind because we had promised too many people too many things, we stopped to consider that there is nothing that doesn't take more than five minutes, and that we had agreed to sixteen in the hour that remained. Practice what we preach: Don't do that.)

Your second goal is the goal for the year. Can a weekly cleanup cope with the house so you can forget all those annual and semiannual cleaning orgies? The answer is yes—and it's to be found in the Weekly Go-Round.

For a Fast Daily Getaway

BASICS FOR CLEANUP IN 15—20 MINUTES

The Bathroom

Clean your way out: Wipe tub or shower walls just before you step out. *Bathers:* spray tub; wipe with a long-handled sponge. *Shower Fans:* Towel-dry walls and chrome after drying yourself.

Take **2 mins 15 secs** to

1. Spray the mirror, sink, vanity, toilet seat and tank top with an all-purpose cleaner also good for glass.

2. Wipe everything down with a paper towel in the same order you sprayed, starting with mirror and ending with toilet.

3. Add toilet bowl cleaner to the bowl and wash with a brush. Leave till you return, or later in the day.

4. Straighten towels and floor mat. Throw away paper towels, remove garbage bag from wastebasket and . . . you're DONE!

The Kitchen

1. Clear and wipe the table. Scrape, rinse, and stack dirty dishes or load in the dishwasher and set on rinse and hold. Leave any sticky pots to soak till later.

2. Wipe off range top, counters and empty wet and dry garbage. Apply a cleanser to stubborn spots and stains and wipe away later, when you return home.

The time for all this: **6 mins 30 secs.** (Under 10 minutes!!). IF you have more time, then vacuum or damp-mop the kitchen floor. Time: **2 mins 30 secs.**

The Living Areas

These may be the places your family or your guests tend to see first. First impressions are lasting ones.

1. Pick up, put away, and straighten any accumulated clutter.

2. Empty ashtrays, wastebaskets.

3. Top dust furniture, straighten cushions, and fluff any loose pillows.

Time: **2 mins 15 secs**

Professional Strategy:
Let cleaning products do most of the work for you. They're made to float loose dirt off a surface, hold it in suspension, and then let you just flush the dirt away!

The Bedroom

1. Straighten the bed (fold down covers neatly if in a hurry).

2. Pick up and put away clothing, books, magazines, cosmetics, jewelry, etc.

Time: **1 to 4 mins**

Add more time for additional areas.

THE STRATEGY

1. You always clear the decks first.

2. Don't make dust after you've cleaned. Do dust-raising chores first. When you dust, work from the top down. *Dust down!*

3. Don't make difficult streaks: When you wash dirty walls, *wash up!*

TWO GREAT GUIDELINES: "Whoever owns the mess should be responsible for cleaning it up."

"Bare is beautiful." Things that sit on your counters, floors, furniture tops (any surfaces) are your number one cleanup enemies.

For the Efficient Weekly Go-Round

The Bathroom

1. Wash the floor.

2. Clean to sanitize the tub, shower, toilet, and sink.

3. Change floor mats and lid cover.

4. Straighten shelves.

5. Wipe-clean light fixtures.

6. Polish chrome.

7. Clean soap dishes.

8. Use special treatments for lime/mineral deposits.

The Kitchen

1. Dispose of leftovers and wipe out refrigerator.

2. Thoroughly clean the floor.

3. Clean and disinfect garbage pail.

4. Clean all major appliance surfaces, counters and sink.

5. Wipe outside of cabinets.

6. Clean range hood and vent.

7. Clean oven, drip pans and surface units if needed.

The Living Areas

1. Dust all furniture and woodwork.

2. Clean glass surfaces, mirrors, table tops, TV screen.

3. Vacuum upholstery, draperies.

4. Vacuum or surface-dust books, picture frames, etc.

5. Vacuum or wash floors.

The Bedrooms

1. Change bed linens.

2. Vacuum or dust-mop floors (under beds, furniture, behind doors).

3. Vacuum or dust drapes, furniture, lamps, windowsills.

4. Clean mirrors.

5. Clean phone.

6. Empty wastebaskets.

 Keep all your gear with you. A multipocket apron is handy.

SPEED-UPS

Keep some cleaning products and equipment on location. You'll be more apt to clean or wipe something immediately if the "tools" are at hand. *Keep these out of the reach of children.*

KEEP IN BATHROOM	KEEP IN KITCHEN	KEEP IN LIVING & BEDROOM AREAS
Roll of paper towels	Paper towels	Lint-free dust cloth
Bowl cleaner	Sponge	Spray cleaner for dusting
Bowl brush	All-purpose spray cleaner	Vacuum or dust mop
Sponge	Dishwashing supplies	Glass cleaner
Glass/all-purpose spray cleaner	Electric broom	Paper towels
	Sponge mop	

You will also cut fetching and carrying to a minimum if you put plastic garbage bags in all wastebaskets to avoid carrying the pail two ways. Keep replacement bags in the bottom of the pail so they are always at hand.

Don't make work for yourself by leaving a job until it's harder to do. (If it looks dirty, clean it!)

YOUR PERSONAL *MUSTS* TO ADD TO OUR TIME-SAVER SCHEDULE

....

....

....

....

....

....

....

....

....

....

....

A toy dust mop works better than a feather duster. It collects dust instead of scattering it, and the handle makes it easier to get at some of those hard-to-reach shelves.

Always clean in one direction, moving through a room left to right, or right to left. Never retrace your steps.

Don't Worry If You're Not Doing It All

Some people live by must-do lists they fret over: things to do daily, weekly, twice a month, monthly, spring and fall, annually. There is no season of rest.

We are recommending that you adopt a streamlined weekly go-round, like the one you just reviewed, tend to a few MUSTS in the name of health and safety, and congratulate yourself on having done everything essential to keeping your house and possessions in good order.

We know that we are flying in the face of motherly and grandmotherly tradition, which clung to "spring tonics" for health and spring cleaning for the soul and the next-door neighbors' approval (followed by another orgy five or six months later: fall cleaning).

There are good reasons why these traditional all-out semiannual house-keeping attacks have gone the way of the dinosaur. Our cleaning methods have changed dramatically. The vacuum cleaner "swallows" the dirt it removes: No need to take rugs outside and thwack them with a hand beater. The air conditioner keeps dirt out. Many of today's lacy curtains machine-wash and dry and rehang without so much as a touch of the iron to them. No need to wait for good dry weather and pull freshly washed and starched curtains into shape on a stretcher. If you give the house its due in weekly attention, you can take any list of traditional annual or semi-annual tasks, and strike out most of them.

Your individual Weekly Go-Round may differ from ours, since you may have some favorite furnishings requiring special attention. Pencil them in.

You'll also consider the layout of your house. Is it best adapted to the room-by-room system in the Go-Round, or would you profit by tackling kitchen and bath as a twosome, as in our Kitchen/Bath Cleanup under K in the ABCs? This latter is a nifty idea for a small house or apartment, since it means that, once you get out the appropriate tools and equipment, you can use them for two jobs at once. It is also a winner in the efficient way it lets cleaning products do the hard work for you.

Consider how your various days are scheduled, too. You may decide that instead of killing a day by doing all your rooms at once, you will add a room a day to your Daily Getaway schedule.

There remains only one concern that may lodge in your mind. You may ask yourself if you are doing your utmost to make your house a safe and healthful place to live. The list of precautions is very short, but we include it because you may see some of these as musts in maintaining your house. So check out our list of musts for health and safety. Note that they are just about the only musts in the entire book!

With your Daily Getaway, plus your Weekly Go-Round, plus any health and safety precautions you've added, you have completed a cleaning plan that should take care of your house, and reassure you the year around.

 To reach cobwebs: Attach a dust cloth to the end of a yardstick with a rubber band.

NOTES

. . . .

. . . .

. . . .

. . . .

Just Be Sure the House Is Safe and Healthy

A TEN-POINT CHECKLIST

To Prevent Fire

1. Test your smoke or heat detector every few months.

2. Keep a fire extinguisher correctly charged.

3. Store combustibles in tight containers and away from heat sources. The list should include rags, paper, plastics, solvents, and chemicals.

4. Check electrical outlets, cords, light fixtures, and appliances for shorts, or any damage. Install ground fault protector outlets in bathrooms, porches, and outdoor lighting appliances. Flickering lights, tripped circuit breakers or blown fuses may warn you of wiring problems.

To Forestall Accidents

5. Wax floors correctly. (It's incorrect waxing that makes them slippery.) Also take care to dry no-wax and glazed ceramic floors thoroughly after washing. They are extremely slippery when wet!

6. Tack down loose carpet edges. Add skid-resistant backing to area rugs, throw rugs and mats.

7. Add glow-in-the-dark switches and night lights to areas where people may venture after dark.

To Avoid Poisoning

8. Keep pesticides, chemicals, cleaning products tightly sealed in labeled containers. Store separately from food products and out of reach of children.

To Protect Air Quality

9. Check and adjust heating systems annually to prevent toxic leaks. The flame on gas ranges should be blue. If it's yellow-tipped, have the range checked and adjusted. Reduce pollutants by improving and using ventilation.

Range and window exhaust fans pull stale air to the outside. Make it a habit to turn on exhaust systems when using oven cleaner or the self-cleaning system in your oven. Vent clothes dryers and check occasionally for clogging and lint buildup.

Keep Flu and Other Infections from Spreading

10. Hand-to-hand contact is a lot more dangerous than kissing, when it comes to passing along colds, etc. Don't forget to sanitize items many people use, like telephones and doorknobs. See the ABCs for information about laundry and cleaning disinfectants.

These "safe ten" conclude our roundup of all the housekeeping chores that belong on your routine list for daily/weekly attention. You should now be able to plan a vacation for the seasons when other people stage annual or semiannual cleaning blitzes.

Enjoy Your Efforts More:
Make Them Show!

One of the exasperating aspects of housekeeping is that no one pays attention to your work.

The better you keep house, the more likely that no one will notice the freshly wiped counter. (And if you draw attention to it: "Oh? Oh, I didn't see that it was all that dirty before.")

Professionals also experience this take-it-for-granted attitude and have developed their own devices to say that they have been around, and done their job. In the hotel bathroom, the last square of toilet tissue will be folded. At night, a chocolate candy may show up on the pillow.

Women who run hometown cleaning businesses have learned that most of their employers like to find their houses "shiny clean." What does that mean? It means that however clean the house may otherwise be, the shiny surfaces should really glisten, and the householder anticipates a nice fresh smell. So cleaners like citrus-scented products are used for the distinctive aroma they leave in the air.

One such cleaner tops off every job by leaving a vase with just one fresh flower in it. It says, "See what a great job I've done."

Many people just naturally wind up a house-straightening with some decorative touch. Fruit artfully set out in a decorative bowl. New soap arranged in a dish in the bathroom. A potted plant moved from its spot by the window to a table where it can be a center of attention.

You hope that your work produces some special pleasure for others: That last touch can heighten their reaction and at the very least it can gratify your need to put your signature on your work.

Fifty Ways to Simplify
Work Around the House

An absolutely carefree house would be one in which nobody tracks in dirt and leaves gear for somebody else to pick up. But this book never did promise to help you remake people.

Here we're listing some of the many useful products developed to ease the housekeeper's burden, along with some other good ideas to make your life more nearly work-free.

Keep Dirt OUT

Dirt creeps in on little cat feet, not as poetically as Carl Sandburg's fog. It creeps through windows and doors that don't quite close, through cracks in foundations—it just sits around, layering its dull and grungy self on shiny spaces, and seeping insidiously into anything with pores or troughs.

So stop it! *Check everywhere for cracks.*

Close windows unless you're airing out the house or enjoying the breeze.

Use your air conditioner. Its filters keep dust out.

People and pets bring dirt in.

Stop that, too! Use doormats everywhere, and keep them in good condition. You need them at your front entry, back entry, the path from the garage, the cellar, maybe even from the kitchen. Every mat should be sturdy and big enough so that people automatically take several steps as they traverse it.

Seal Off What You Can

You'll both prevent dirt and avoid work if you seal surfaces like concrete floors, use varnish or polyurethane on unfinished wood floors and even tables and other work-surfaces you use a lot.

Also consider a smooth resilient floor in your kitchen, as opposed to a carpet. It is easier to clean.

Don't Let Dirt Show

Pick medium colors for your decorative scheme—at least where dirt will show the most. Avoid lights, avoid darks: medium colors show less dirt and fewer spots. And if you are addicted to carpeting in rooms where people eat and drink, look at some of the multicolor patterns that can provide camouflage for an occasional spot that won't come out.

Repel Dirt

Be sure your kitchen range is equipped with a vented cooking exhaust.

Use soil repellent on everything you can. Repellents work on upholstery fabrics, draperies, carpets. Use mildew inhibitors. Wax floors correctly.

There Is No Such Thing as a Self-Cleaning House, But . . .

Think how much you're worth, and invest all you can to save your valuable time and energy. The self-cleaning oven, self-defrosting refrigerator, and automatic-defrost refrigerators make kitchens more fun and less work than ever before.

Elves to Work While You Rest or Enjoy Yourself

To save precious time, most seriously consider the dishwasher, the new automated ranges, etc.

Other Time-Tested Work-Savers

The double sink has been a boon to washerwomen since they rub-a-dubbed laundry on a board in the tub, and to all those who grew up having to help with dishes. It's still a godsend.

Built-ins are another boon our grandparents knew well as work-savers. After all, they have only three sides . . . maybe only two . . . maybe only ONE to wipe down, compared with the attention free-standing units demand.

New-fangled Work-Savers

It's impossible to list here all the machines and devices and products designed for you.

Do you realize that once every year some 200,000 people descend on the city of Chicago to consider you, your desires, your problems? There for the housewares show, they are the manufacturers who spend millions of dollars to develop products to clean the house, along with small-time inventors who aim to make it big with their brainstorms; Mom and Pop store owners interested in your patronage, along with representatives from the giant retail chains that sell household work-savers.

Surely when you visit the dealers where you'll find our choices you will come upon still more helpful and tempting tools and products.

The Nifty Fifty Plus

We decided to limit ourselves to fifty work-saving concepts, and did pretty well to keep the list to sixty, we think.

Ways to Get the Family's Cooperation

1. Install a spigot near the backdoor, so everybody can get a drink, or wash off dirty tools (or sandy feet) without coming inside.

2. Put in an old-fashioned mud room so everybody can shed dirty boots without tracking mud into the house.

3. If you can't have a mud room, use old bath mats or disposable foil trays for muddy boots.

4. Supply plastic baskets to receive gear in snowy weather.

5. Put wastebaskets in every room.

6. Have plenty of hangers and towel racks.

7. Dump the things people leave lying around in one closet (or box or drawer). If they don't retrieve their belongings at week's end, they must pay one dollar for each item they want back, or it will be given or thrown away.

Ways to Eliminate Dirt (Almost) Entirely

8. Built-ins present fewer surfaces to get dirty.

9. Humidifiers cut down dirt-inviting static, so do antistatic finishes and antistatic sprays.

10. Dehumidifiers help to prevent mildew.

11. Air purifiers trap dirt particles.

12. Vacuum cleaners remove dirt (and do away with it)—a central vacuum system is the most efficient, if you can install one.

13. A kitchen range fan disposes of something like two hundred pounds of grease annually.

How to Keep Dirt Out and Clutter Under Control

14. Use mats and scrapers at all entrances.

15. Avoid clutter-catchers like tables near the door.

Decorating for Less Work

16. Buy low-pile medium color carpets.

17. Use carpet treads on stairs rather than full carpet.

18. Use scrubbable paint and patterned washable wallpaper.

19. High-gloss finishes for woodwork, trims, and switchplates cut down cleaning.

20. Try Lucite or ceramic switchplates.

21. PVC patio furniture may fit into your family room.

22. Fiberglass cushions are highly soil-resistant.

23. Laminated plastic tops are useful on children's furniture. Glass or Plexiglas are also protective covers and can be used for wood furniture in adult living spaces.

24. Smooth surfaces are always easier to handle than rough ones, and nonporous materials are more impervious to soil than porous ones. Use sealers (varnish, polyurethane) on floors and furniture surfaces that must take heavy use.

25. Install no-wax or glazed tile floors where you can. Consider grout in a dark color. (If yours is light, there is a do-it-yourself stain on the market.)

26. Stain-resistant Formica is a boon in the bath.

27. Shower curtains are more easily cleaned than installed doors.

28. Marble sills at the bathroom door are easily washed.

29. On the other hand, you may opt for *no* doorsills throughout the house so that nothing obstructs the rolling carts you use to wheel around food and drinks or to tote your cleaning supplies from room to room.

30. Venetian blinds may not be your answer for every window, as they are harder to clean than ordinary window shades.

31. Built-in storage prevents clutter and presents fewer surfaces to clean. Also consider under-cabinet appliances and any other wall-mounted units you can accommodate.

Ways to Contain Mess, and Wear and Tear

32. Use a rubber mat for petfood dishes. It can keep the dishes from being nosed around, and save the floor from yucky crumbs.

33. Coasters or no-sweat sleeves for drinking glasses preserve your fine wood surfaces, and can eliminate some cleanup on any surface.

34. Paper doilies or napkins look pretty, and can protect wooden, fiber, or papier-mâché dishes or trays you use for serving refreshments.

35. Arm covers on upholstered furniture (shades of grandma's anti-macassars) can eliminate the need for frequent furniture shampoos.

36. Trivets, tiles, and wine caddies protect your dining table or side-board.

37. But they should be felt-bottomed so as not to scratch. In almost any variety store or hardware store you will find packages of self-stick felt rounds you can apply yourself. At the same time, take a look at the self-stick rubber products useful for application on chair backs that rub against a wall.

Make Work Last Longer

38. Protect cleaned fabric with Scotchgard.

39. Try silver polish with tarnish-delay ingredients.

40. Use antifog glass/mirror cleaners.

41. A coat of liquid wax or silicone makes plastic surfaces more impervious to soil.

42. A light coat of liquid wax serves the same purpose on painted woodwork. (Silicone prevents easy repainting!)

43. Keep clean clothes clean in proper garment bags.

44. Drawer liners and shelf papers protect freshly washed and dried drawers and shelves. (While you're cutting these to fit, cut two layers. Then when the top paper is soiled remove only that layer.)

Time and Energy Savers

45. Water-softening equipment. It makes every single job of laundry, dishwashing, cleaning, bathing, hair shampooing, and bathroom cleaning easier.

46. Double sinks let you wash in one tub, rinse and air dry in the other. (No changing water all the time.)

47. Garbage disposer. (Need we say how or why?)

48. An electric scrub brush is a handy, fast worker.

49. The mini-vac (battery-powered, hand-held vacuum) is ideal for after-meal cleanup in the dining room.

50. Disposables of all kinds, including diapers.

51. Microwave ovens. The cleanup is quick, especially with some of the disposables you'll use for cooking and serving.

52. Kick stools.

53. Tongs and grabbers.

54. Long-handled anything.

55. Toilet bowl sanitizers.

56. Carts you can roll from room to room with food, drinks, hobby projects, cleaning supplies, whatever. Or baskets or totes set aside for the same purpose. (Carts with big wheels go over carpeted floors.)

57. Oversize casters on heavy furniture, especially beds.

58. Treated mops and dustcloths.

59. Those multifingered Venetian blind cleaners.

60. The wet-dry vacuum that picks up both dry dirt and liquids, if you have large areas with resilient floor covering.

61. Many households are replacing the standard bedspread with quilts, comforters, or futons to speed up bedmaking.

62. Clean as you go! It takes a lot less time to remove new dirt than old, and to clean and put away stuff as you use it, than to clean and store the pile-up you can accumulate.

The ABCs of Housekeeping:
How to Care for Your Possessions to Get the Most Use and Pleasure from Them

The ABCs

You can do everything by all the standard rules and—oops!—something goes awry.

When that happens, look up the answer to your problem in our ABCs.

Here is where we also get down to the now-and-then beauty treatments some of your especially prized possessions may need if they are to stay handsome and functional.

Here also you'll find the troubleshooters that may save the day (and a repair bill) when a favorite appliance acts up.

You may well know how to launder, iron, cope with floors and furniture, etc. But in case you aren't onto all the tricks that simplify these chores, here are Mini Manuals on these subjects, all loaded with trouble-savers.

These ABCs deal with bugs and slippery floors, waterbeds and sleeping bags and yellowing and pianos and hundreds of other subjects.

As we noted earlier in this book, if you go to the annual housewares show you will find congregated there two hundred thousand people engaged in making or selling household products. For most of them this is a lifetime occupation.

So don't feel guilty if you don't know everything about housekeeping or can't keep all of it in your head. This is why we decided that our hundreds of subjects and hundreds of handy tips ought to be accessible—A! B! C!—with the flip of a page.

So here you are.

ABRASIVES

For our great-grandmothers, sand was the abrasive of choice for scouring their wood floors and stone doorsteps. Abrasives are the age-old means of removing dirt by rubbing, wearing away the buildup of food particles, tarnish, grease, and stains under attack.

Sandpaper is a handy abrasive. As is steel wool, for some tasks, plastic and nylon meshes for others.

Then there are the powders, pastes, and liquids—commercial products like Ajax and Comet and Soft Scrub and the polishes for silver and other metals.

Whiting, pumice, rottenstone, cigar ash, small pebbles, and gunshot are other abrasives that polish as well as clean.

Baking soda is a mild abrasive.

You will find many specially designed products for use on possessions you treasure. Among these are mild abrasives or liquid cleaners for fiberglass and other shiny surfaces.

Go easy with all coarse abrasives. Regular use can scratch the finish on your bathtub or kitchen appliances, causing them to soil faster and stain deeper. Scratches on plastic ware, glass, some nonstick cookware finishes, painted woodwork, and highly polished and plated metals also make them harder to clean.

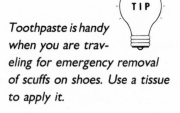

TIP

Toothpaste is handy when you are traveling for emergency removal of scuffs on shoes. Use a tissue to apply it.

ABSORBENT FINISHES

Diapers hold more moisture and also dry more quickly with these finishes. So do towels, underwear, sanitary products, and surgical dressings.

Sportswear designed to be comfortable in hot, humid weather may be treated to help the fiber wick, so moisture travels from the skin surface to the fabric surface, where it more readily evaporates.

ABSORBENTS

Every housekeeper needs absorbents like cornstarch, cornmeal, French chalk, talc, talcum powder, fuller's earth, baking soda, kitty litter. All are effective stain removers, especially on anything that cannot be rubbed or flushed. Rugs, carpets, upholstery, artificial flowers—these are typical candidates for cleaning with such powdery substances.

The trick is to apply the powder (or paste made from the powder) to a stain, allow it to absorb the liquid, and then dry so you can brush or vacuum off the residue.

Or, with subjects like artificial flowers, to shake them in cornmeal, allowing it to absorb the accumulated dirt.

Baking soda both removes stains and absorbs odors.

Other handy absorbents for wicking stains are white paper towels, soft cloths, and tissue.

TIP

Kitty litter is a good absorbent for grease or oil accumulations in your garage or driveway.

ACETATE

Like other man-made fibers with low absorbency, acetates dry quickly and require little or no ironing.

But they wrinkle easily, dissolve in acetone, acetic acid, and other chemicals in this family.

While 100 percent acetate fabric requires dry cleaning, some acetates hand-wash.

If they are solution-dyed, they provide color fastness to sunlight, perspiration, air contaminants, and washing.

The general formula for washing: Warm (not hot) water, mild suds, gentle handling (don't twist or wring). Don't soak colored items. Dry at low temperature or drip dry.

Press with special care—while damp, on the wrong side, with cool iron. If finishing on the right side, use a pressing cloth. Don't use steam. Hang to dry completely.

CAUTION

Never use nail polish remover or perfumes containing acetone or other organic solvents on acetate items.

ACETIC ACID

Acetic acid is a mild disinfectant and stain remover, neutralizing stains caused by alkalis such as ammonia. White vinegar (which is principally acetic acid and water) can be used as a substitute.

ACETONE Acetone is a solvent widely used in paint and varnish removers, and also a component of nail polish remover. It may be safely used on natural fibers and on most synthetics (the exceptions are acetate and triacetate).

Note: It is poisonous and its fumes are toxic. Use it only in well-ventilated areas.

Instructions for its use are included with specific stains in the Master Stain Removal Section.

ACIDS Acids act as stain removers, take care of hard water deposits, and remove rust stains.

Vinegar and lemon juice cope with hard water deposits on glassware, rust stains in sinks, and tarnish on brass and copper. These two very mild acids also counteract alkaline oven cleaners.

Cream of tartar sweetens coffee makers and brightens aluminum.

Cautions on Some Acids

The potentially injurious ones like oxalic acid are found in rust removers and some toilet bowl cleaners. Sodium bisulphate, dilute hydrochloric acid, and dilute sulfuric acid also show up in some toilet bowl cleaners.

All are poisonous. All can injure skin and eyes and damage clothing, leather, and some metals.

So be sure to follow the instructions on the container.

Dispose of cloths and brushes you use to apply oxalic acid, so you won't transfer the acid to kitchen utensils and dishes, and ingest the poisonous residue.

Soak metal items you are cleaning with acid in non-metal containers such as plastic or glass.

ACRYLIC FIBERS Acrylic fibers alone or blended with wool, rayon, or cotton turn

up in fleece fabrics, blankets, carpets, home knitting yarns, sportswear, and work clothes.

They do not readily absorb moisture. Characteristically, then,
they are static-prone, feel hot in hot weather, and dry quickly—
to a virtually wrinkle-free state. Acrylics have a tendency to pill.

You can either machine-wash or hand-wash acrylics.

To wash delicate items by hand, use warm water, with a fabric
softener in every third or fourth washing. (Reduces static electricity!) Gently squeeze out water, smooth or shake out garment,
and let dry on a nonrust hanger. (Except for sweaters, which
should be dried flat.)

Machine-wash in warm water and add a fabric softener during
the final rinse cycle.

Machine-dry at low temperature setting. Remove from dryer
as soon as tumbling cycle is completed.

If ironing is required, use moderately warm iron.

ACRYLIC PLASTICS These colorless, transparent plastics transmit ultraviolet light better than glass. They are combustible, and some can craze from
too much heat. But they are weather-resistant and also resist acids
and solvents. Acrylics are found in everything from appliance hous-
ings to piano keys. For cleaning instructions, see Plastic (Thermoplastic).

ADHESIVE TAPE See Carpet Stain Removal Guide; Master Stain Removal Section.
RESIDUE

AEROSOLS Take care with these pressurized containers. Never leave them
on a kitchen range, radiator, furnace, in direct sunlight, or near
other heat sources. Don't smoke while you're spraying. Before
discarding a container, hold the valve open until all the contents
and gas have escaped. Never puncture an empty can or toss it

into a fire or incinerator because even the gas remaining in an apparently empty container can explode when heat causes it to expand.

AIR CONDITIONERS Your air-conditioning system does more than cool your home. It lowers humidity and, by moving air through filters, removes dust and dirt at the same time.

Dirty air filters reduce the efficiency of the unit and run up your utility bill, so change or clean filters often. They can become clogged within a month or so of operation.

If your system has disposable filters (as most central units do), check them every two months, and replace if necessary. Some can be vacuumed gently with the dust brush attachment on your vacuum cleaner for very temporary maintenance. Permanent filters, common in window units, should be washed monthly with detergent and water. Dip filter up and down in a sink full of sudsy water, then rinse well by holding it under cool running water from the faucet.

Check use and care instructions and under no circumstances run an air conditioner without the filter.

Central Systems

The Air Conditioning & Refrigeration Institute suggests that "preventive maintenance is the least expensive kind" for central systems. Have your system inspected by an authorized service technician in spring, before the cooling season begins, or in midwinter if you live in a warm climate. Don't put maintenance off for a period longer than three years.

For all systems, keep the area around the unit clean (including grass and leaves near exterior central units). Ask your dealer or manufacturer for a system start-up checklist.

ALCOHOL This book suggests rubbing alcohol or denatured alcohol (70 percent or 90 percent concentration) as a solvent for stain removal. It is a good, safe cleaner for many surfaces from which you need to remove grease or glue. It is also useful as a disinfectant (for thermometers).

Always test a fabric for color-fastness before using alcohol on it because alcohol fades some dyes. And if you use it on acetate, dilute it with two parts of water to one part alcohol. Do not use on silk. And do not use perfumed or colored alcohol for these jobs.

Denatured alcohol is both poisonous and flammable, so observe cautions on label.

ALCOHOLIC BEVERAGE STAINS

See Carpet Stain Removal Guide; Wood Floor Troubleshooters; Master Stain Removal Section.

ALKALIS

These do away with oily dirt.

Mild Alkalis: These include baking soda, a handy answer, mixed with water, to clean glass, wall tile, and porcelain enamels. This mix also works on china and plastic dishes stained with tea or coffee.

Moderate Strength: Household ammonia, with 5 to 10 percent ammonia gas in water, is a standard cleaner for kitchen range burners and ovens; also windows and mirrors.

The addition of soap or detergent produces sudsy ammonia to clean garbage pails, kitchen range burners, and sinks.

Borax is another alkali in the moderate column, practical for woodwork, walls, and sinks.

Strong Alkalis: Trisodium phosphate (TSP), often an ingredient in powdered cleansers. It is a favorite for cleaning walls, woodwork, and resilient floors (except linoleum).

Very Strong: Lye (sodium hydroxide, also called caustic soda) has been a household staple since colonial days. Notably, today, it's used in drain and oven cleaners.

TIP

Alcohol is a handy cleaner for the silicone caulking around bathroom tubs. It also shines chrome.

The key point to remember is that the function of alkalis is to remove oil. They remove oil from skin: so wear gloves. They strip oil from linoleum and oil-based paints, making them crack or peel. They can darken aluminum. Preventive measure: use mild alkaline solutions when you can, and rinse well to remove all the cleaner from any surface.

ALL-FABRIC BLEACH

See Bleaches; Laundry Aids in the Laundry Mini Manual.

ALLOY

An alloy is a combination of two or more metals. Like pewter, nickel, bronze.

ALUMINUM

Aluminum resists rust but can be darkened by alkalis, damaged by hydrochloric acid, and scratched or punctured by sharp utensils.

To clean, wash with hot water and detergent, by hand or in the dishwasher. Rinse and polish dry. *Do not* use abrasives, strong soaps, or detergents containing alkalis, which can cause the aluminum to pit. In some cases dishwasher cleaning may darken aluminum. If this bothers you, wash your aluminum utensils by hand. Glass cleaners and household cleaners containing ammonia may also darken aluminum. For more information, see Cookware (Aluminum).

ALUMINUM, ANODIZED

This is a finish, sometimes with color added, applied to baking pans, pot lids, and appliance trim. It also gives a "copper" look to molds and kitchen tools.

To clean: Use hot soapy water, rinse, and dry. *Do not* use abrasives or scouring pads. (It scratches easily.) *Do not* place anodized aluminum in the oven or dishwasher (color may fade) unless recommended by the manufacturer.

ALUMINUM POTS See Cookware (Aluminum).

AMMONIA Household ammonia is an essential on any cleaning shelf. An alkali containing 5 to 10 percent ammonia gas in water, it cleans range burners and ovens, windows and mirrors, and is often a component of oven and all-purpose cleaning products. Plain ammonia (without added color or fragrance) is also a mild bleach, and useful in stain removal. Sudsy ammonia is simply ammonia with soap or detergent added, handy for cleaning garbage pails, kitchen range burners and sinks.

Don't use ammonia on acetate, Dacron, or triacetate, and dilute it with an equal amount of water if you use it on wool or silk.

If it changes dye color, rinse the color-changed area thoroughly with water and apply a few drops of white vinegar. Then rinse with water again.

Ammonia is poisonous and irritates skin and eyes. It can take oil from linoleum and oil-based paints, causing them to crack or peel, and can darken aluminum. Use a mild ammonia solution, when that will do the job, rinsing quickly and well to remove it.

ANDIRONS Very fine steel wool does a good job on neglected brass andirons and fire sets, but it's a time-taker to use. Fine emery cloth works faster, but be sure you rub the metal in only one direction (not round and round). Finish up with a brass polish. Some commercial products do not require rinsing. (Check the manufacturer's directions.)

For further information, see Brass; Iron.

ANGORA True angora is Angora goat or rabbit hair.

Dry cleaning is the safest procedure on all angoras, to avoid shrinkage. Garments should be turned inside out before they are dry-cleaned. Always dry soft wool knitwear at room temperature.

Pilling or balling may occur, especially at points of wear, since the soft wool yarns are so fragile. See Pilling.

ANTIPERSPIRANT STAINS   See Master Stain Removal Section (Deodorants).

ANTIQUES   Our antiques suffer from the same hazards as our other possessions—too much heat, too much cold, too much light, fumes, conditions that dry them out or encourage mildew, wear and tear, and, of course, dirt.

We are better off than the people who originally owned them, since we can control temperature and humidity with contemporary air conditioning, and some of our newer cleaning methods are more gentle.

If your routine cleaning methods, gently and carefully executed, are inadequate for your antiques, seek advice from experts. Begin with the curator at your local museum. Such a specialist may be able to suggest truly knowledgeable antiques dealers, restorers, or conservators who make a business of caring for art and antiques collections.

Three centers for conservation are:

The American Institute for Conservation
of Historic and Artistic Works
3545 Williamsburg Lane N.W.
Washington, D.C. 20008

The Chicago Conservation Center
Center Arts Building, Suite 701
730 N. Franklin Street
Chicago, Illinois 60610
Barry R. Bauman, Director, Painting Conservator

Washington Conservation Studio
4230 Howard Avenue
Kensington, Maryland 20895
Justine Wimsatt, President

See also Paintings.

ANTISEPTIC/ ANTIBACTERIAL FINISHES   These resist the bacteria that cause problems like perspiration odor; they eliminate mildew odors, minimize diaper rash, and curtail the spread of disease and infection. They show up on socks and shoe linings (to retard athlete's foot reinfection), in infants' wear and bedding, health products, and a variety of home furnishings subject to mildew.

Note that chlorine bleach may remove these finishes. You can treat fabrics yourself, with such antibacterial products as Borateem (which is sodium perborate).

For further information on sanitizing household procedures, see Disinfectants.

ANTISNAG FINISHES   Some soft knits, especially girls' and women's wear, are treated to resist snagging. The finish reduces snagging, provides water repellency, and reduces oily spotting and staining.

ANTISTATIC FINISHES   See Static.

ANTS   The surest way to attack ants is to destroy their nest. But if you can't locate it, use insecticides near the places where ants enter the house—along cracks in baseboards, window frames, doorsills, and foundations.

Use sprays containing propoxur, diazinon, malathion, chlorpy-rifos, and pyrethrin or resmethrin aerosols. New bait products are popular because they are child-proof and easy to use.

APPLIANCE TROUBLESHOOTERS See Mini Manual on next page.

ARAMID (Nomex, Kevlar) is the man-made fiber that produces new resil-ient, flame-retardant, and abrasion-resistant fabrics with only moderate-to-low absorbency. Du Pont recommends either dry cleaning or laundering for its Nomex products, claiming the per-manent flame-resistance and high temperature resistance will both survive such cleaning.

Du Pont offers a few additional tips.

- Spot greasy stains with a solvent spot cleaner before washing.
- Wash such garments by themselves so they won't pick up lint, with the potential for flammable surface fuzz pickup.
- Use hot water with heavy-duty detergents such as Tide, Cheer, All, and Wisk, and rinse well.
- Garments will be more comfortable if you use a fabric soft-ener or antistatic product (like Downy or Cling Free).
- Dry at hot or high temperature (remove and place on a hanger while still hot). Line dry if you wish. Touch up with a hot or steam iron if needed. Starching is not recommended.

ARMETALE Made by Wilton, this is a fusion of ten different metals, and is featured in tableware that is wholly ovenproof.

Hand-wash with a mild detergent. (Dishwasher cleaning or harsh detergents may damage the pieces.)

If food stains occur, polish out with Goddard's Glow, says the manufacturer, and wash. Surface scratches are considered to be part of the natural aging of the dinnerware pieces.

Appliance Troubleshooters

A MINI MANUAL

Today's appliances are generally trouble-free and easy to maintain. However, the day they go on the blink always seems to be the day you have a houseful of company, it is a holiday or weekend, or the repair center is closed. Don't go into breakdown yourself. Forty percent of all appliance repair service calls could be avoided, says the Association of Home Appliance Manufacturers. At that rate you may be able to do a quick fix yourself—and save money, to boot!

THE BEFORE-YOU-DO-ANYTHING-ELSE CHECKLIST

In fact, before you ever pick up the phone to call a repairman, check the following save-the-day suggestions. If they don't work, then turn to our ABC listing on the appliance that seems to be in trouble.

Particularly if a large appliance goes belly-up, do a quick but careful check on the following.

Switches: Double check to be sure that the ON switch or button is really on.

Plugs: Is the plug firmly in the outlet? If it's loose you can bend the prongs slightly outward with pliers (too much bending will break the prong). If the plug continues to fall out, the receptacle or plug may have to be changed. If dirty prongs are giving you a poor electrical connection, clean them with a piece of fine sandpaper. *Don't* use water. Wet prongs will short circuit the appliance. Has the appliance disconnected itself by "walking" away from the wall? Level it so it won't shimmy or wiggle away.

Circuit Breakers and Fuses: An electrical overload may have tripped the appliance circuit or blown a fuse. Change the fuse or reset the circuit breaker.

Outlets: Check to see if the outlet is really working. If you plug in a lamp and it doesn't light, you may blame the problem on the outlet, not the appliance.

If worn or torn cords are the troublemakers, better get professional help to replace them. (You can avoid some such repairs by habitually grasping the plug, not the cord, when you disconnect your appliance, and keeping the cord looped or flat rather than kinked.)

Overload Protectors: Motor driven appliances (dishwashers, dryers, washers) have "overload protectors" on the motor. The appliance will automatically turn itself off if an overload occurs and overheating results. Some appliances have a button to push to reset the motor, and others reset themselves after a cool-down period. (Check your use and care manual.)

For troubleshooters on small appliances, see the entry immediately following this. For major appliances (e.g. dishwashers, refrigerators, etc.) see individual listings.

GENERAL CARE FOR
SMALL ELECTRICS

Keep use and care books. These are your best guides.

- Before cleaning disconnect cord from outlet.
- Clean washable parts with hot sudsy water after each use. Rinse and dry thoroughly.
- Use a soap-filled steel wool pad to remove stubborn stains.
- Pitting and darkening of aluminum may occur because acid or highly salted foods remained in the pan for long periods of time.
- For aluminum interiors, boil a solution of 2 tablespoons of cream of tartar to 2 quarts of water for twenty minutes.
- Season nonstick finishes by rubbing with a paper towel soaked with unsalted shortening or oil.
- To remove discoloration from nonstick finishes, use nylon, wooden, or plastic-coated tools. Boil a solution of 1 cup water, ½ cup liquid household bleach, and 2 tablespoons of baking soda in the appliance for ten minutes. Re-season with oil (as above).
- Silver cleaner or other commercial cleaner may be used to clean shiny exteriors.
- Remove grease stains or fingerprints with denatured alcohol.

Do not immerse any electrical appliance unless it is marked "immersible" or manufacturer recommends.

ARTIFICIAL FURS   See Furs, Synthetic.

ASBESTOS   Asbestos was widely used in fireplace gas logs, vinyl flooring, door gaskets for furnaces, ranges and ovens, in stove mats and ironing-board covers and some appliances, and in insulation (in walls and ceilings, around hot water and steam pipes, in cement sheets around wood-burning stoves). Then, in the late 1970s, it was shown to cause cancer of the lung and stomach, especially among asbestos workers.

You should avoid exposure to asbestos. If you undertake any renovation that might release asbestos particles, do not attempt to dust, sweep or vacuum any dust or dirt, which may contain tiny asbestos fibers. Get professional help.

The U.S. Consumer Products Safety Commission publishes an up-to-date booklet, "Asbestos in the Home," and maintains a hotline through which you can obtain it: 800-638-CPSC (2772). Or write to the Commission in Washington, D.C. 20207.

ASHTRAYS   Spray furniture polish over hard-to-clean ashtrays like those made of silver or pewter. Ashes then dump out without sticking, and there is no residue of odor or ash. Rewax when needed.

ASPHALT/RUBBER (Synthetic)   These resilient floorings require the same care as vinyl floors.

- Vacuum or dust-mop daily to remove loose dirt before it scratches the floor or becomes ground-in.
- Damp-mop when the floor begins to look dirty. First vacuum, then go over it with a dampened sponge mop and warm water. Mop a small area at a time, rinse and wring out the mop often. If the area is large, also change water often so you won't redeposit the dirt back onto the floor.

- Wash once a week, first vacuuming the floor to take up loose dirt. Avoid harsh, strong detergents and scouring powders, which can damage the flooring.

Special Cautions

Asphalt tile may soften or bleed color in contact with grease, oil, or solvents.

Rubber tile can deteriorate if exposed to strong sunlight. A coat of wax offers some protection. Do not use a paste or solvent-based liquid wax, however. Ask your dealer to recommend a cleaner.

ASPHALT STAINS   See Carpet Stain Removal Guide; Vinyl Flooring Stain Removal Guide; Master Stain Removal Section.

AUDIO EQUIPMENT   Stereo Cassette—Player

Clean the tape head frequently with a cotton swab or cloth dipped in denatured alcohol. (Sony Corporation suggests cleaning after every ten hours of use.)

Radio Cassette—Player

Clean heads and the path of the tape after each ten hours of operation. Clean tape path before every recording for the best possible quality. Be sure newly cleaned areas are dry before inserting a cassette.

Demagnetize heads and tape path with a commercially available head demagnetizer after twenty to thirty hours of use. Built-up magnetism may cause hiss and loss of high frequencies.

If a portable radio will not be used for a long period of time, remove the batteries to avoid damage from leakage and corrosion.

CAUTION

Clean cabinet, panel, and controls with a mild detergent solution. Do not use abrasive pads, scouring powder or alcohol or benzine solvents on the cabinet.

Car Stereo Cassettes

Heads and tape path should be cleaned with a cotton swab dipped in denatured alcohol. Direct sunlight, dust and high temperatures can cause the cassette shells to warp and tapes to stretch. Store the tapes in their cases to protect them, and always remove cassettes from the player when not in use (especially if you leave the car with the windows closed).

Store tapes carefully: even the heat build-up in a glove compartment can warp them.

Turntables

Clean the cabinet with a dry soft cloth, using a mild detergent if it is stained. Avoid solvent cleaners.

Clean the stylus with a soft brush. Do not use your fingertip. (Commercial stylus cleaners are available.)

AUTOMATIC DRYER   See Dryers.

AUTOMATIC WASHER   See Washing Machines.

B

BABY FORMULA STAINS   See Master Stain Removal Section (Dairy).

BAKELITE   See Plastics.

BAKING SODA (Bicarbonate of soda)   This is a chemical cousin to washing soda, but unlike the relative that stars as a cleaner, baking soda excels as a bleach, a freshener, a deodorant, a dentifrice, an antacid (taken with a physician's guidance), a useful adjunct to chlorine in stabilizing swimming pool water, etc.

As a deodorant, it stops litterbox odor, keeps dishwashers smelling good, absorbs odors in refrigerators and freezers.

It can extinguish flames if sprinkled at the base of a kitchen fire. It may be patted on underarms and elsewhere as a personal deodorant. It is convenient for cleaning and polishing appliances, countertops, and cabinets. You will find dozens of uses for it in this book.

BAMBOO   See Wicker.

BATHROOM   See Fast Daily Getaway and Weekly Go-Round (pages 14-18), Kitchen/Bath Mini Manual, Sinks and Tubs, Toilet Bowls for cleaning procedures.

BATHTUB   See Sinks and Tubs.

BEDBUGS   These small brown pests arrive in your house in clothing, baggage, laundry packages, or secondhand furniture. They feed by piercing the skin and sucking blood, leaving a telltale lump that itches and burns. Use DDVP (Vapona), pyrethrin or malathion insecticides, spraying bed springs lightly but thoroughly. Also treat the sides and edges of mattresses and overstuffed furniture and cracks in floors and baseboards, where they also like to hide. Pyrethrin sprays induce bedbugs to leave their cracks, crevices and other hideouts, so they are especially effective. Repeat treatment if bugs persist: you may need to apply every thirty days.

BEDSPREADS, COVERLETS, DUST RUFFLES   Launder washable spreads regularly to keep them fresh and dust-free (and hygienic, if they are being used by someone who is ill).

A commercial laundromat may be needed to launder king and queen-size spreads.

If you are hand-laundering such bulky items, try accordion-folding them as you put them to soak. To dry, spread them over two parallel clotheslines.

Bedspreads that require dry cleaning or are troublesome to wash might well be removed from the bed each night so they'll stay clean longer.

In every case, fabric type and filler content will determine how you handle spreads. See appropriate listings for Quilts, Comforters, Pile fabrics, Chenille, Corduroy, and other fabrics.

BEER STAINS   See Carpet Stain Removal Guide; Master Stain Removal Section (Alcoholic Beverages).

BEETLES   Beetles infesting foods, like whole grains, cereal products, flour, dried fruits, dried pet foods, etc., may be found under Pantry Pests. For information on Carpet Beetles, see Moths.

BERRY STAINS   See Carpet Stain Removal Guide; Master Stain Removal Section (Fruit).

BEVERAGE STAINS   See Master Stain Removal Section.

BICARBONATE OF SODA   See Baking Soda.

BLANKETS   To hand launder

Fill a bathtub with lukewarm water and detergent. Accordion-fold the blanket and place it in the tub to allow sudsy water to work its way through the folds. Work the blanket up and down for about five minutes. Do not rub. Rinse three times in warm water, or until the rinse water is clear of soap. Add a cup of white vinegar to the final rinse water for extra softness. Squeeze excess water from the blanket without twisting.

Dry in the shade by stretching the blanket over two parallel lines spread two to three feet apart. Shape the blanket as closely as possible to its original size.

To machine-launder

Follow the care label. If there is none, clean as follows.

Fill the machine with liquid laundry detergent and warm water. Add the blanket so it loosely surrounds the agitator. Set the machine on the soak cycle. At the end of the cycle, agitate the blanket on Gentle for about one minute. Rinse twice in warm water. Two cups of white vinegar added to the washer during the last rinse cycle will leave your cotton and wool blankets free of soapy odors and produce a softer and fluffier nap.

Most blankets can be tumble-dried. Place the blanket in the dryer with two or three towels for about ten minutes. If possible, finish by line-drying. If the blanket is made of wool or if you are uncertain about possible shrinkage, use the line-drying tips given above.

BLANKETS, ELECTRIC

Follow manufacturer's directions. They are most helpful. If you have lost them, observe the following rules.

Do not dry-clean. Dry-cleaning solvents harm the wiring.

Machine-wash for a short time, generally one to five minutes. Dissolve a mild detergent in lukewarm water before putting the blanket in the washer, distributing it evenly in the machine. Avoid bleach.

Use a cold water rinse and spin cycle. Do not use a wringer.

Hand wash by soaking the blanket for fifteen minutes in detergent and lukewarm water. Squeeze suds through the blanket. Don't twist or wring it. Rinse in cold water, twice or more.

Drying: To line dry, drape the blanket over two parallel clothes-lines, gently stretching into shape. Don't use clothespins.

If you machine-dry at all, preheat the dryer at medium temperature, add the blanket and let it tumble for ten minutes, no more. You can damage the thermostat and shrink the blanket if you dry it completely by machine. Finish the process by line drying as above.

Storing: Don't store electric blankets with heavy objects or other blankets on top of them. Moth preventives are damaging to the wiring (and are unnecessary with synthetics).

For safety's sake, do not lie on top of an electric blanket when it's on. You can get burned; you can damage the wiring. Turn it off when it's not in use. Don't tuck in the wired area of the blanket. Don't use pins. Electric blankets are inappropriate for infants or the handicapped, and keep small children and pets from playing on them.

BLEACHES

Nature has given us sunlight as the most pervasive bleaching agent of all.

The two most common man-made products are chlorine and all-fabric (peroxy- or oxygen) bleach, based on a sodium perborate or sodium or potassium monopersulfate.

Bleaches do not remove dirt. They whiten, fade color, and remove stains. Chlorine bleaches also act as disinfectants.

You can identify a product containing chlorine bleach by any label boasting bleaching action or listing sodium hypochlorite as an ingredient or indicating it is "chlorinated."

Chlorine bleach can dull shiny finishes on sinks, bathtubs, and other porcelain enamel surfaces. Note that it's an alkali and will darken aluminum and make linoleum brittle.

For other bleaching agents, especially useful in stain removal, see Color Remover, Hydrogen Peroxide. See also Laundry Mini Manual, Laundry Aids for correct use of bleaches and Master Product List for representative brand names.

Mixing bleach with a toilet bowl cleaner or rust remover produces a harmful gas, and under some conditions, using bleach and ammonia together forms dangerous chemical compounds that can ignite.

BLENDER

It's a cinch to clean a blender jar on its base. Fill the jar halfway with warm water and add $\frac{1}{2}$ teaspoon liquid dishwashing detergent. Turn the blender on low and let it spin for about half a minute. Rinse and dry. Most jars are dishwasher safe.

Clean the base housing with detergent and warm water, or use an all-purpose liquid cleaner. Never immerse base in water.

Knobs and push buttons may need to be cleaned with a cotton swab dipped in cleaning solution.

Troubleshooting

If the blender is sluggish or not spinning, check the control buttons, knobs, and timer. Then remove the blender jar and reseat on the base. Blenders operate at their best if only two-thirds or less full.

BLINDS

See Venetian Blinds.

BLOOD STAINS

See Grout Stain Removal Guide, Tile Floor Stain Removal; Master Stain Removal Section.

BLOOM	See Furniture Troubleshooters.
BLUE STAINS ON LAUNDRY	See Laundry Troubleshooters.
BLUEBERRY STAINS	See Master Stain Removal Section (Fruit).
BLUING FOR LAUNDRY	See Laundry Aids in Laundry Mini Manual.
BONDED FABRICS	See Laminated Fabrics.

BOOK LICE (Or Psocids)

These small, soft-bodied, grayish insects thrive on humidity and warm temperatures. They show up in starch, cereals, flour, and sugar. Also in paper, bookbindings, and wallpaper. (They feed on the sizing in paper.)

To prevent infestation, store food in tight, moisture-proof containers, and books and papers in dry warm areas, periodically checking them for damage.

To treat, ventilate and dry infested areas. Use a household formulation (or dust) of malathion on shelves. Pyrethrin and rotenone insecticides are also recommended.

BOOKS

Books require occasional dusting—gentle dusting. Never try to clean them by banging them together. The dusting brush of your vacuum cleaner is a good tool, or run a soft brush (like a shaving brush) along the top edge, holding the book firmly by the front edges to keep dust from being driven right back into it.

Stack oversized books flat, since they may not support their own weight. All others should stand upright, straight up, not leaning at angles, but loose enough on the shelf so you won't damage the bindings when you remove them.

A book's enemies are too much dry heat, which damages leather-backed books and makes the bindings of clothbound books brittle, and dampness, which can cause mildew or small brown spots (foxing).

BOOTS See Shoes.

BORAX Borax is an alkali of moderate strength, good for cleaning woodwork, walls, and sinks. It is poisonous and irritates skin and eyes.

BOTTLES, BABY See Glassware.

BOTTLES, THERMOS See Thermos.

BRASS An alloy of copper and zinc that may also contain other elements, brass is easily shaped into ornamental forms. The color varies from almost white to bronze. It is corrosion-resistant, but will tarnish over time.

To Clean

Glass Wax can help prevent tarnish on brass.

Shiny: Use a commercial metal cleaner made for brass. (Brasso). Test on an inconspicuous spot before using. If too harsh, see Antique, below.

Lacquered: Brass that has been lacquered for protection against corrosion and tarnish should not be polished, soaked, or washed

To polish a brass doorknob without removing the entire lock from the door, cut a hole the size of the fixture flange in a piece of cardboard. Hold shield in place with strips of double-faced adhesive and the polishing can be done without soiling the area around the knob.

in hot water. Just dust with a soft cloth. Or stick with lukewarm sudsy water, rinse with tepid water, and dry. To remove damaged lacquer rub with a soft cloth dipped in denatured alcohol.

Antique: Test before using any polish on antique brass. Some polishes remove the desirable mellowness of age. You may wish to try the recipe from the Cooperative Extension Services of the Northeastern States.

Polish for Soft Finish: Make a paste of fine whiting or rotten-stone and boiled linseed oil. Caution: Purchase boiled linseed oil at paint or hardware store—do not boil it yourself.

Wash brass in hot soapy water. Wipe on paste with a soft cloth. Rub to remove light tarnish. Polish with a soft, dry cloth, frequently changing the cleaning surface of the cloth.

BRICK

Brick tends to be porous, so grease, grime, ashes, and dust can give rise to occasional cleaning problems.

To clean, remove loose dust, ashes, and soil with the dust brush attachment on your vacuum cleaner. Grease and smoke stains can be removed or reduced by scrubbing with a solution of 1 cup detergent-based liquid household cleaner to 1 quart water. Too much detergent will leave a filmy residue on the brick that is difficult to rinse off. Rinse with clear water.

For hard to remove stains, try a mixture of trisodium phosphate (available at hardware stores). Follow manufacturer's instructions. Muriatic acid can also be used, but with extreme caution—or better yet, by a professional.

BROCADES, EMBROIDERIES, LACES

Brocades may be made of any yarns, including genuine gold and silver threads. Content determines care! But one rule applies for all these decorative materials: to preserve their prominent raised designs, always press on the wrong side and use steam with care. (A dry iron may be best.)

BRONZE   Bronze is a very hard, acid-resistant alloy found in art objects as well as machine parts. It is sometimes confused with brass because of color similarities.

To clean, dust often with a clean, soft cloth, so dirt won't settle into the applied surface. Use a small paint brush or soft toothbrush to clean crevices. Wash with a mixture of salt water (3 tablespoons salt to 10 quarts water). Rub lightly.

Lacquered bronze may be washed in lukewarm soapy water, rinsed, and dried.

A professional should be engaged to clean and restore heavily soiled or crusted bronze pieces.

BRUSHES AND BROOMS   All brooms should be washed with plain water periodically, if only to keep the fibers flexible, as well as to clean them. Always store with the head up, so as not to bend the fibers.

All household brushes, likewise, should be rinsed before you store them—always bristle side up.

Nylon bristle brushes are ideal for kitchen use because they can stand very hot water. An executive in the brush manufacturing business, Joyce Libman, vice-president of The Libman Company, notes that brooms and brushes with polypropylene bristles also have their special uses: since they can't be damaged by harsh chemicals, they are ideal for toilet bowl cleaning, applying cement sealer and roofing compounds, etc.

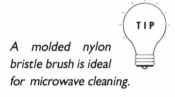

A molded nylon bristle brush is ideal for microwave cleaning.

Paint Brushes

Rule No. 1 is to clean a paintbrush immediately after use. If you're interrupted for just a short time, leave the brush in the paint. For a longer period, protect it from air by wrapping it in a double thickness of aluminum foil or plastic, twisting this tight around the handle. Soak the brush in water if you're using a water-based paint.

Soak it in turpentine, mineral spirits, or thinner if you're working with oil paint.

To clean when you're through painting, first remove excess paint with a scraper, then place the brush in turpentine, mineral spirits, or thinner for oil-based paint, water for water-based paint. Work it against the bottom of the container as it soaks, squeezing the bristles between thumb and forefinger to loosen paint in the center of the brush, brushing it on newspapers to work off paint.

Then wash the brush with powdered soap, liquid detergent, or cleaning powder and rinse well. Finally, let it dry, wrap it in foil, and store it on its side or hang it up.

If you are using a paint roller, remove the roller from its handle and follow the same procedure. Hang the roller; do not lay it on its end or nap.

Hairbrushes

Soak for a few minutes in a solution of baking soda and warm water, swish around in solution, rinse under running water and air dry. Or fill a basin with 1 tablespoon detergent, $\frac{1}{2}$ cup borax and warm water, swish around, rinse, and dry.

BURNS   See Carpet Troubleshooters; Cookware (under the type of utensil damaged); Wood Floor Troubleshooters (Cigarette Burns); Master Stain Removal Section (Scorch).

BUTCHER BLOCK/ CHOPPING BLOCK   Wood is porous and will warp or crack if exposed to excessive moisture. However, sanitation demands that wood surfaces used for food preparation be kept clean.

Clean chopping blocks after each use with a nylon scrubber dipped in detergent and hot water. Rinse well and dry immediately and thoroughly.

To remove stains and disinfect, wipe with a mild solution of chlorine bleach and water, rinse, and dry.

Odors can be removed by rubbing with a slice of lemon wrapped in cheesecloth or gauze. Or sprinkle the board with baking soda and rub with a damp sponge. Rinse with clear water and dry.

To preserve the wood, apply a coat of mineral oil to the surface, let it stand for five minutes or so, then rub with a soft lint-free cloth. If dry areas appear, repeat the process. Several thin coats of oil will give better results than a single heavy coat.

BUTTER STAINS See Carpet Stain Removal Guide; Master Stain Removal Section (Grease).

CALCIMINE   Calcimine is a water-based wall finish, much like whitewash, that cannot be cleaned. When dingy, remove it, and refinish the surface.

CAMEL HAIR   The wool-like underhair of the Bactrian camel of Asia makes fine soft fabrics. All-camel hair fabrics are expensive and not too common. Many combine camel hair with wool. Dry-clean. See Wool.

CAN OPENERS   Electric can openers manufactured within the last eight to ten years generally have removable cutting blades to make cleaning easier. Remember to unplug before cleaning.

To clean the blade, remove it, and soak in hot soapy water or place in the top rack of the dishwasher. Wash the magnetic lid holder with a detergent-soaked toothbrush, handling it carefully if it is attached to the cutting blade.

Brush metal filings off the cutting wheel, and the small ledge beneath it, with a dry toothbrush. Then scrub the wheel with detergent and water.

Wipe the plastic housing with a damp sponge dipped in detergent or a liquid cleaner.

CANDLES   To clean: Wipe with denatured alcohol.

To control dripping: Keep candles in the refrigerator if you would like them to drip less.

To cope with wax residue: Spray with no-stick cooking spray. Or apply a dab of petroleum jelly to the inside of candle holders so that wax will be easy to remove.

CANDLEWAX STAINS   See Carpet Stain Removal Guide; Furniture Troubleshooters; Master Stain Removal Section.

CANDLEWICK   See Chenille.

CANDY (SUGAR) STAINS   See Carpet Stain Removal Guide.

CANE   See Wicker.

CARBON PAPER STAINS   See Master Stain Removal Section.

CARPET BEETLES   See Moths.

CARPET CARE   See Mini Manual on next page.

CASHMERE   The downy hair of the Kashmir goat is usually blended with fibers, except in sweaters. The fabrics, soft and beautiful but delicate, cannot take hard wear and are susceptible to abrasion. Observe care labels. Unless the fabric is preshrunk, shrinkage may occur when you wash or dry-clean it at home. Always dry soft wool knitware at room temperature. Follow care labels on imitation cashmere. For washable cashmeres, see Wool.

CAST IRON   See Cookware (Cast Iron).

CATSUP STAINS   See Carpet Stain Removal Guide; Master Stain Removal Section.

Carpet Care

A MINI MANUAL

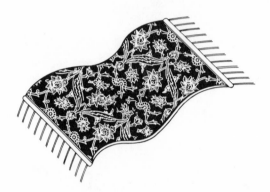

Weekly vacuuming should suffice, unless you have some very heavy traffic areas.

Weekly vacuuming *is* important, however. According to the Hoover Company, "A carpet can hold its own weight in dirt and still appear clean." That not only does terrible things to the way carpets eventually look and wear, but means that the trapped dirt can be spread around as people and pets stir it up—and keep your room from looking as clean as it deserves.

Rotate area rugs and relocate furniture occasionally to prevent uneven wear.

You can never over-vacuum a carpet. Be slow and thorough and pay attention to the carpeted areas under furniture.

The vacuum cleaner crevice tool helps in corners, and you'll be using it for upholstery anyway.

If your kitchen or bath is carpeted, you may need to deodorize and disinfect the carpeting from time to time. Use a spray (Lysol) to disinfect and a deodorizer formulated to cope with carpet odors.

To absorb carpet odors sprinkle with baking soda, wait fifteen minutes, and vacuum. For problem odors let baking soda remain overnight, then vacuum. Use only on dry carpet, test for colorfastness.

CARPET SHAMPOOS
(Do-It-Yourself)

Carpets may be cleaned professionally or you can attempt the job yourself by renting a carpet-cleaning machine. If you choose to do it yourself, follow the carpet manufacturer's recommendations on the cleaning solution and method of operation.

Shampoo strategy: Don't allow the floor to become too wet. Moisture will damage the carpet backing. Moisture will damage the floor beneath.

Before you begin

1. Test the detergent. Pour a little on a plate, wait until it dries. If the residue feels tacky or greasy, it may well remain that way on your carpet and can act as an adhesive, causing the carpet to resoil very quickly.

2. Check carpet seams. Shampoo brushes can catch in loose seams and distort or damage your carpet. Poor seams need professional repair.

3. Look for pulled yarn. Cleaning brushes can pull loose yarn ends higher than the level of the carpet and cause the carpet to run. Clip uneven yarn pulls before you begin.

4. Check carpet edges. Carpet should be securely tacked down. Loose carpet can be pulled, distorted and damaged by the cleaning machine.

5. If your carpet is wool, select a cleaning product recommended for wool.

When you shampoo carpet, hang long draperies out of the way on a wire coat hanger suspended from the drapery rods.

Carpet Stain Removal

Most carpets today are nylon, and a prompt, quick swipe with a damp cloth can be the easy answer to many stains.

If you have a serious staining problem, the stain as well as the stain-removal solvent can soak through the carpet into the backing. The trick is to use as little solvent as possible (even when it's just water) and blot both stain and solvent until all moisture is absorbed.

Some household chemicals can cause permanent stains on carpets. They include: acne medicines, bleaches, medicine, insecticides, and liquid plant food. Use them all with caution.

They may be responsible for those "mystery spots" that turn up. (What has actually caused the mystery is the delayed staining from a spill that occurred a day or even a week or two ago.)

CARPET STAIN REMOVAL GUIDE

Directions

Pretest spot or stain removal treatment on an inconspicuous area of the carpet.

Use caution: some chemicals when used in combination can damage carpet. Do not apply solutions directly to the carpet—use a clean white paper towel. Never wet the carpet through to the backing.

If more than one stain treatment procedure is suggested, try the second only if the first does not remove the stain.

Group A
asphalt
butter
furniture polish (grease)
ink: ballpoint
lipstick
mascara
paint: oil
tar

1. Apply a commercial spot remover (Carbona) to a dampened towel and blot stain. Repeat if necessary.

2. Apply water with a dampened towel, blot up moisture with layers of white paper towels.

Group B
India ink
marking pen
shoe polish

1. Follow directions for Group A.

2. Apply a detergent solution of 1 teaspoon dishwashing detergent to 1 cup warm water with a damp towel. Leave five minutes and blot.

3. Apply a solution of 4 tablespoons hydrogen peroxide to 1 tablespoon sudsy ammonia. Apply undiluted white vinegar with a damp white paper towel (to neutralize ammonia). Blot, absorb with weighted white paper towels.

Group C
Mercurochrome
Merthiolate
dyes
red wine

Scrape or blot excess stain. Follow directions for Group B—beginning with Step 2.

Group D
beer
candy (sugar)
chocolate
glue (white)
ice cream
mayonnaise
milk
mud
paint (latex)
wine (white)

1. Scrape or blot excess stain. Apply a detergent solution of 1 teaspoon dishwashing detergent to 1 cup warm water with a damp towel and blot up stain. Repeat if necessary.

2. Apply undiluted, sudsy ammonia with a damp towel. Blot with white vinegar on a damp towel.

3. Apply water with a damp sponge, blot up moisture with layers of weighted white paper towels.

Group E
berries
coffee
alcohol
tea

1. Follow directions for Group D. Let stand five minutes and blot excess moisture with weighted white paper towels.

2. Apply 4 tablespoons hydrogen peroxide to 1 tablespoon sudsy ammonia with a damp paper towel. Let stand thirty minutes under weighted white paper towels. Repeat until stain removal is complete. Apply white vinegar, blot up moisture with weighted white paper towels.

Group F
candle wax

Scrape excess wax with a dull knife.
Cover stain with brown paper and apply a warm iron to melt and absorb wax residue.

Group G
feces
vomit

1. Scrape or blot excess stain. Apply dry baking soda to absorb residue; vacuum. Apply water with a damp sponge to remove excess baking soda.

2. Unless you are working on wool, apply a solution of 1 teaspoon enzyme pre-soak (Axion, Biz) to 1 cup warm water with a damp towel. Rinse with water-dampened sponge, blot up moisture with weighted white paper towels.

Group H
ketchup
fruit juice
fruit drinks
mustard
pet food
soft drinks

1. Follow directions for Group G.

2. Follow directions for Group B.

3. Follow directions for Group E—starting with Step 2.

Group I
cooking oil

1. Follow directions for Group A.

2. Follow directions for Group G.

Group J
foundation (makeup)
unknown stains

1. Follow directions for Group A.

2. Follow directions for Group D.

Group K
nail polish

Apply a nonoily nailpolish remover with a cotton swab. Push softened nail polish to the center of the stain with a clean towel and pick up the residue. Repeat.

URINE STAINS: A SPECIAL PROBLEM

Most urine stains can be removed or reduced if you go to work on them immediately. According to the Carpet and Rug Institute, the degree of success depends on urine content, the dye in the carpet, and the time lapse between your removal attempt and when the staining occurred.

To Remove:

1. Blot excess liquid with white paper towels.

2. Flush stained area with clear water and absorb with paper towels till dry.

3. Apply a solution of 1 teaspoon detergent to 1 cup water; work into carpet pile.

4. Absorb with layers of white paper towels and flush with water.

5. Absorb with weighted white paper towels till dry.

If some stain still remains, apply a solution of equal parts white vinegar and water, let stand five minutes. Absorb dry. Place a new layer of white paper towels over the area and weigh down with a heavy object. Replace towels as often as necessary until moisture is removed. Urine that is not removed can produce a reaction stain later.

If urine has caused a loss of color, the area may have to be professionally dyed, or cut out and replaced.

Neutralize urine odors by dampening the affected spot and sprinkling borax over it. Rub in borax, let dry, and vacuum or brush to remove the dried borax.

CARPET TROUBLESHOOTERS

These cope with problems other than dirt and stains.

Fading: All carpets lose some color over time. Fading can be reduced or delayed by (1) frequent laundering, (2) changing air filters in heating and air conditioning systems, (3) use of a dehumidifier to reduce high humidity, and (4) limiting exposure to direct sunlight.

Shedding: This is normal in cut pile. Vacuuming eventually removes the loose fibers with no harm to the carpet. Shedding may also occur after professional cleaning.

Buckles and puckers: Ripples that develop after a while may be caused by (1) dampness between carpet and floor, the result of high humidity, (2) distortion caused by low-density padding, or (3) poor installation. Have the carpet restretched by a professional carpet installer.

Pulling or wheeling heavy items over carpets may also stretch the carpet and produce ripples. These stretch marks are harder to remove. Protect your carpet with a board when moving heavy items.

Corn rows: These generally occur in the high traffic paths of thick carpet. Persistent vacuuming in the same direction can cause them. To remove, brush with a pet-grooming tool and vacuum with a beater-bar cleaner, frequently varying the cleaning strokes of the vacuum.

Good underpadding increases the life of your carpet.

Footprints in deep pile carpets. Remove them temporarily with a pet-grooming brush and a vacuum with a beater-bar brush.

Shading is normal. It is caused by light reflecting off the carpet tufts and is considered an artistic touch, not a defect.

Pile crushing, usually a compacting with use, can be removed or minimized by brushing the carpet in the opposite direction from the way the pile lies. Vacuum with a beater-bar cleaner.

Pilling: Carefully scissor off these small balls of tangled fiber and lint.

Dents are usually caused by heavy furniture. Relocate the furniture occasionally. Brush dented area with a pet-grooming tool.

To remove, steam the dented area. Hold an iron a few inches from the carpet, then brush tufts up with fingertips. Do not allow the iron to touch the carpet.

Sprouts are tufts that stick up higher than the rest of the pile. Clip with scissors.

Snags are caused by tufts pulled from the carpet. Clip off with scissors. Do not yank—you may cause a long run. Your carpet dealer may be able to have the tufts retufted or reglued.

Burns: The charred tips of lightly burned carpet fibers can be clipped carefully with fingernail scissors. A deep burn needs professional repair.

Fuzzing, most often occurring in older loop pile carpeting, is caused by embedded soil and grit. Clip off the fuzzed fibers. Fuzzing can be reduced by more frequent vacuuming.

Static: Some carpet has static protection built in. To reduce static, (1) increase room humidity, (2) apply temporary antistatic treatment (see your carpet retailer), and (3) shampoo periodically.

Mildew preys on natural-fiber carpets and rugs. Mildew damage (dry rot) can remove up to 90 percent of a natural fiber's strength in as little as two weeks. Mildew can be detected by a musty odor, and the best chance of eliminating it is to stop its growth.

1. Use a dehumidifier to reduce the moisture in the air.

2. Open windows and use a fan to circulate air over the entire carpet.

3. Allow artificial light and sunlight to shine on the carpet. If you live in an area subject to mildew, consider carpets of man-made fibers.

For more information, see Mildew.

CEILINGS   See Walls.

CEMENT, UNTREATED   Basements and playrooms (interior floors) should be vacuumed, then scrubbed with a scrub brush or stiff broom, using hot water and scouring powder or heavy-duty detergent. Rinse and let dry. Exterior floors (patios, porches, garages) should be swept before scrubbing and hosed off for the final rinse. Add a coat of liquid wax to repel soil and reduce dust.

Stains

Greasy stains are hard to remove completely. The best way is to absorb as much of the residue as possible. Use an absorbent like kitty litter or fuller's earth and lime. Sprinkle over the stain, and let it remain a few hours or overnight. Sweep absorbent into a dustpan to remove. Then scrub the stain as above. If the stain remains, try applying dishwashing detergent directly to the stain. Let the detergent stand for fifteen minutes or so. Rinse with boiling water.

CEMENT GROUT   See Grout.

CENTIPEDES AND MILLIPEDES   These many-legged wormlike insects feed on other insects—cockroaches, flies, spiders, moths, etc. Best leave them alone unless they are a definite nuisance. Direct spray from a household insect bomb will kill individual insects. Propoxur, diazinon, malathion, or carbaryl sprays are effective pesticides.

CERAMIC COOKTOPS   See Cooktops.

CERAMIC TILE   See Tile, Ceramic; Tile Floors.

CEREAL PESTS   See Pantry Pests.

CHAMOIS   Wash with warm soapy water. (Detergents affect the natural oils in the skin.) Rinse well in clean water, squeeze (don't wring) out excess water, and dry away from heat and sunlight. Rub dry chamois against itself to soften it.

CHANDELIERS   Chandeliers are gorgeous, but they can be a lot of hard, tedious work to maintain. To limit the task of cleaning them to every six months or so, dust them weekly with a clean soft cloth.

The safest way to clean a chandelier is to move your dining table out of the way, and lay a drop cloth or plastic tablecloth on the floor beneath the fixture.

Use a step stool to reach the fixture. You may also use a five-foot painter's ladder. The paint can tray will hold your cleaning solution, and you won't have so much climbing to do.

To clean

Remove any glass globes and crystals that can be detached from the chandelier and soak them in a plastic dishpan filled with hot water and ammonia with a tablespoon or two of white vinegar added. Wipe each piece clean, rinse in clear water, and dry with a lint-free towel. Place the pieces on a soft towel until you are ready to reinstall them.

If the rest of the chandelier still attached to the ceiling is glass, use the same cleaning solution as above. Wipe it clean, then rinse with a dampened paper towel and dry. If the remaining portion of the fixture is metal, use an appropriate metal polish and buff

TROUBLE SHOOTER

While cleaning, always move the stool around the fixture. Don't turn the chandelier. If you turn it as you clean or dust it, the ballast will unscrew from the electric box in the ceiling and the chandelier will fall.

TIP

Wear rubber gloves to prevent soapy glass pieces from slipping out of your hands.

to shine. If glass cleaner should come in contact with the metal, wipe it off immediately. For more information about metal cleaners, check Brass, Copper, Chrome, etc.

Many professional house cleaning services also clean chandeliers (see your Yellow Pages).

CHENILLE

Chenille loungewear, rugs, or bedspreads should be given a short gentle wash, then regular rinse and spin cycles, with fabric softener in the last rinse. Pile fabric items, like chenille, should be cleaned inside out.

They are lintmakers, so keep them separate from other laundry items.

A dryer helps to fluff up chenille items, but remove them while still slightly damp. Shake and brush. If you line dry chenille, you will achieve fluffier tufts if you hang the item wrong side out so the tufts rub against each other in the wind.

Do not iron.

CHEWING GUM RESIDUE

See Carpet Stain Removal Guide; Grout Stain Removal Guide; Wood Floor Troubleshooters; Master Stain Removal Section.

CHIMNEYS

If you heat with a wood stove, your chimney will need cleaning at least once a year, and possibly as often as once every two months, says the National Chimney Sweep Guild. Wood stove fires will build up a tarry deposit in your chimney—not just the soot that fires in an open fireplace produce.

As for your fireplace chimney, it demands less frequent cleaning, depending on how much you use it. One well-accepted rule is that the chimney doesn't need cleaning until the creosote deposit reaches an eighth to a quarter of an inch.

Many authorities recommend a professional checkup and

professional cleaning as far better, cleaner, and safer than do-it-yourself efforts.

You can locate professionals in the Yellow Pages under "Chimney cleaners." Note that some are certified by the National Chimney Sweep Guild.

CHINA AND EARTHENWARE

China can go into the dishwasher. Remember, it's the water that moves, not the dishes. If your china is heat-sensitive, put it in the top rack.

If you're unsure that it's dishwasher safe, hand wash it, using a dishpan or a rubber mat on the bottom of the sink to cushion against breakage.

Prevent staining by rinsing items like coffee and tea cups directly after they're used. Some foods injure china if allowed to remain in it for long periods. Protect china from extreme heat or cold, and don't use good china for food storage.

Tips on fine china

When you stack it, use a paper napkin or cloth between plates to keep the unglazed underside of one from scratching the glazed surface of the one beneath. Don't hang fine china cups on hooks. Wire hangers can damage the rims of platters.

As china ages, the glaze may wear and crazing, a network of fine cracks, may develop. There is no cure for this, but you may be able to minimize the stained appearance by soaking the china for a day or two in a strong bleach solution.

Earthenware is more porous than china, so it is more likely to chip or crack.

TIP

To remove the film of glue that remains from store labels on vases and other decorative containers, first remove any paper that sticks to the glue with a small brush. Then cover the area with transparent tape and the sticky film comes off neatly.

TIP

An equal mixture of salt and white vinegar will clean coffee and tea stains from china cups.

CHINTZ

This is a glazed cotton fabric, characteristically printed with a floral design. Wax and starch glazes will wash out in laundering. If the glaze is a resin finish, it should last through washing or dry cleaning. Iron on the right side. Unglazed chintz is called cretonne.

CHLORINE BLEACH   See Bleaches; Laundry Mini Manual; Laundry Aids.

CHOCOLATE STAINS   See Carpet Stain Removal Guide; Master Stain Removal Section.

CHOPPING BLOCK   See Butcher Block.

CHROME   Also known as chromium, this is an extremely hard metal commonly used as an applied finish on appliances, utensils, backsplash panels, and handles of major appliances. You'll find it also on oven and refrigerator racks.

Although it cleans well, the highly polished surface is easily scratched, can be discolored by high heat, and is subject to etching by strong oven cleaners.

To clean

Wipe with a commercial liquid glass cleaner or denatured alcohol or a damp sponge sprinkled with baking soda. Do not use abrasive cleaners or steel wool, which will scratch the highly polished finish. For general cleaning, wash with detergent and water, rinse, and polish dry. Commercial polish is available.

Chrome Plumbing Fixtures: When mineral deposits clog shower heads, remove the heads and soak in a pan, with enough white vinegar to cover them. Rinse with cold water.

CIRÉ   This wet-look finish is a glaze achieved by slightly melting a man-made fiber, like nylon, to create a shiny surface and increase water repellency.

CLAY COOKERS, UNGLAZED

An unglazed clay cooker is a highly porous terra cotta earthenware vessel. When heated, water-soaked clay absorbs moisture and releases it as steam.

Clay cookers should be cooled to room temperature before cleaning. Then wash the cooker with a solution of baking soda or salt mixed with hot water. Scrub with a stiff brush. Dry before storing.

Do not wash unglazed clay cookers with soap, detergent, or cleansers. These cleaning items are absorbed into the porous surface of the clay.

CLOSETS

If you shut closet doors to keep dirt out, you may find closets need very infrequent cleaning. In any case, if you vacuum or sweep the closet floor when you clean a room, always then shut the door.

Here are hints for closet-cleaning, if you tackle this as a job marking the change of seasons:

1. Take out all the clothes and sort them into four piles: those to be washed or dry-cleaned; those to be fixed; those to be given away; those to throw away.

2. Brush the closet walls with a cloth-covered broom (fasten the cloth with a safety pin so it won't slide off). Or, if it is not too awkward, use your vacuum cleaner, since it does a superior job of picking up insect larvae.

3. Then, with the cloth off, sweep the floor with the bare broom. (Or vacuum.)

4. Arm yourself with two buckets and two cloths: with the one cloth and a bucket of warm sudsy water, wash shelves, woodwork, and clothes rod. Rinse with a clean cloth dampened from the second bucket of warm, clear rinse water. Let dry.

5. Wring a cloth out of the sudsy water. Wipe the floor with it.

TIP

If you have trouble cleaning the back walls and corners of deep cabinets, use a long-handled tub-cleaning sponge mop. You can sit or kneel on the floor and scrub away. It is also great for wiping up spots on the kitchen and bathroom floors.

Rinse the floor with a damp clean cloth. Let dry.

Then—clothes go back, with the ones you wear most often in the handiest location. Hats go on the shelves, in boxes. Extra shoes go on racks or in boxes.

CLOTHES DRYER   See Dryer.

COCKROACHES   There are 3,500 different kinds of cockroaches in the world. The German roach (our best known cockroach) hides by day in sheltered dark places and comes out at night to feed. The Asian cockroach, which arrived in Florida a few years ago, threatens to invade the East Coast up to New York, plus the states that rim the Gulf Coast, Mexico, and the Pacific. The Asian cockroach flies and likes light.

All cockroaches contaminate food and utensils, spread filth, and give off an unpleasant odor. And all eat almost anything: food, of course; they also chew bookbindings, stamps, paper, and even starched clothing.

Good housekeeping is your first defense against roaches. Kitchen cleanup is essential. So is vacuuming, which can remove cockroach eggs that aren't killed by chemicals. But even the best housekeepers are plagued with roaches—they come in on grocery bags and firewood, find their way through cracks in screens and doors, through the spaces around pipes, etc.

Your second best defense is repairing leaks; sealing openings where pipes or wires pass through walls, floors, or ceilings; caulking cracks in walls, window sills, and foundations; maintaining tight-fitting doors and windows.

Third, use insecticides. Effective ones contain chlorpyrifos (Dursban), diazinon, dichlorvos (DDVP, Vapona), malathion (household grade), propoxur (Baygon), and pyrethrins. To these, some manufacturers are adding ingredients that alter the growth and breeding patterns of the roach—less toxic "birth control" products. One of the first manufacturers to combine a conventional insecticide with a hormonal ingredient claimed that this "one-two" punch could knock out roaches virtually overnight, with roach-free protection for up to four months.

Boric acid has long been a housekeeper's favorite because it isn't as toxic as other insecticides. You simply apply a thin film of boric acid dust at a 99 percent concentration to roach hideouts or runways. As the cockroaches walk over the dust they pick it up on their antennae, legs, and feet; ingest the dust when they groom themselves; and die three to ten days later. A thorough job of boric acid dusting takes time and effort, but it pays off. The U. S. Environmental Protection Agency estimates that the treatment can be effective for six months to two years, and uses the system in its own Washington, D.C., offices.

Boric acid is about as toxic as aspirin and dangerous only if taken in huge amounts. But the EPA warns against mixing it with sugar, grease, or shortening, since these concoctions attract cats, dogs, and kids as well as roaches. Such a mixture also reduces the concentration and efficacy of the boric acid. You are also advised to keep boric acid off houseplants.

Cockroach bait trays are popular since they are very easy to use, they are sealed to prevent children and pets from readily coming in contact with the poison, and they are safe to use around food. They come with the claim that you will see noticeable results within a week, and a roach-free environment for several months.

Cockroach traps are also available.

Precautions: If you use roach spray, don't let children or pets near treated surfaces until spray has dried. Follow label instructions. Don't contaminate food, water, dishes, utensils, or countertops where you prepare food. If you treat shelves containing food or dishes, cover them with shelf paper before replacing the contents.

If roaches are a persistent problem, you should use professional pest control, although this alone is unlikely to banish these pests.

COCOA STAINS

See Carpet Stain Removal Guide; Master Stain Removal Section (Chocolate).

COFFEE MAKER, AUTOMATIC DRIP

Wash the carafe, lid, and basket in detergent and water, by hand, or in the upper rack of the dishwasher. Machine-washing may fade the plastic parts. Polish with a soft dry cloth to restore the color.

Once a month, flush out mineral deposits with a solution of $1/4$ cup white vinegar, adding enough cold water to reach the fill line in the water tank. Slide the basket with a paper filter into place. Switch the coffeemaker to the ON or "brew/warm" setting. When the carafe is half-full, switch to off and pour liquid back into the water tank. Let the liquid cool fifteen minutes and run through the drip cycle again. Discard solution, wash, and dry.

Never use abrasives or metal scouring pads.

TIP

To keep the coffee grounds out of the brew, place your finger or a sewing thimble over the stem when filling.

COFFEE MAKER, PERCOLATOR

Disconnect the percolator before cleaning. Wash the inside and the basket after each use with hot soapy water. Take care not to immerse the electric terminal in water. A narrow brush or pipe cleaner is handy to clean the spout, stem, and water-level gauge.

To eliminate hard-water deposits and stale odors in aluminum coffee makers, clean the inside of the pot monthly. Use a solution of 6 cups water to 1 tablespoon of white vinegar or baking soda or cream of tartar. Percolate for ten minutes and rinse clean.

For stainless steel and glass percolators, fill the pot with water and add 1 teaspoon borax for each cup. Perk this mixture for a few minutes and let stand for twenty minutes. (Do not use borax on aluminum, which it may darken.)

Troubleshooter

If the percolator doesn't operate, unplug and reseat the stem into the pot. If it still won't work, remove the stem and clean according to the tips above.

COFFEE STAINS See Carpet Stain Removal Guide; Grout Stain Removal Guide; Master Stain Removal Section.

COLOR REMOVER The most readily available form of color remover is the chemical hydrosulfite, a packaged product designed to remove color (or stains) from washable fabrics that can tolerate hot water. The package instructions are detailed and specific, for both a washer method to whiten dingy whites, and a range-top method with water hot enough to remove dyes (generally in preparation for redyeing).

The products work best on cotton and rayon. They are not recommended for fabrics that won't wash, nor for glass or metal fibers. Wool should not be subjected to water hotter than tap water (140° F/60° C) and care instructions should be observed on other fabrics, including nylon and other synthetics. You must not use or store color remover in metal containers.

These products are all eye irritants and harmful if swallowed.

CAUTION

Package instructions also cover first aid procedures. Keep them and observe them carefully.

COMFORTERS More and more of today's comforters are designed for easy care. Popular fillers like polyester fiberfill and down are machine-washable. So is cotton batting, though it can be lumpy, and thus harder to handle. Polyester fiberfill dries fastest. Many come with zipper covers, enabling you to skip frequent cleaning of the comforter itself.

The shell fabric determines whether the comforter should be machine-washed and dried or dry-cleaned. You are best advised to follow the care label directions, which take this into account, along with the fact that home equipment can't always cope with such bulky items.

You can have worn comforters refurbished. Repair services will save your old down, adding more if necessary, and also clean and repair covers, or provide new ones.

For further information on handling items of like construction, see Down Coats and Vests and other Quilted listings.

COMPACT DISCS   The Electronic Industries Association says that, if compact discs are handled and stored properly, they will theoretically last forever.

Their pattern of microscopic pits, protected by a coat of plastic, is read by a very low-powered laser beam located inside the compact disc player. Since the playing surface thus never comes in contact with a solid object, like a phonograph stylus, there is no wear or distortion.

Care

Do not finger the playing surface. Store compact discs in their containers when not in use.

To Clean

Remove dust and fingerprints with a clean, soft lint-free cloth dipped sparingly in denatured alcohol. Wipe with straight strokes from the center of the disc to the edge. Do not use a circular motion.

Never use a solvent or abrasive cleaner. If you have a disc collection, you may want to invest in one of the cassette disc cleaning kits.

COMPUTERS   The best care for your computer is to protect it.

Cover keyboard and disk drives with a static-free dust cover when not in use.

Avoid static discharge. If your computer is in a carpeted area, purchase an antistatic mat or antistatic spray for the carpet. Discharge your own static electricity by touching something metal before touching the computer.

Clean environment. Computers are allergic to smoke, excessive heat, humidity, and dust. Make sure there is free air circulation around the unit to avoid heat build-up. (Be sure you don't block the air vents.)

To clean, dust keyboard weekly with a lint-free cloth or the soft brush attachment of your vacuum cleaner. If necessary, spray the cloth with an antistatic cleaner available from your dealer. Disk-head cleaning kits are available for cleaning disk drives.

CONCRETE

See Cement, Floors.

COOKTOPS, GLASS CERAMIC

An electric cooking unit with a ceramic (pyroceram) cooking surface is not only durable but highly resistant to thermal and impact shocks.

To clean

The best strategy is to use the cleaner recommended by the manufacturer. However, a very mild abrasive cleanser works well. Wipe the entire unit after each use, taking up food spatters while the cooktop is still warm (not hot).

Stains. Even though the surface is stain-resistant, it may not be stain-proof. Certain foods can cause discoloration when the unit is heated. If you use the top as counter space or for food preparation, wipe it clean before turning on the heating elements. The outside surface of cookware should be clean and dry before it goes on the cooktop. The mineral content of the water in some areas can cause staining problems. Zud has been recommended by a few manufacturers to remove stains. But check use and care book.

COOKWARE   See Mini Manual on next page.

COPPER   An expensive metal used as a finish or base material, copper turns up in home plumbing or wiring systems, as the base for cookware, or as a finish on stainless steel. It is an excellent conductor of heat and electricity, gives a high luster when polished, but tarnishes readily.

To clean

Shiny: Use a commercial copper cleaner, purchased at grocery or hardware stores. Test before cleaning the entire item.

Soft: See cleaner recipe under Brass, antique.

Lacquered: Newer decorative copper accessories may be lacquered to ward off tarnish. Do not polish or clean lacquered copper with hot water or abrasive cleaning products. Simply wash with tepid, soapy water, rinse, and dry. If lacquer finish deteriorates, and you want to remove it, rub with a soft cloth dipped in denatured alcohol. This leaves the copper unprotected, and polishing will be needed after lacquer is removed.

Green rust is a copper carbonate that is the result of corrosion. A piece of lemon dipped in salt (or hot vinegar with salt) will clean it. Buttermilk is another old-fashioned remedy. Wash and dry immediately after treatment.

Storing copperware: If you put some utensils to infrequent use, you might try a home-grown polish saver. After polishing decorative copper, give it a good coating of hairspray. This will preserve the shine for a long time. Just wash it off when the time comes for repolishing.

COPPER POTS   See Cookware (Copper).

Cookware

A MINI MANUAL

Whether you are using a sparkling new set of cookware or grandmother's favorite cast-iron skillet, a small amount of knowhow and an even smaller amount of effort will extend the life and attractiveness of your cookware.

ALUMINUM

Lightweight yet sturdy aluminum pans are excellent conductors of heat, and most are manufactured in one piece, eliminating seams and hard-to-clean crevices.

Thickness or gauge determines the quality (and cost) of aluminum utensils. The smaller the gauge number (8), the thicker the aluminum. The larger the gauge (20), the thinner the aluminum. Thin gauge aluminum may warp or dent.

Care

Wash new aluminum utensils before using for the first time to remove manufacturing oils.

To eliminate water spots, dry immediately after washing.

Undissolved salt or acid produces pitting. To prevent, bring liquids to a boil before adding salt, then stir to dissolve.

Aluminum stains easily when combined with some minerals found in water and foods.

To remove such stains and discoloration, boil a solution of 3 table-spoons of cream of tartar (or lemon juice or white vinegar) and one quart of water for ten minutes. Lightly scrub with a soap-filled pad.

To prevent such staining, select the wash/natural dry cycle on the dishwasher or wash by hand. (The high heat of the dishwasher dry cycle may increase staining.)

Remove burned-on food by filling the pan with water and simmering until burned particles loosen; scour if necessary, then wash.

Cooking foods containing acid (tomatoes, rhubarb) will remove stains naturally.

Borax, used dry, is a good nonabrasive cleaner. Just rub it on with a damp dishcloth. Rinse thoroughly.

For nonstick finish, see end of this Mini Manual. For anodized aluminum finish, see Aluminum in ABCs.

CAST IRON

The cast-iron cookware of today is a far cry from the cast iron molded into rice bowls by the Chinese nearly three thousand years ago. Naturally finished cast-iron cookware is used for skillets, roasters, Dutch ovens, broilers, griddles, muffin tins, and cornbread pans. Cast iron is excellent for browning, stewing, baking, and frying. Because of its heavy weight, it heats slowly and holds heat well. A good choice for foods needing a long cooking time.

Care

Cast iron is pre-seasoned and should not be washed in strong detergents or scoured.

To prevent rusting, wash in warm sudsy water, rinse, and wipe dry immediately.

 To speed up drying time, use the heat from range or oven.

Coat newly cleaned cookware with unsalted shortening. Before each use, wipe the inside with a paper towel.

 Storing cast-iron utensils with their lids on causes "sweating," which invites rust damage.

To reseason, scour inside thoroughly, wash with soap and water, and dry. Coat with unsalted shortening, heat in a moderate (325° F/163° C) oven for two hours. Wipe off excess grease with a paper towel.

COPPER

Copper is one of the oldest cooking materials known to man. Its uniform heat conductivity distributes heat evenly in range-top cookware. Copper fully deserves its reputation as a "keep-warm" element in a serving dish.

Copper may discolor in direct contact with food. Although such discoloration is not dangerous to health, the cooking surface of copper cookware is therefore usually lined with a stainless, tin, or nonstick finish.

Or copper is sandwiched between layers of stainless steel, to take advantage of its conductivity while minimizing staining problems.

Care

Wash in hot sudsy water, rinse, and polish dry with a soft cloth.

Polish with a paste mixture of flour, salt, lemon juice, and ammonia, or a mixture of flour and vinegar.

Soak off burned-on food with a solution of detergent and water, then polish with a commercial copper cleaner.

 Don't throw away worn tin-lined copperware. It can be "retinned" professionally. This is less expensive than purchasing new utensils.

GLASS AND GLASS/CERAMIC

Glass and glass ceramic are popular materials for today's cook-and-serve utensils. Some heat-resistant glass utensils are strictly for range-top use; others are designed solely for oven use. Glass and glass ceramic ovenware offers such excellent heat retention that you can cut cooking time and reduce oven temperatures by 25° F/14° C.

Care

Glass and glass ceramic baking dishes that go from refrigerator or freezer to the oven should be allowed to warm to room temperature before being placed in a hot oven.

Clean with hot sudsy water by hand or in the dishwasher.

Burned-on foods may be removed by soaking in a detergent solution overnight. To clean burned-on foods from the outside, or rim, immerse the dish in a detergent solution or soak in white vinegar and water, and scrub with a nylon net pad.

Avoid sharp tools and abrasive cleansers or scouring pads.

PLASTIC

Plastic cookware, now the product of space-age technology, is highly resistant to heat and highly durable. All plastic cookware is dishwasher-safe, stain-resistant, and easy to clean. Do not use in conventional ovens. All plastic ware currently on the market is designed for microwave only.

To remove burned-on foods, soak in detergent and water, and scrub with a nylon or plastic pad.

Do not use abrasive cleansers, pads, solvents, or sharp kitchen tools.

Nonstick coated ovenware will go from freezer to microwave to table.

PORCELAIN ON METAL

Porcelain enamel is essentially a highly durable glass used originally as a medium for making fine jewelry. Eventually it became a coating for such utensils as coffee pots, roasting pans, and saucepans, offering an unlimited choice of color and designs. Porcelain enamel cookware is highly scratch- and stain-resistant. It is practically immune to fading, peeling, or chemical damage. If abused, it will chip.

Normal cleaning requires only warm sudsy water or washing in the dishwasher.

Burned-on foods may be removed by either soaking or scrubbing with a nonabrasive cleanser.

Borax is a good nonabrasive dry cleaner. Rub on with a damp cloth and rinse.

For nonstick finish, see end of this Mini Manual.

STAINLESS STEEL

Stainless steel will not tarnish or corrode permanently, and it is highly resistant to wear. Bakeware is usually solid stainless steel. But in range-top utensils, where good heat conduction is required, stainless steel may be combined with conductors like copper, aluminum, or carbon steel.

Care

Wash by hand or in the dishwasher. Prompt drying prevents water spots.

Burned-on foods may be removed by soaking in hot sudsy water and scrubbing with a nylon pad.

Use a commercial stainless-steel cleaner to remove stubborn burns that may stain the inside. This procedure also copes with stains produced by cooking starchy foods like rice, potatoes, and peas, and with color changes caused by high-temperature cooking.

For nonstick finish, see end of this Mini Manual.

TIN

Tin plating dates back to sixteenth-century Germany. Tin-plated steel is both durable and scratch-resistant, and it is still used effectively today, especially for baking.

Very little care is needed for this economical bakeware. Just wash it in warm sudsy water, by hand, or in the dishwasher. Burned-on or crusted-on foods can be removed with soaking or scouring.

NONSTICK FINISHES

These fluorocarbon finishes like Teflon and SilverStone have taken a good deal of drudgery out of the pot washer's life. They require little special care.

High temperatures will cause discoloration of these finishes and shorten their life. Use medium to low heat for cooking.

TIP *If you must use high cooking temperatures, Du Pont recommends pre-heating on medium heat first.*

Use nylon, plastic, wooden, or rubber cooking tools; avoid metal.

Machine- or hand-wash with detergent and hot water. Use plastic mesh pads for spots—not steel wool or coarse scouring pads. Season with a thin coat of cooking oil before reusing.

Stains: To remove stains, mix ½ cup chlorine bleach, 1 tablespoon white vinegar in 1 cup of water. Simmer ten minutes, wash, rinse, and dry.

Or substitute 2 tablespoons of baking soda for vinegar.

For SilverStone, use one of these cleaning methods:

1. Make up a solution of ¼ cup Dip-It to 1 quart of water, and simmer in pan for twenty minutes.

2. Combine 3 tablespoons oxygen bleach (Snowy) with 1 teaspoon liquid dish detergent (Ivory) and 1 cup of water, and simmer in pan for fifteen minutes.

3. Combine 3 tablespoons dishwasher detergent (Cascade) with 1 cup of water and simmer fifteen minutes.

Baking: When baking foods high in sugar or low in fat, grease the nonstick pans lightly. Do not season angel food cake pans.

CORDUROY This napped fabric goes back to the eighteenth century, when servants wore "poor man's velvet" (*cord du roi,* meaning "King's cord"). Made from flax and cotton, it was a durable and economical substitute for the more royal fabric.

Most corduroy today is cotton (or cotton blended with polyester or nylon for even greater durability) and is a cinch to wash, but with the designer corduroys now on the market, and many special finishes, better check the care label.

Washing

Wash inside out to reduce abrasion and to keep lint from adhering to the pile.

You want to forestall wrinkling. So wash and dry in small loads, never wring or twist and use a permanent press cycle on both washer and dryer for cotton/polyester blends. Add a fabric softener to the final rinse to help fluff the pile and make any touch-up ironing easier. Pick a wash-water temperature to suit both the color of the item and the degree of soil.

Drying

Machine-drying restores fluffiness and helps eliminate any need for ironing, but remove items from dryer while they are slightly damp, so as to maintain fluff and prevent wrinkling.

Air dry, then fluff the pile by brushing in one direction.

Ironing

This is rarely needed, but if it is, steam the item, holding the iron slightly above the nap. Or you can press on the wrong side over a terry towel, preferably with a steam iron. Use no pressure, going with the ribs and using a lifting motion. Then brush the pile on the right side to raise it.

TIP

If your corduroy becomes wrinkled, hang it in the bathroom with a roomful of steam for about an hour. Then let it dry. Or blow steam on the garment from your steam iron.

CORK FLOORS See Wood and Cork.

COSMETIC STAINS See Carpet Stain Removal Guide; Master Stain Removal Section.

COTTON Cotton is a favorite around the world. In cool weather the close weaves are quite warm, as are those with flannel or pile construction. In hot, muggy weather cotton's capacity for absorbing moisture makes it cool to wear. That hydrophilic character also keeps cottons free from static cling.

Cottons wear well, don't pill. Most can take severe washing procedures, making the fiber ideal for diapers and other items requiring a truly hot water wash. (All-cotton fabrics can be boiled, if you wish.) When you find "Dry-Clean Only" labels on cottons, says Cotton Incorporated, they are dictated by the trim and construction of the item, its dye content, or findings (i.e., the binding, lining, facing, buttons, ribbons—any materials used in the making or trimming). Many 100 percent cotton fabrics tend to wrinkle in wearing and shrink in washing.

Care of Untreated Cottons

All colorfast cottons wash, and unless they are delicate in weave (chiffons, organdies, e.g.), they machine-wash and dry. Untreated cottons are actually stronger when wet.

You may be pleased to know that pure (untreated) cotton shirts are available, for consumers who don't mind ironing, or have a neighborhood laundry to patronize. If you tackle the job yourself, iron cottons while they're still damp, on either side.

Care of Cotton Blends and Finishes

Cotton's popularity has prompted the textile industry to develop a galaxy of finishes and blends to make it more soil-resistant, fire-retardant, resistant to mildew and to shrinkage.

Once "wash-and-wear" was introduced in the 1950s, promising a "no iron" future, hard-working homemakers demanded more easy-care fabrics, including cottons that might go without ironing. These wash and wear, permanent press, and durable press cottons are important in the market.

In *blends,* just zero in on the fiber that requires the gentlest treatment, and follow those gentle-treatment specifications for washing, drying, and ironing. Polyester/cotton blends are more durable and wrinkle-resistant than most 100 percent cottons.

The *resin finishes* that make cotton wrinkle-resistant also make it wear out more quickly. Use gentler laundry procedures to save on wear. Avoid excessive use of chlorine bleach.

Mercerized cottons (treated with a caustic soda bath to improve cotton's luster and smoothness) are easier to iron and don't pick up soil as readily as other cottons. They require no special care.

There are really very few differences between today's wash-and-wear cottons, and those designated as "permanent press" and "durable press." They are all easy-care fabrics that eliminate most if not all ironing.

Washing/Drying Durable Press Fabrics

Wash with warm water as suggested, with a mild detergent. Use little or no bleach (chlorine may yellow cotton).

Dry with care. The trick to successful handling of these finishes lies in the drying process. "What we most need is a dryer that will unload itself," says one textile scientist. Overdrying increases abrasion. Leaving clothes in the dryer after the dry cycle makes wrinkles.

Pretreat oily stains on durable press fabrics just as you do other wrinkle-resistant, crease-resistant, and soil-release fabrics.

Cottons treated to repel water require thorough rinsing to

TIP

Never wring treated cotton fabric when hand-washing it. Just rinse and hang it to drip-dry, or you'll create wrinkles.

insure that all the soap and detergent is thoroughly flushed out. (Procter & Gamble adds that using a fabric softener, then pressing a garment thoroughly, help maintain water-repellency.)

For care of flame-retardant or water-repellent finishes, note directions under these entries.

Cotton Knits

With machine knits, heed care labels.

Firm knits have dimensional stability, they should hold their shape without blocking. More fragile, loose knits will almost certainly require blocking. Roll them while still wet in a towel to remove excess moisture. Then spread them out flat, shaping them to their original contours, and air dry.

CRAYON STAINS See Wood Floor Troubleshooters; Master Stain Removal Section.

CREAM OF TARTAR This is a mild acid you may have on hand to make frostings and candies and to beat egg whites. It is also handy for sweetening coffee pots and brightening aluminum.

CREAM-BASED FOOD STAINS See Master Stain Removal Section (Dairy).

CREASE-RESISTANT FINISHES See Wrinkle-resistant.

CREPE These fabrics, characteristically crinkled or grainy on the surface, range from lightweight sheers like chiffons to heavy satin-backed fabrics. The crepe effect is achieved by a high level of twist in the yarn. The fiber content determines correct care. Heavier crepes have some tendency to shrink when damp, and they can lose their distinctive crepey finish when pressed. Your best bet is to place them face down on a turkish towel and press very lightly, using very little moisture or steam. This also works for ribbed fabrics.

CRYSTAL   This glassware is not true rock crystal, but any clear, colorless glass, and often lead glass. Lead glass is heavier, rings when tapped, and abrasives will scratch it. See Glassware for care.

CURTAINS   See Draperies.

CUSHIONS   See Pillows, Upholstery.

D

DAIRY PRODUCT STAINS   See Carpet Stain Removal Guide; Master Stain Removal Section.

DECALS   To remove decals, "paint" them with several coats of white vinegar. Let the vinegar soak in for a few minutes, then slide off as much of the decal as possible and wash off the rest.

Or use a heat lamp over a decal for five to ten minutes and peel off.

DENIM   Back in the 1850s, when a man named Levi went west to sell tents to gold miners, he found that miners needed pants more than they needed tents. So he used his supply of tent fabric to make really strong pants, so comfortable and inexpensive and long-wearing that his designs for jeans make them the mainstay of many casual wardrobes today.

Denim was once 100 percent cotton, a combination of blue yarns in the warp and white yarns in the filling, that traditionally shrank and faded after washing, and stretched as a garment grew older. Now denim comes in various colors and also in blends that aim to do away with the shrinking, fading, and stretching.

Shrinkage: If there's no guarantee on shrinkage, better buy a size larger.

Color control: Do you prewash jeans to make them more comfortable, remove excess sizing, and prevent the color from running (bleeding) or crocking (rubbing off on your hands, or worse, on your sofa)? If so, use hot water with detergent and dry in a hot dryer. Several washes may be necessary, with a generous dose of fabric softener.

Regular Washing

Just machine-wash denim in warm water—white and pastel jeans with light-colored clothes; dark ones with other darks; reds separately.

Don't bleach, unless you want to take out color.

Tumble dry and remove promptly from the dryer.

If you iron jeans, press with a steam iron.

When a blend's fiber content is over 50 percent synthetic, it requires little or no ironing.

TIP

If you want jeans to fade, machine-wash them separately, using the hottest possible water, and chlorine bleach.

DEODORANT STAINS See Master Stain Removal Section.

DEODORANTS See Carpet Care; Odors.

DETERGENTS See Laundry Mini Manual; Laundry Aids. See product listings in Master Product List.

DIAPERS Diapers have improved a hundredfold since grandma was a new mother. Today's parents have a wide selection of diaper products from which to choose—disposable, fitted or unfitted paper/plastic, or cloth. The choice often depends on whether your goal is to save time, money, or energy. Of course, whatever the choice, keeping baby clean and comfortable is a major priority. If you have selected cloth diapers, and will be laundering them at home rather than renting them from a diaper service, read on.

Cotton cloth diapers are available in soft gauze, which is inexpensive, lightweight, and dries quickly; birdseye, which is firmer than gauze and lasts longer, and is more expensive; or flannel, good for soaking up moisture, but heavy and requiring longer drying time.

Care

Rinse soiled diapers in the toilet bowl and then soak in a covered diaper pail filled with water mixed with 2 tablespoons borax or ½ cup white vinegar. Machine-launder separately in hot soapy water. Use a very mild detergent or soap flakes (Lux or Ivory). The use of harsh detergents and bleaches can irritate baby's skin. Rinse at least twice to insure all soap residue will be removed. Dry on the line or in the dryer.

Johnson & Johnson suggests boiling diapers every few weeks to protect baby from ammonia-forming bacteria. After boiling, rinse in a mild antiseptic (1 cup white vinegar) and water.

DISHWASHERS

Whether built-in, portable, or convertible, the dishwasher has been a major task-fighter for the American household. A four-person family washes, on average, 340 tons of dishes in a lifetime. That works out to fifty-two eight-hour days a year if they are washed by hand.

Dishwashers are truly self-cleaning appliances, so you are spared practically all care for this time- and labor-saving aid.

But staining may be a problem in hard-water areas.

Remember that the flatware basket in your dishwasher can be moved. Use it next to your cutlery drawer when unloading.

- Add 1 teaspoon citric acid crystals (from the drug store) to the dishwasher and run through one wash cycle. Follow with a full detergent-added wash. If staining is severe, increase the amount of citric acid.
- Reduce mineral deposits by adding a stain/rust remover (Lime-A-Way). One cup to a complete wash cycle. Repeat if necessary.
- Minimize odors by adding a handful of baking soda to the bottom of the dishwasher while running a load of dishes.

Sprinkle a handful of baking soda on the bottom of the dishwasher to absorb odors from dishes left all day.

DISHWASHING

See Mini Manual on next page.

Dishwashing

A MINI MANUAL

TO GET A GREAT HEAD START

1. Presoak pots, pans, and cooking utensils while having your meal.

2. After eating, scrape the dishes into a plastic receptacle near the sink.

3. Wash the pots and pans left soaking at the beginning of the meal, place in drain rack, and rinse with very hot water. Put the silverware in a pan of clean sudsy water and soak while drying and storing the cookware.

LOADING THE DISHWASHER

- Prerinsing dishes is not necessary, but you don't want to use your dishwasher as a garbage disposer, so scraping is wise.
- If you have a partial load and don't plan to run the dishwasher until the next day, use the "Rinse and Hold" cycle.

- Small, lightweight items go on the top rack.
- So do plastics, if they're dishwasher-safe. If you have a lot of plastic items, the "Wash Only" or Crystal/China setting is the safest. This cycle overrides the dry cycle and the heating element will not activate and melt the plastic.
- You don't know if something is dishwasher-safe? If you think it may be heat-sensitive, place it on the top rack.
- Large dishes, heavy items, pots, pans, and utensils go on the bottom rack.
- Place soiled surfaces to the center.
- Don't nest. Load one item per set of prongs.
- Silverware goes randomly in the silverware basket in both up and down positions.
- Don't block the movement of the sprayer arms. (Check pot handles.)

ALL-PURPOSE DISHWASHING TIPS

- If glassware shows a cloudy film, rub with a sponge soaked in white vinegar.
- Coffee and tea stains in china cups and plasticware can be minimized by rinsing or washing immediately after use. If stains remain, remove by washing cups in a solution of 3 tablespoons baking soda and 1 quart hot water.
- Greasy areas that remain on (or in) pans will turn black when the pans are used again.
- Do not soak cast-iron cookware. See Cookware (Cast Iron).
- If you are short on counter space, stack dishes near the sink on a folding tray.

Place dish drain rack on the side of the sink closest to dish storage area.

- Keep all dishwashing material in a small plastic pan and place near the sink while washing dishes to avoid extra hunting and pecking under the sink when special problems arise.

Cupcake papers save cleaning regular muffin pans.

When you use a double boiler, put marbles in the pan along with the water. When the water boils down, the marbles make such a racket that you'll never forget you have a pot on the stove—and wind up with a scorched pan.

Soak pan in ice water before scalding milk, to prevent scorching.

HAND WASHING STRATEGIES

1. Follow the correct work-saving order:

- Glassware
- Silverware
- Dishes
- Serving pieces

2. Change water and detergent as often as necessary. When dishwater cools off, or becomes greasy, or when suds disappear.
Hot rinse water speeds up air-drying.

3. Use a dishpan. You can fill the sink with water and wash dishes without one, but the quickest way to change water and detergent is to empty and refill a dishpan. It also acts as a cushion against breakage. If you don't have room to store a dishpan, use a rubber mat in the sink to protect both the dishes and sink finish.

WORK-SAVING EQUIPMENT

An All-Purpose, Liquid Dishwashing Detergent will handle most dishwashing needs.

Beyond that, there are many useful aids you may want to consider.

Metal Cleaners work on problem food stains or burned-on food.

Two Sink Cleansers are useful. An abrasive cleanser (mild, medium or hard) to scour sink and counter stains after dishwashing. A mild liquid or spray cleanser to generally clean and disinfect sink and counters.

A Scraper removes loose food soils from dishes and pans. It can even eliminate the need for prerinsing.

Scrubbers remove crusty food residues. Plastic mesh, rough-surfaced sponges, steel wool pads, and soap-filled pads cope with the finishes on virtually all dishes, pans, and utensils.

Dishmop and Sponges get into glassware, cups, and storage jars, also crevices fingers cannot reach.

A Cotton (lint-free) Dishtowel polish-dries items that will water spot if left to air dry.

A Drain Rack with a Tray:

1. Air-dries dishes, eliminating hand drying.

2. Collects excess water from the dishes and returns it to the sink. (You don't have to wipe down the counter and maybe the floor after the dishes are done.)

3. Enables you to give dishes a very hot water rinse after they're all done. This speeds up air drying—and you needn't stop to rinse each dish after you wash it.

DISHWASHER TROUBLESHOOTERS

Water Spotting. To minimize, use a rinse agent made for dishwashers.

Etching caused by very soft water combined with an alkaline detergent. Use less detergent and less heat.

Spotting and Filming: To eliminate, try adding more detergent and increasing the water temperature as well as adding a commercial dishwasher rinse agent.

Calcium Deposits and Lime Film Inside the Dishwasher: To clean such deposits run the dishwasher on "Rinse and Hold" and add ½ cup of white vinegar during the fill period.

Poorly cleaned dishes. Check for possible causes:

Is the water source blocked?

Are large items blocking small?

Are spray arms restricted?

Proper amount of detergent?

Old or caked detergent?

Water too cold? If soft, too hot?

To prevent caking, store dishwasher detergent in tightly closed container. Caked detergent can cause "sand" deposits on dishes.

Packaged water softeners and detergents not made specifically for dishwashers will cause unwanted high sudsing that could spill out onto the kitchen floor.

DISINFECTANTS
(Sanitizers)

Sanitizing is part of any normal cleaning procedure, but especially important in the common cold season, or if you have illness in your house.

There are many disinfectant products designed to kill bacteria, preventing the spread of skin, respiratory, intestinal, and kidney infections. As they kill bacteria, they also destroy odors.

Routinely, they are used for cleaning tubs, showers, toilet bowls, bathroom sinks, and ceramic or plastic bathroom tile. They are also used in laundering and dishwashing.

When disinfecting laundry, use bleach for bleachable items. Quaternary (e.g., Roccal, available at swimming pool supply outlets), pine oil, or phenolic (e.g., Pine-Sol) disinfectants are suitable for nonbleachables.

Hot water is most effective. (Liquid chlorine bleach is less effective in cold water, and all-fabric bleach also loses effectiveness the lower the water temperature.)

When using a laundromat, a germ killer is a good idea. Illness in somebody else's family can be passed along if the washing machine is not disinfected before you use it. Wipe off the surface of the machine with a disinfectant before using it; add disinfectant to the wash cycle.

Don't forget to sanitize doorknobs, switchplates, the telephone receiver, and other items everybody handles. To keep from spreading other bacteria, don't put packages or other items (like a handbag) on the floor, and then on the kitchen or dining table. (They are carrying the same bacteria as your shoes!)

Never use chlorine bleach with a toilet bowl cleaner or rust remover, because this produces a harmful gas. You may also produce harmful chemical compounds by mixing chlorine bleach and ammonia.

See Getaway (p. 14), Garbage Pails, Kitchen/Bath Mini Manual, Tile (Ceramic), and Toilet Bowls for correct use of disinfectants in various areas.

Caution: Sanitizers are all poisonous. Like pesticides, they are registered by the U.S. Environmental Protection Agency, and you use them unlawfully if you fail to follow label directions. Note that containers specify limitations on use, and give first-aid information in case anybody accidentally swallows the contents.

DISKETTES   See Floppy Disks.

DISPOSERS   Garbage disposers should be flushed out every other week. This will keep odor-causing, soft food waste from collecting in the trap under the disposer.

To flush, fill sink half to three-quarters full of cold water. Open drain and let the water flow through the disposer.

To keep the disposer clean and fresh-smelling, pour a handful of baking soda into the disposer drain weekly. To eliminate odors, occasionally grind up the peel of citrus fruits.

DOUGH CLEANER   For nonwashable paint, lamp shades, window shades, and wall coverings you can make a cleaner as follows. In the top of a double boiler combine

> 2 cups flour
>
> 4 teaspoons baking soda
>
> 1 1/4 cups water
>
> 2 1/2 tablespoons ammonia

Cover and simmer over very low heat about 1 1/2 hours. Remove from heat and leave covered until cool enough to handle. (Yield: 1 1/4 cups)

Take a small amount of dough and clean the wall from the top down. As the surface of the dough becomes soiled, knead it to the inside as you are cleaning. When the dough no longer cleans, begin with a new amount of dough. Brush or vacuum away crumbs from the dough.

DOWN COATS AND VESTS   Since down is the light, fluffy undercoating that protects geese and ducks from the cold, it is obviously washable. Down items need dry cleaning only if the outer fabric won't wash, or their construction stands in the way.

To Wash: Follow the procedure for delicates. Avoid enzymes and heavy-duty detergents.

Rinse several times if necessary, since residues cause down to clump together. Avoid wrinkling by removing the garment from the washer as soon as possible.

Keep a down item separate from other clothes, since it has a distinct odor when wet, and you want to avoid transferring the smell.

To Dry: Use the regular cycle and "Delicate" temperature setting. To help open down clusters, put a couple of clean tennis balls in the dryer with the garment, and tumble dry thoroughly. Dry bath towels added to the dryer can also improve the tumbling action and shorten drying time.

Dry thoroughly, if you don't want to invite mildew, but don't overdry, since too much heat can melt nylon zippers.

To Dry-Clean: If dry cleaning is in order, take the garment to a professional dry cleaner expert in handling down-filled items. Do not, however, plan to alternate cleaning methods, because dry cleaning is likely to remove oil from the feathers, making them brittle, and apt to break in automatic washing.

DRAINS To keep bathroom and kitchen drains fresh smelling, pour a few generous handfuls of baking soda down them every month or so.

To unclog stopped-up drains, use a commercial product (with caution) or a plunger. If neither is available, here are other methods to try.

- Flush the drain with boiling water.
- Dissolve a pound of washing soda in 3 gallons of boiling water and pour into the drain.
- Pour ¼ to ½ box of baking soda down the drain. Add ½ cup of white vinegar. Cover drain tightly for a few minutes and flush with cold water.

DRAPERIES AND CURTAINS

The life expectancy of lined draperies is five years; unlined, four years; and sheers, three years. Exposure to sunlight may shorten these life expectancies, depending on the fiber composition. Buy fabrics resistant to sun-fading, always clean matching draperies at the same time, and try to switch draperies from window to window so all fade equally.

Draperies hung near heating and air conditioning vents and open windows are subject to fume-fading and exposed to greasy soil that can damage fabrics. Faded areas may not show until you wash or clean the draperies, and you can't do much about this unless you employ exhaust fans to remove vapors from the house.

Cleaning

Vacuum draperies with dusting brush attachment monthly, especially along the tops and hems where dust tends to cling.

Treat stains immediately.

If draperies are only slightly soiled, freshen by tumbling in a dryer set on "Air-Fluff" with no heat. For heavier soil, wash according to label or hang tag instructions.

Wash or dry-clean all draperies or curtains at least once a year. To aid in soil removal, shake out before washing or sending to the dry cleaner.

Check curtains before washing by gently pulling the fabric to determine its condition. If your washable curtains are damaged, launder them using a delicate or gentle cycle. Or wash them in a pillow case or mesh bag.

When machine-washing, don't crowd. Crowding results in poor soil removal and excess wrinkling.

To avoid or lessen ironing, tumble till damp dry and hang. If you can, slip a curtain rod through the bottom hem to ensure their drying unwrinkled.

Follow care label instructions for both draperies and curtains. (See individual fabrics—Nylon, Polyester, Rayon, Glass Fibers, Velvet, etc.)

TROUBLE SHOOTER

When pulling sheer curtains onto a rod, you can forestall snagging by applying plastic tape to the ends of the rod.

DRY CLEANING

Using a dry cleaner is sometimes the economical way to go. It is the safest way. Dry-cleaning solvents are most effective in removing grease and oil. They preserve colors that may be damaged in laundering and maintain size in items that may shrink in washing. To remove water-soluble soils (sugar, syrup, orange juice, coffee stains), the dry cleaner adds a surfactant and a small amount of water to the usual solvent.

The professional dry cleaner is not dependent on a hand iron, but uses steam and air—often blown through garments hung on airforms, so no creases are created or press marks or shiny areas. For tailored garments, flat bed pressing is available.

Custom dry cleaning differs from regular dry cleaning in the greater attention given to each article. Some fragile items are cleaned by hand, linings may be hand-pressed, knits measured and blocked, etc.

Economy dry cleaning is bulk cleaning. Prespotting, inspection, and finishing procedures are usually omitted. It's satisfactory for blankets and sweaters and other items that require no special finishing.

Coin-operated ("coin-op") dry cleaning with do-it-yourself equipment is a way to cut cleaning costs when you have sturdy clothes that aren't heavily soiled or stained and don't require pressing. (There is less temperature control in coin-operated dry cleaning.) Sort clothes according to color (it is false economy to clean lights with darks and end up with color transfer). Clean large household items separately from smaller articles. Prespot your cleaning before you leave home, unless your coin-op establishment has appropriate supplies on hand.

Can all clothes be dry-cleaned? Most machine-washable clothes can be safely dry-cleaned, says the Iowa State University Extension Service. But they warn against flocked designs sealed on with adhesives, polyurethane finishes, or fabrics with olefin, vinyl, spandex, or rubber content. Repeated steam pressing may also shrink clothes of synthetic fibers. For more information, check fiber listings.

To Get the Best Work
from Your Dry Cleaner

1. Clean soiled items promptly.

2. Point out any spots and stains to the cleaner and tell him if you tried to remove them yourself.

3. Protect your clothes from hair spray, perfume, still-damp anti-perspirants or deodorants—they all can damage fabric.

4. Remove salad oil stains promptly. Heat and age will make them permanent.

5. Tell the cleaner when you have spilled tea, coffee, soda, liquor, or fruit juices on a garment even if no stain shows. These substances contain tannin, and if the garments aren't prespotted you will wind up with tan or yellow spots when they are exposed to heat and dry-cleaning solvent.

6. If there is a chafed area that has lost color or luster (particularly with silks) ask your cleaner if he can give it a restorative finish.

7. Use the dry cleaner's special services. Cleaners can restore rain-repellent finishes. Many offer repair and reweaving services and attempt restretching draperies which have shrunk. Some will take down your draperies and rehang them after cleaning and refinishing.

DRY SPOTTER   A dry spotter removes many stains. It is prepared, according to the Pacific Northwest Extension Service, by mixing one part coconut oil (from health food and drug stores) and eight parts dry-cleaning solvent. Tightly cap the container to keep the dry-cleaning solvent from evaporating. (If you cannot obtain coconut oil, use mineral oil instead.)

Dry-cleaning solvent is poisonous, and may be flammable as well. So use with care.

DRYERS Lint buildup is your main concern in dryer care. Clean the lint filter each and every time you dry a load of clothes. Clean out the lint duct twice a year to prevent clogging. Do not, under any circumstances, operate the machine without the lint filter in place.

Protect the surface finish. Wipe spills immediately, especially those involving stain removal and pretreatment products. Wash the exterior with a liquid all-purpose cleaner or detergent and water. Rinse and dry. You need to wipe the appliance clean once a month—more often if you use the top of the dryer for a laundry folding or sorting table.

Caution: Never use the dryer for items that contain wax or paint or that have been treated with cleaning solvents until you have washed and air dried them to remove all solvent residue.

Dryer Troubleshooters

Dryer won't run/won't heat

- Door is not closed completely.
- Reset start button.
- Dry cycle is not set correctly.
- If gas, check turn-on valve.
- Electric dryers work on two different circuits. If your electric is fuse control, rather than circuit breaker, make sure both fuses are working.

Poor drying

- Lint filter is clogged.
- Lint exhaust duct is clogged.
- If it is a "time dry," the control should be set for more than fifteen minutes.
- Load's too small. Add towels to help tumble action.
- Dryer load is too large.

TIP

For pet lovers: If clothes are full of cat or dog hairs but do not otherwise need cleaning, spray lightly with water and with an antistatic spray. Then run them through the permanent-press cycle of the dryer at medium temperature. Animal hair winds up in the lint trap.

Dry time is too long

- Lint filter or lint exhaust duct is clogged.
- A cold-water rinse will increase drying time.
- If control is set for synthetics, there is a longer dry time at a lower heat, plus a cool-down period.
- A slow wash spin is causing excessive moisture in load.
- Dryer load is too large.
- Dryer is located in an unheated area (garage, basement).
- Electric dryers operating on less than 220/240 volts take longer to dry clothes.

Timer starts and stops

- Dryer may be set at a "custom dry cycle." Control will not move until load is partially dry.

Clothes yellow in dryer

- Poor washing: detergent or oily dirt has not been removed from wash load during rinse. (See Laundry Troubleshooters.)

DURABLE PRESS (Permanent Press)

Durable press fabrics resist wrinkling during wear and laundering. They retain pleats or creases heat-set at the time of manufacture.

Most durable press items blend polyester (or other man-made) fibers with natural fibers, but resin finishes on natural fibers give naturals the same sort of easy-care and wrinkle- and shrink-resistant attributes we associate with man-made fibers. However, the wear-life of durable press cotton is greatly reduced.

TIP

(1) Durable press fabrics tend to retain oily stains, requiring pretreatment before laundering. (2) Wrinkles can be set-in by mishandling during the laundering process.

Washing

Use the durable press cycle on washer. Provide a cold rinse before spinning. Do not wring or spin while warm. (If hand washing, rinse in cold water and squeeze gently.) If the label so cautions, avoid chlorine bleach.

To reduce wrinkling, tumble clothes with a damp towel in a dryer for a few minutes at the durable press setting. Remove clothes from the dryer immediately and hang on hangers right away.

Drying

Dryer heat and tumbling may remove some wrinkles caused by washing. True no-iron results can be obtained only by tumble-drying. Line dried items are more likely to need pressing.

Note: Experts now use "durable press" in preference to "per-manent press" since the permanency of the finish depends on the fibers, yarn, and construction—not to mention the care you give your clothes.

DUST CLOTHS

Your vacuum cleaner is a superior tool for removing surface dust, because it does away with it entirely. You will never see it again (if you are careful about emptying the dust bag).

But dust cloths that attract and hold dust are also effective.

You can buy treated cloths or make some yourself. Here are two recipes from the Cooperative Extension Services of the Northeastern States.

Dustless Dust Cloth for Wood with an Oil Finish

Place 1 teaspoon boiled linseed oil, 2 tablespoons gum turpentine, and 2 tablespoons warm water in a pint-sized glass jar with cover and screw top. Add three or four 18-inch square soft lintless cloths (e.g. cheesecloth). Cover tightly, turn upside down, and leave overnight.

Store the cloth in the glass jar with screw top lightly on. It should last several months. When it seems dry to you, add a few drops of warm water before re-storing.

Dustless Dust Cloth
for Waxed Furniture

Buy boiled linseed oil; don't try boiling it yourself. Dustless dust cloths are flammable. Keep in tightly covered jars.

Combine 1 tablespoon boiled linseed oil and 1 quart of warm water and cut three or four 18-inch squares from lintless cloth like cheesecloth. Then dampen, and dip into the linseed oil mixture. Wring out dry. Hang up and dry thoroughly.

Store in a tightly covered and labeled jar.

When these cloths become soiled you can wash and repeat treatment.

DYE STAINS ON CERAMIC TILE

See Grout Stain Removal Guide.

DYE TRANSFER STAINS

See Master Stain Removal Section.

E

EARTHENWARE　See China.

EGG STAINS　See Master Stain Removal Section.

ELECTRIC APPLIANCES, SMALL　See Appliance Mini Manual.

ELECTRIC BLANKET　See Blankets, Electric.

ELECTRIC BULBS　See Lights.

ELECTRIC RANGE　See Ranges.

ELECTRIC SCRUB BRUSH (Hand Held)　This laborsaver is usually equipped with two sizes of brushes, for flat surfaces and hard-to-reach corners.

To clean the brushes, remove them from the unit and soak in a pan of water and dishwashing detergent. Rinse, shake off excess water, and store. Clean the base or plastic housing by wiping with a sponge dampened with a mild soap and warm water; rinse and dry.

This powerful cleaning tool may cause surface damage if used with abrasive cleansers. If you are uncertain, test cleanser and scrubber in an inconspicuous spot. Never operate the unit under water or under running tap water.

TIP

Use your electric mini scrubber dry to scrape mud from the soles of shoes and boots.

Troubleshooter

Cleaner spinoff: Reduce by using less cleaner. Turn the appliance off while in contact with the surface you are cleaning. Black &

Decker suggests using a cardboard shield to protect other surfaces you do not wish to clean with the scrub brush.

ELECTRIC SKILLETS/ FRYPANS
These countertop appliances not only fry; some will boil, keep foods warm, and even bake.

After use, disconnect the temperature control probe (if removable) and wipe it clean with a damp cloth. Never submerge the probe in water. Do not immerse the skillet either, unless the appliance is marked "Immersible," usually on the underside of the pan.

To avoid warping, allow the pan to cool before cleaning or soaking. Some immersibles are dishwasher-safe. Check before using this cleaning method.

Wash both the skillet and the lid in hot sudsy water. Remove stubborn food spots by soaking in soapy water, then rubbing with a nylon scrub pad and a mild powdered cleanser or baking soda. Do not use scouring cleansers on the pin terminal (control outlet area). Also refrain from using such cleansers on pans with colored or anodized exteriors. Rinse thoroughly and dry.

Occasionally aluminum skillets may darken from exposure to hard water, strong detergents, and some foods. These stains are harmless. You can lighten them by cooking either apples or tomatoes in the frypan. For more information, see Cookware (Aluminum, Stainless Steel).

EMERY CLOTH
Emery cloth has an abrasive surface derived from corundum. It is available at hardware stores, graded from coarse to fine.

ENAMEL, ACRYLIC
This coating, often on the metal exteriors of refrigerator-freezers and laundry appliances, resists stains and cleans easily. However, acrylic enamel has poor resistance to high temperatures (above 180° F/82° C).

To clean, use warm, sudsy water or baking soda and water. Rinse with clear water and wipe dry. Protect and shine with a thin coat of kitchen wax (Jubilee) or silicone wax (Star brite). Avoid cleaning agents containing strong solvents, abrasives, or ammonia.

ENAMEL, ALKYD

This coating on metal cabinets and refrigerator-freezer liners isn't as durable as acrylic enamel.

It's easily cleaned, but observe the cautions listed for acrylic enamel. (See Enamel, Acrylic.)

ENAMEL, BAKED

According to the Porcelain Enamel Institute, baked enamel is technically any baked-on organic finish. (See Enamel, Acrylic; Alkyd.)

ENAMEL, PORCELAIN

This is a glass finish applied to metal, most frequently to steel. You'll find it as an interior and exterior finish on major appliances, cookware, sinks, and other plumbing fixtures. It's very durable, nonporous, stain- and scratch-resistant, burn- and rustproof. It is a poor conductor of heat and can chip under heavy impact.

To clean, just wipe or sponge with hot, soapy water or a liquid all-purpose household cleaner. Rinse with clear water and dry. It can also be cleaned with a solution of baking soda and water. Polish with a liquid kitchen/appliance wax (Jubilee, Star brite) to repel soil if desired.

ENZYME PRESOAKS

See Laundry Mini Manual, Laundry Aids.

EXHAUST FANS/ RANGE HOODS

An average kitchen range generates upwards of 200 pounds of cooking grease over time. So a well-maintained exhaust system can save you hours of cleaning.

We should say the kitchen exhaust system should be cleaned thoroughly each week, but we won't. To reduce some of the heavier cleaning later, give the fan exterior a quick weekly once-over with a solution of washing soda to reduce the grease and the chance of grease fires.

Every month or two, the fan needs more than a lick and a promise. To clean it thoroughly, turn the exhaust fan to the off position and let it cool. Soak removable parts in a dishpan filled with a grease-cutting cleaner (Grease Relief) and warm water for ten to fifteen minutes. While the parts soak, dip a sponge into the cleaning solution and wipe, rinse, and dry the permanently installed sections of the system. Then scrub the soaking parts to remove any remaining grease and dirt, rinse with clear water, and dry.

If you own a ductless exhaust fan (one that does not filter smoke and grease to the outside), replace the filter with a new one every three to four months.

EYEGLASSES The Optical Laboratories Association recommends cleaning your eyeglasses at least once, and better yet twice, a day with warm water and a mild soap. You can also use one of the available eyeglass cleaning solutions. Always dry with a very soft, clean cloth. Plastic lenses are subject to scratching, so it is best to rinse them on both sides with clear running water.

Designer glasses, tinted glasses, and eyeglasses with wire or rimless frames need special attention. Check with your eyecare specialist for instructions.

FABRIC SOFTENERS

These laundry aids reduce static cling and wrinkling in the dryer. They also impart a feeling of softness and fluffiness to laundered fabrics. If you must iron, use fabric softener to make ironing easier.

Three fabric softeners are available. All give fairly similar results. The difference lies in the point at which the softener is added to the laundry.

Rinse-added Softeners (Downy, Final Touch) are added during the final rinse. They work well in any water temperature, cold to hot.

Rinse-added softeners can produce greasy stains on wash. To avoid, dilute softener in water before adding it to the machine, even if your washer has a special rinse dispenser. If stains do occur, rub with a bar of laundry soap and rewash the article.

Wash-added Softeners (Rain Barrel) go into the laundry at the same time as the detergent. If you forget it at the beginning of the fill cycle, you can put it in during the final rinse. Just remember to dilute it with water first.

If a wash-added softener is used to excess, wash loads may become dingy or develop an oily feeling. If this happens avoid using a softener for two or three washings.

Dryer-added Softeners are either sheets or packets impregnated with softener (Cling Free, Bounce). They are tossed into the dryer with the clothes at the beginning of the dry cycle.

As with all softeners, greasy stains can occur. To remove, follow the directions given above for rinse-added softener stains.

For fabric softener stains, see Master Stain Removal Section.

FANS

Fans in constant use should be lubricated weekly with two or three drops of electric motor oil. Newer fans may be permanently oiled by the manufacturer; check instruction booklet.

Occasionally disconnect fan from outlet and wipe blades and base with a damp cloth. Before storing at the end of the cooling season, remove grease buildup with sudsy water, rinse and dry thoroughly. See Exhaust Fans.

FEATHERS   See Down Coats, Quilts, Sleeping Bags.

FECES STAINS   See Carpet Stain Removal Guide; Master Stain Removal Section (Urine).

FELT   Felt is a nonwoven fabric made from fur, wool, or mohair sometimes mixed with cotton, jute, or rayon. Both mildew and moths may be a problem with felt, as with any wool-containing product. Brushing and steaming may freshen it.

FIBERFILL OUTERWEAR   Polyester fiberfill insulation for cold-weather wear is odorless, nonallergenic, machine washable, and fast-drying. You will find some garments that require dry cleaning because of their shell fabric or trim.

The recent news in this field is the development of liners providing exceptional warmth without bulk, in all sorts of outerwear, gloves, hats, footwear, etc. (e.g., Thinsulate, Thermolite). The possibilities for sleek design with these new thin insulators do not interfere with function. It is claimed that these insulators block loss of body heat even when damp, that they may be warmer after washing and dry cleaning.

To wash and dry fiberfill, use a mild soap and low suds detergent, warm water, and a permanent press or gentle cycle. Button up or close zippers before washing and tumble drying. The tumbling action is important. Manufacturers suggest extra care if your washer or dryer is fully loaded and some recommend laundromat washing.

Use a low heat setting for drying and to avoid wrinkling, remove the garment immediately following the drying cycle, and place it on a hanger.

FIBERGLASS These spun-glass filaments show up in fireproof textiles, acid-resistant fabrics and draperies, or as a reinforcement for some bathroom plumbing fixtures, shower doors, and walls. Fiberglass is also used in home and appliance insulation.

To clean, use a detergent and water solution or general household cleaner (Top Job). Or wipe with a damp sponge sprinkled with baking soda, rinse, and dry. For very difficult cleaning problems, you may want to try a professional fiberglass cleaner, available at marinas and boating supply stores.

Note: Do not launder fiberglass textiles in washing machines, or dry in tumble dryers, because glass fibers are brittle and will fragment. For more information on fabrics, see Glass Fibers.

FINGERNAIL POLISH SPOTS See Carpet Stain Removal Guide; Grout Stain Removal Guide; Master Stain Removal Section (Nail Polish).

FIRE EXTINGUISHERS Fire extinguishers should be recharged after any use.

Inspect the unit at least once a year, weighing it from time to time to see if it has been partially discharged.

A dry chemical extinguisher (containing powder) should be turned upside down or shaken once a month to keep the powder from solidifying. It may need to be recharged completely every year or so. An extinguisher service or local fire station can discharge—and recharge—it.

Don't keep an extinguisher so close to the range (or wherever a fire might start) that heat or flames will keep you from grabbing it.

CAUTION

FIREBRATS See Silverfish.

FIREPLACE   Fireplace cleaning raises lots of dusty dirt, so tackle it first if you are going to do any other cleaning in the room, and make sure ashes are completely cool before disposing of them.

To Clean

Spread newspaper in front of the fireplace hearth to protect carpet and floor. Stand any unburned logs on end at the back corners of the fireplace. Remove andirons and vacuum or dust, and apply a coat of metal cleaner/polish if needed.

If your fireplace has an ash dump (a hole at the rear of the fireplace covered with a metal trapdoor), open the trapdoor and sweep the ashes into the dump. If your fireplace does not have an ash dump, sweep the ashes onto a small shovel or dust pan and then into a paper bag. Vacuum the inside of the fireplace and hearth. Buff andirons to polish.

To clean the exterior surface of the fireplace, see Brick, Marble, etc.

For general cleanliness and safety, choose a firescreen that completely covers the fireplace opening to keep sparks from flying out. Use a hearth apron so ashes and coals won't land on the floor.

FLAME-RETARDANT FINISHES   All children's sleepwear, sizes 0-14, is now manufactured with flame-resistant cotton or treated synthetic fabrics. Federal standards require garments to maintain flame resistance through fifty washings.

Other clothing and household textiles are often available with flame-retardant finishes, and carpets and rugs, mattresses and mattress pads must pass flammability tests to be sold in the United States. The Upholstery Furniture Action Council sponsors a gold hang-tag to designate upholstery constructed or treated to resist damage from smoldering cigarettes.

"Flame-resistant" does not mean that a fabric won't burn at all, but merely that it won't support a flame.

To Maintain Flame-Resistance

1. Thorough soil removal is a must. For clothing that has acquired oily dirt (baby lotion), wash in hot water and use more detergent than the recommended amount.

2. Do not use soap in hard water areas, and if you live in a place where phosphate-built detergents are banned, the Consumer Product Safety Commission recommends a nonphosphate heavy-duty liquid detergent, rather than soap or a carbonate-built detergent.

You may not harm most flame-resistant garments by using bleach or fabric softener on them, but such products are not recommended. Note that care labels also may warn against using commercial laundries.

FLEAS

Fleas in the house usually come from cats and dogs, who pick them up outdoors. The fleas lay eggs on the pets, the eggs drop off into the carpet or furniture—and you have an infestation!

Sprays or foggers are recommended for these pests.

To fumigate an infested area, use a fogger. Before you activate it, cover or clear away any exposed food in the area, as well as dishes, cookware, food-processing equipment, and food-preparation surfaces; cover fish tanks; and remove any birds or other pets. Close off the area and leave it for several hours. On your return, vacuum the area thoroughly to remove dead insects. Then empty the vacuum bag and spray it with pesticide, or discard disposable vacuum bags.

If you don't wish to fumigate, spray floors and other surfaces that may be infested, keeping the spray away from food and water and food-serving or eating areas.

Once you have treated the inside of the house, you want to be sure your pet is free of fleas. Wash and dry the pet outdoors, then treat it with a flea killer intended for use on pets. Follow

Fogger sprays are flammable. Turn off the gas if your range has a pilot light.

CAUTION

directions carefully. They generally warn you against spraying the pet's head, rectal area, and any open wounds, and prohibit use of such products on puppies or kittens. If your animal is sensitive to the pesticide, bathe the pet immediately. Call a veterinarian if symptoms persist.

Other methods include integrating pesticide and nonpesticide methods—called integrated pest management. An example of this is a "birth control" insecticide that interrupts the flea's life cycle, preventing the young from growing into adults capable of reproduction, thus extending the period before you may need to repeat insecticide treatments.

Commercial flea powders are available, as are flea collars. Follow label directions.

FLEECE

Fleece is a luxurious fabric characterized by a thick, deeply napped surface, valued for warmth without weight. The term "fleece," says the Wool Bureau, correctly applies only to wool fabrics, though there are so-called fleeces of other fibers—cotton, acrylic, and other man-mades. Care is determined by fiber involved.

FLIES

Flies are filthy. They live in garbage, human wastes, and manure, and they carry diseases like typhoid and dysentery.

Discourage them by keeping food covered, screen your windows and doors, keep a fly swatter handy, and use it.

If you're really plagued, use an insecticide spray. Ask for one containing: DDVP (Vapona); Ronnel with pyrethrins; or malathion with pyrethrins. Wash your hands after using the spray.

"No Pest" strips are also helpful.

FLOCKING ON FABRICS

Flocked designs are produced by gluing soft fibers onto a fabric surface. Some are more durable than others, so heed labels! If you dry-clean a flocked item, consult your professional cleaner. Dry-cleaning solvents can remove or damage the adhesive.

FLOORS   See Mini Manual on next page.

FLOPPY DISKS   Computer disks cannot be cleaned. However, here are DOs and
(Computer Diskettes)   DON'Ts to help you protect diskettes and the data on them

- Store in their envelopes.
- Use a felt-tip pen for writing on the label. When you relabel, peel off the old label. Don't stick a new one on top of the old. Keep fingers off the magnetic surface. Hold the disk by the label portion.
- Avoid bending. Insert the disk in the disk drive with care. Don't force or jam.
- Keep disks away from magnetic fields (e.g., stereos and TV speakers). Don't expose to heat, sunlight, liquid, dust, or smoke.

FLUSHING   Flushing is a technique for treating stains by pouring a solvent through stained fabric.

If you are dealing with a sturdy washable fabric, just lay the stained area over a bowl and pour water on it from six inches or more above.

If you are dealing with a delicate or nonwashable fabric, first loosen the stain and then finish the job by flushing to take out the remaining stain *and* stain remover.

Put absorbent material under the stained fabric, apply the correct remover with an eyedropper or any container that allows very slow pouring, applying it no faster than it can be soaked up. Work in as small an area as possible. If you are treating a stain and a fabric on which water may be used, give the fabric a final water rinse.

Floors

Dirt plays the very devil with floors and carpets. Grit scratches floors, and when it's embedded in carpet, it can actually cut the fibers. The easiest ways are the best ways to cope with this unwanted dirt.

AVOID WORK

1. Keep dirt out: Use mats and scrapers at your doors to prevent tracked-in dirt.

2. Keep dirt off: Use a tarp or newspapers when you have a messy job to do.

3. Take up spills as soon as you can.

ONCE A DAY

Vacuum or dust mop to catch loose dirt. Take a quick damp mop to bath and kitchen floors.

The best technique for damp mopping is to use a dampened sponge mop and warm water, working a small space at a time. Rinse and wring out the mop frequently.

Use two buckets—one for mopping and one for rinsing the mop, and change water frequently so you don't redistribute the dirt.

ONCE A WEEK

Nonwashable Floors: The vacuum cleaner is your workhorse. Use the floor attachment on all wood and cork floors.

While you're about it, vacuum the carpet, too, doing a slow and thorough job and using the crevice tool on the parts that slide under the furniture.

Washable Floors. Just wash with a product designed for the type of floor you have. For more information, see the Master Product List.

If you're faithful with these simple routines, you should have few problems year-round. Information on the less-frequent jobs of waxing and polishing and shampooing is found under Tile, Vinyl and Wood Floors and Carpet Shampoos, as are the remedies for stains and other problems that may occur with flooring and floor coverings.

Rule of Thumb: If the floor would not be damaged by water, use a water-based cleaner. If the floor could be damaged by water, use a solvent-based cleaner (paste wax).

FOAM RUBBER   Foam rubber is light, mildew-proof and nonallergenic.

Foam mattresses take much the same care you give any mattress—except that they never require turning.

Washable foam cushions should be washed in their zipper casings, preferably by hand, since this material is weak when wet.

Never use mineral spirits solvents on foam rubber. Heat is also damaging. If you must speed up drying, try an electric fan.

See Pillows, Upholstery.

FOOD COLORING   See Master Stain Removal Section (Fruit).

FOOD PROCESSOR   Unplug the food processor from electric outlet before cleaning. Rinse blades and bowls immediately after use to make cleanup easier.

Use the dishwasher, or hand wash all removable parts in hot sudsy water. Wipe the base with a damp cloth or a nonabrasive liquid cleaner. Do not use scouring pads or cleansers. Do not allow plastic blades or bowls to soak in boiling water or remain in water for long periods of time. Cutting blades have been permanently sharpened by the manufacturer. Do not attempt to sharpen them yourself.

A coating of vegetable cooking oil sprayed on the processor blades will make cleanup easier.

FOOD STAINS   See Carpet Stain Removal Guide, Grout Stain Removal Guide, and individual foods in Master Stain Removal Section.

FORMICA   See Plastics (Laminated).

FOUNDATION GARMENT   See Spandex.

FREEZER See Refrigerator/Freezer.

FRENCH CHALK French chalk is an absorbent powder—actually a fine-grained variety of talc—recommended in stain-removal procedures. Available at drugstores.

FRUIT FLIES Fruit flies are best controlled by discarding garbage regularly. Always discard spoiled fruit, and don't eat sprayed fruit.

FRUIT/ JUICE STAINS See Carpet Stain Removal Guide, Grout Stain Removal Guide, Master Stain Removal Section (Fruit).

FRYING PAN See Cookware (Aluminum, Cast Iron, Copper, Stainless Steel, etc.), Electric Skillet.

FULLER'S EARTH This is a mineral substance that absorbs colors, removing them from oils. It is available from drugstores and is used in combination with cleaning fluid to make a paste. In fact, it is often found in commercial cleaning products, which you may find convenient to use.

FURNITURE (WOOD) See Mini Manual on next page.

FURNITURE POLISH See Furniture Mini Manual, Master Product List.

Furniture (Wood)

A MINI MANUAL

Remove dust from wood furniture with a clean, soft cloth moistened with furniture polish. This cloth holds dust and thus helps to avoid scratches that can occur with dry dusting.

Clean with a wax-based polish. Wax polishes protect with a hard, dry surface finish, whereas oily polishes attract and trap soil. Don't worry about wax buildup—today's furniture polishes are self-removing. (Old polish comes off with dirt and grime with each new application.) This regimen should keep your furniture in good condition.

 Use coasters to prevent rings and marks on wood furniture.

For care of chrome or plastic furniture, see Chrome; Plastics; and Plastics (Laminated).

For upholstery care, see Upholstery.

REMEDIAL CLEANING

If your furniture needs a very thorough cleaning, here are approved methods.

1. Wax and polish small areas at a time, rubbing with the grain, using at least two clean, soft cloths—one saturated with paste, one to buff.

2. Furniture can also be cleaned with mineral spirits or naphtha, available at hardware or paint stores.

These products are flammable and should be used only in a well-ventilated room.

Saturate cleaning cloth with solvent.
Rub saturated cloth over a small area in a circular motion.
Wipe with a clean dry cloth.
Repeat until dry cloth shows no sign of soil.
Apply polish—rubbing with the grain.

3. A third good idea is to protect wood surfaces with a coat of polish or wax to guard against spills and other soil. Rewax when sheen becomes dull.

4. Once a year, go over it first with turpentine, then beeswax (bowling alley wax).

An application of paste wax can hide minor scratches and wear.

A paste of mayonnaise and cigarette ashes also works on marks caused by heat, says Jodi Martin, a Merry Maid in Loveland, Colorado.

For Extensive Damage

Employ a professional furniture refinisher. The Consumer Services Center of Johnson Wax tells us that home furnishings can be the fourth largest investment a family undertakes in its lifetime. Taking care of furniture can benefit your pocketbook.

TROUBLESHOOTERS

Here are do-it-yourself techniques for minor problems.

Scratches: Camouflage by rubbing scratches out and then recoloring.

1. Remove polish. (See cleaning method above.)

2. Dip a #0000 steel wool pad in paste wax. Rub gently with the grain and buff with a clean cloth.

3. Restore the color with a color wax stick for furniture (available at hardware stores). Or apply a paste shoe polish to match the color of the finish with a cotton swab and buff.

Conceal nicks in mahogany and other dark wood furniture by polishing abrasion with the meat of a walnut.

White Marks: These are caused by either hot items or spilled liquids. Repair by using the steps listed for scratches.

Bloom: Varnished woodwork or furniture sometimes takes on a cloudy cast. If it hasn't worked through the varnish, you can renew the luster by rubbing the surface with a soft lintless cloth wrung out of a solution of a tablespoon of white vinegar in a quart of lukewarm water. When rubbing, follow the grain of the wood. Finish by wiping with a soft dry cloth.

Alcohol: Blot spill. Do not rub. Allow the stain to dry for twenty-four hours. Hide the damage by rubbing the spot out and then restoring, following the steps listed for scratches.

Cracking/Crazing: Usually caused by extreme changes in humidity and/or temperature or normal aging. This damage cannot be repaired (except by refinishing the entire piece of furniture). Slow down the process by filling in cracks with a paste wax. Avoid liquid or spray polishes that seep under the finish.

Nailpolish Remover: See Alcohol, above.

Paint: For water base, remove with a water dampened cloth. For oil base, scrape gently with a plastic credit card. Cover residue of oil base paint with boiled linseed oil. Let stand until paint softens. Wipe with a cloth dampened with more linseed oil. Remove residue from dried water base paint with the rub-out technique (see Scratches). (*Note:* Purchase boiled linseed oil. Do not attempt to boil it yourself.)

Candle Wax: You can quickly and safely remove candle wax from wood furniture with a hand-held hair dryer held slightly above the drips. The heat softens the wax, which can then be wiped away with a paper towel, leaving no scratches.

NOTES

....

....

....

....

FURNITURE POLISH STAINS   See Carpet Stain Removal Guide.

FURS   The best way to keep furs in good condition is to have them professionally cleaned and stored every summer. Professional fur cleaning (unlike regular dry cleaning) not only removes the soil, but keeps the leather soft and the fur lustrous.

If your fur gets wet, don't worry. Rain and snow rarely harm fur. Simply give it a shake and hang to dry, away from heat, in a place where there is good air circulation. When dry, shake it out again. Never comb or brush the fur. If by chance it is soaked through, take it to your furrier for proper treatment.

The Fur Information Council offers some dos and don'ts.

1. If you use a cover, store in a cloth bag, never plastic. (Plastic dries out leather.)

2. Never hang furs close to a heat source.

3. Give furs enough closet room to prevent crushing.

4. Hang on a broad-shouldered hanger away from light. (Over-exposure to light can oxidize or change the color.) Use a cloth cover if you can't otherwise shield the garment.

5. Never mothproof furs with a chemical spray. If moths are a problem, store furs with a professional furrier.

6. Don't pin jewelry or flowers to your furs; avoid wearing heavy jewelry that will rub against them.

7. Don't apply cologne or perfume to fur. The alcohol will dry the leather and stiffen guard hairs.

FURS, SYNTHETIC (Deep Pile Fabrics)   Most of these require dry cleaning, especially fake fur coats and other apparel. In fact, some should go to a furrier for cleaning.

They are durable, mothproof, mildew-resistant, and resistant to acids, alkalis, and abrasion. They are also flame-resistant if mod-acrylic fiber is used (but easily damaged by hot cigarette ashes or hot radiator surfaces.) They are more static-prone than real fur.

If fake fur garments get wet from rain or snow, shake out to remove excess moisture and dry at room temperature. Hang on padded hangers and store in a cool, dry uncrowded closet (or at your furrier's).

Washable items should be handled gently. The Man-Made Fiber Producers Association suggests you should machine-wash mod-acrylics with these properties in warm water, with a fabric softener added during the final rinse cycle. If a dryer is used, they suggest a low setting, and removing articles as soon as the tumbling has stopped. You may prefer to line dry, brushing gently to fluff up the pile. If you're dealing with an item so large that the weight of water may stretch it, lay it on a towel and pat to remove as much moisture as possible. Then stretch to its original measurements. Shake the item occasionally while it's drying. If it looks shaggy and matted when dry, brush gently against the pile and then with it, or brush or comb it gently to fluff it up.

In the absence of care tags suggesting machine care, avoid machine-drying. This is because some fibers will flatten, turn brittle or melt if they come in contact with excess heat. Also avoid coin-op dry cleaning.

To spot clean, stroke lightly with the nap with a damp cloth. Avoid a circular motion, because you may thus just rub the spot in deeper and cause the fibers to mat.

Pressing is generally not recommended, because you surely don't want the pile to mat. But if you do press, use a dry iron rather than steam, on the wrong side.

FUSE See Appliances.

TIP

A wire pet brush may be handy on items like slippers, bathroom rugs, hoods, etc.

G

GARBAGE DISPOSER   See Disposers.

GARBAGE PAILS   Garbage pails and wastebaskets should be emptied daily and cleaned and deodorized frequently. Once a week is ideal. Once a month if you line your waste can with a plastic garbage bag.

To clean and disinfect, fill the garbage pail with 1 gallon warm water and ¼ cup liquid disinfectant cleaner (Spic and Span Pine). Scrub the bottom and sides with a long-handled brush. Wipe the cover clean with a sponge dipped in the same solution.

To deodorize, rinse the pail thoroughly with clear warm water to which a handful of baking soda or ¼ cup borax has been added. Or rinse, dry, and spray with a disinfectant deodorizer (Lysol).

To control flies around outdoor garbage pails, wrap fruit, peelings, and other wet garbage in newspaper, hose out cans that have contained any liquid garbage, and keep lids tightly in place. If flies persist, spray cans inside and out with insecticide and attach pest strips to the garbage pail lid.

See also Disinfectants, Flies, Odors.

GAS RANGE   See Ranges.

GAS WATER HEATER   See Water Heater.

GESSO   Those ornate old picture frames that appear to be intricately carved wood are gesso, a hard plasterlike material on wood molding. If you must clean a gesso frame, treat it gently.

First vacuum it. Then, following the advice of the Cooperative Extension Services of the Northeastern States, clean it painstakingly one section (one or two inches square) at a time, finishing each section before you go on to the next.

Rub each section with a slice of fresh lemon, using the cut edge to get into the crevices, then sponge immediately with a solution of soda and water (1 tablespoon of baking soda in 1 pint water). This immediate sponging is very important: there is a danger of dissolving any gold leaf or gilding if you don't neutralize the lemon with the soda solution.

Dry thoroughly with soft cloths. Use cotton-tipped swabs or an orange stick wrapped with cotton to absorb moisture in the crevices.

Repeat process if necessary.

GIRDLES   See Spandex.

GLASS   To clean regular household glass and mirrors, add two or three tablespoons of ammonia to a quart of water, wash, rinse with clear water, and dry with a lint-free towel. Or use a commercial cleaner and buff dry with a lint-free cloth or paper towel. For more information on glass items and glass containers, see Cookware (Glass), Glassware, Windows. For special techniques with mirrors and items framed under glass, see Mirrors.

GLASS, CERAMIC
(Pyroceram)   This glass substance, transformed into a crystalline material, is usually opaque white in color, and shows up in freezer-to-oven cookware, some range cooktops, and heat-resistant counters. It is a nonporous material unaffected by acids or alkalis.

To clean, see Cooktops, Glass Ceramic.

GLASS, HEAT-RESISTANT (Borosilicate)

Heat-resistant cookware and bakeware can withstand reasonable changes in temperature without cracking or breaking.

To clean, you need only hot water and detergent. If the glass appears cloudy or streaked, soak in a solution of $1/2$ cup white vinegar to 1 gallon of water, rewash in detergent, rinse, and dry. For more information, see Cookware (Glass).

GLASS AND GLASS / CERAMIC COOKWARE

See Cookware (Glass).

GLASS FIBERS

Curtains and draperies are the principal items produced with textiles featuring glass fibers. These fibers are strong and resist most chemicals, mildew, moths, and sunlight. They don't burn, don't stretch much, neither do they shrink. They don't absorb moisture and are resistant to soil and stains and wrinkles.

The fabrics are brittle, however, and tend to break along creases, where rubbing occurs.

Therefore:

Do not machine-wash, or tumble dry.

Do not dry-clean (the solvent may damage dyes).

Hand wash, and do not rub, wring, fold, or iron, as the fibers may break.

To clean, place items in water with mild detergent. Soak fifteen to thirty minutes; swish gently to remove soil. Or, if soil contains no oil or grease, just hang curtains or draperies on the line outdoors, and hose them down.

You may use chlorine bleach on white fabrics. Otherwise, no bleach on fiberglass.

Hang curtains or draperies over a hanger or clothesline and drip dry until excess water is out. Rehang at windows while still damp; do not iron.

CAUTION

Do not wash anything else with fiberglass because it may shed small particles that will lodge in garments and cause skin irritation when worn. Rinse the washtub thoroughly when you are through.

GLASSES See Eyeglasses.

GLASSWARE

Glassware for everyday use may be washed in the dishwasher or by hand, using hot water and detergent. Be careful when washing cut glass or lead glass crystal in the dishwasher, especially if water supply is very hard or very soft. For more information see the Dishwashing Mini Manual.

Wash fragile pieces individually, holding stemware by the base of the bowl, not the stem. Use hot water and detergent, rinse well (twice if needed), and buff dry with a lint-free towel.

Protect glassware by using a plastic dishpan, rubber mat, or toweling on the bottom of the sink. Use a plastic-coated rack for draining and avoid chipping by covering the faucet with a rubber cap. Rubber gloves help you to hold onto slippery, soapy glass.

Store drinking glasses and glass containers in rows. Don't stack or nest or crowd. Don't attempt to pry, twist, or pull stuck glasses apart. Dip the outer glass in very warm water (heat expands the glass), and they will slide apart.

Glass will break if subjected to extremes in temperature. So don't plunge cold glassware into hot water.

Avoid stains and hard-to-remove residue by rinsing glass containers after use. Rinse hard-to-clean cruets and small-necked containers with diluted ammonia before washing. North Dakota Cooperative Extension Service suggests removing surface discoloration inside small-necked containers by adding uncooked rice and white vinegar and shaking vigorously.

For flower vases, rinse with a solution of water and chlorine bleach.

Stains in glass *coffee makers* respond to a teaspoon of baking soda in the rinse water.

Lime deposits can be removed by adding tea leaves to the bottom of the container and filling with a solution of white vinegar and water.

For surface residue, try rubbing the glass with a slice of lemon

TIP

Add a teaspoon of borax to the rinse water for extra shine.

TROUBLE SHOOTER

Sticky film residue from labels on glassware comes off with nailpolish remover.

TIP

Remove the unsightly deposit in a goldfish bowl by rubbing it with a cloth in white vinegar. Then rinse well.

TIP

Put a metal spoon in an ice-filled glass when pouring hot tea, coffee, and so forth. The metal absorbs some of the heat.

or wash with a white vinegar solution.

For information about glass cookware, see Cookware Mini Manual (Glass).

GLAZED FABRICS   See Chintz, Ciré.

GLAZED TILE   See Ceramic Mosaic under Tile.

GLOVES   Machine-wash washable fabric gloves, following directions for their fiber content. Or wear them while you hand wash them, rubbing detergent into palms and fingertips. Remove the gloves, rinse, and roll in an absorbent towel to remove extra moisture. (Always wash dark gloves separately, since they may bleed color.)

Washable leather gloves are often treated with additives to keep them supple, and these additives may be extracted by the dry cleaner's solvents. So don't dry-clean them. Wash with lukewarm to cool, mild soap suds. Change water till gloves are clean.

Wash them on the hand, except for doeskin and chamois gloves. Then rinse in clear, lukewarm water.

Blot excess water from gloves with towels. Never wring them or dry them on the radiator. Shape them gently and dry flat at room temperature.

When dry, soften them by rubbing with your moistened fingers. The oils in your skin actually help to keep gloves in condition.

Wash wool gloves as you would any wool item, tracing the pattern on paper and working the washed gloves, while still wet, to fit the pattern when you dry them.

GLUE   Try a little white vinegar to soften the hardened glue for easier removal.

See Carpet Stain Removal Guide and Master Stain Removal Section for removal methods.

GLYCERINE Glycerine acts as a lubricant to soften stains. Combined with liquid detergent and water, it produces a "wet spotter" for washable fabrics. It can sometimes help to remove ballpoint ink. Available in drug stores.

GRANITE Polished granite on your kitchen counter responds to the same regular care as polished marble. Just wipe it off with a mild detergent and water, rinse, and buff with a soft cloth.

Because of its unique crystalline structure, granite is more absorptive than marble, and stains deep in the stone are virtually impossible to get out. Consult a local dealer in granite or other stone products for professional help.

The Marble Institute of America publishes an inexpensive booklet on the care of granite, as well as marble. See Marble.

GRAPE STAINS See Master Stain Removal Section (Fruit).

GRASS STAINS See Master Stain Removal Section.

GRAVY STAINS See Master Stain Removal Section.

GRAY/YELLOW BUILDUP ON RESILIENT FLOORS See Vinyl Flooring Troubleshooters.

GREASE STAINS See Carpet Stain Removal Guide; Cement; Grout Stain Removal Guide; Tile, Floor Stain Removal; Wall-Covering Troubleshooters; Wood Floor Troubleshooters; Master Stain Removal Section.

GREASY STAINS ON LAUNDRY	See Laundry Troubleshooters; Master Stain Removal Section.

GRILLS—INDOOR These enable us to have outdoor-food flavor all year round, no matter what the weather. However, indoor grilling would not be possible without a ventilating system to remove smoke and odors. For best results a grill range should be vented to the outside.

Cleaning

Clean grates after each use with detergent, using a nylon or plastic scrubber, or wash in the dishwasher.

Cleaning the grill element is easy because the high-wattage element burns off most food soil. Never immerse in water.

Clean grill rocks frequently with detergent or in the dishwasher.

Clean grill basin after each heavy use. (See Enamel, Porcelain.)

Grease Removal

Excess grease collects in a drip tray or remote drip collector. It should be checked often and emptied frequently.

Care

1. Wash grates before first-time use. Use hot, sudsy water, rinse, and dry.

2. Condition grates with vegetable oil or nonstick spray-on vegetable coating. Repeat after each cleaning.

3. Spray grill rocks as well as grates with a nonstick vegetable spray to prevent food residue from sticking.

4. Trim excess fat from meats to prevent cleaning and flare-up problems.

GROOMING ACCESSORIES Toss combs, hair clips, washable makeup applicators, and brushes into a solution of baking soda and warm water. Soak for a few minutes, swish in solution, rinse under running water, and air dry. Or, fill a basin with 1 tablespoon detergent, ½ cup borax, and warm water. Swish grooming accessories in the sudsy water, rinse, and dry.

GROUT Cement

Soiled White or Standard Gray: To brighten, scrub with a powder cleanser (Ajax, Comet) and rinse thoroughly.

For stains, apply undiluted chlorine bleach and rinse thoroughly. Or apply a paste of powdered cleanser and water to stain, allowing it to remain overnight. Scrub, rinse, and dry.

Colored: Bleaching may fade such grout, so pretest cleaning methods in an inconspicuous spot.

Use methods listed above, rinsing completely to avoid cleanser residue.

Rubber Silicone

1. Apply undiluted chlorine bleach.

2. Wipe off with a damp sponge after grout appears uniformly white.

3. Rinse well.

If stain remains, cut out with a razor blade and regrout following manufacturer's instructions.

TIP

To remove silicone rubber grout from tile surfaces, wipe down with denatured alcohol.

GROUT STAIN REMOVAL GUIDE

The following treatments have been recommended by American Olean and the Tile Council of America. They work well for both ceramic tile and grout.

Stain	Treatment
Coffee, Tea Fruit Juices Lipstick	Household cleanser in hot water, followed by hydrogen peroxide or chlorine bleach. Rinse, dry.
Blood	Hydrogen peroxide or household bleach.
Fingernail polish	Dissolve with polish remover. Apply chlorine bleach, rinse, and dry.
Grease and Fats	Spic and Span and warm water.
Ink and Dye	Apply chlorine bleach; let stand until stain disappears, keep surface wet continuously. Rinse and dry.
Iodine	Scrub with ammonia. Rinse and dry.
Mercurochrome	Chlorine bleach.
Mildew	Use an instant mildew stain remover. Or scrub with ammonia (for tile) and scouring powder (for grout). Wash with bleach if needed. Rinse and dry.
Chewing gum, wax, tar	Chill with ice cube and scrape away residue with a dull knife. Remove the rest with (nonflammable) paint stripper; rinse and dry.

GUM STAINS   See Carpet Stain Removal Guide; Grout Stain Removal Guide; Master Stain Removal Section (Adhesives).

HANDBAGS

Leather and reptile bags are best treated with cream polish, following package directions. (Use neutral shade; colored wax can stain clothes.) To clean leather, try wiping with white vinegar, touch up scuffs with an indelible felt-tip marker. Reptile bags can be wiped with cool water.

Test cleaning solutions on the handle or in a corner.

Suede should be brushed with a wire suede brush. An art gum eraser (or fine sandpaper) will remove spots.

Metallics may be wiped with cool water. When they're new, you might spray with acrylic art fixative.

Patent or vinyl bags can be cleaned with white vinegar applied with just-damp terry or cheesecloth. They may be shined with Liquid Glass Cleaner or Pledge.

Fabric bags may be cleaned with a shampoo sold for use on upholstery. Spray with Scotchgard when brand-new.

TIP

To treat stains on leather, blot spot with baking soda or talcum powder to absorb stain, then have professionally cleaned.

TIP

Never store bags in plastic. It dries out leather and promotes mildew and rot. Wrap and stuff with tissue paper.

HARD WATER

See Water Quality.

HEAT REGISTERS

See Radiators.

HEATERS
(Electric Space Units)

To clean, unplug unit from wall outlet. Vacuum grillwork and heating elements, using the dust-brush attachment. Clean exterior surface with a damp cloth dipped in a mild, sudsy detergent and water solution, rinse, and dry.

Rule number one for portables is to refrain from using them in the bathroom to avoid the shock hazard to bathers.

A heat lamp in your bathroom ceiling fixture is a safe alternative space heater in this room.

HEATING PADS   See Blanket, Electric.

**HOLIDAY
COUNTDOWN**   See Mini Manual on next page.

HOSIERY   Wash pantyhose and women's stockings in warm water and detergent, rinse well, drip dry. Do not bleach. If necessary, rub heels and toes together gently to remove stains or soil. You very likely hand wash these delicate items. If you machine-wash them, protect them with a drawstring mesh bag to minimize snagging.

To Prevent Snags: Wearing gloves can keep hosiery from catching in your jewelry and fingernails. Soften your hands with a little lotion before pulling on pantyhose. Some claim that hose will wear longer if you wash new pairs before wearing them. You can help smooth the fibers by using a fabric softener when you launder them.

Washable Wool: Launder wool hose inside out on the normal cycle with warm water and mild detergent. Rinse and dry at normal temperature. Tumble dry fifteen to twenty minutes (don't let wool get bone-dry).

Socks: Socks will keep their shape and resilience if you wash them after each wearing. But beware of excessive hot drying since this can ruin the stretch fibers in sock tops.

TIP

To pretreat white sports socks, use a heavy-duty laundry detergent and soak for five minutes.

HOT PLATES   Clean the metal or enamel base of the hot plate with a cloth or sponge dipped in hot, sudsy water, rinse, and dry. When the unit is completely cool, wipe off excessive grease or spills from the heating elements with a dry cloth. Turn the control to high to burn off any remaining food spills. Use a soft brush to remove burned-on food particles.

HOUSEFLY   See Flies.

Holiday Countdown

A MINI MANUAL

Christmas and Chanukah are occasions so dear and familiar to many of us that we just follow the patterns we grew up with. An inner clock tells us when to start bustling about in preparation for these holidays.

But every year, in some families, the traditions are passed along. Someone new must take over the responsibilities and ready the house and the people, the food and the drink and the cheerful paraphernalia that make year's end a joyous season.

This, then, is a checklist for the newcomers—or for old hands who'd like to pass it along to any helpers they can involve in the doings. It assumes that you may be planning one big feast as a holiday climax.

NOVEMBER

Weeks 1–2

- Finish catalogue shopping.
- Buy the gifts you must mail.
- Buy mailing supplies: stamps, wrappings.
- Collect boxes for shipping.
- Mail overseas gifts.
- Buy cards, stamps.

Weeks 3–4

- Mail overseas cards.
- Address other cards.
- Mail out-of-town gifts.

DECEMBER

Week 1

- Mail all cards.
- Buy extra kitchen supplies: detergent, paper towels, toilet tissue, plastic bags, cleaning and polishing products.
- Make holiday guest list.
- Dig out recipes, make menus.
- Mail or phone invitations.
- Buy food staples: flour, sugars, extracts, candied fruits, shortening, oils, herbs, spices, crackers, nonperishable dairy products.

Dec. 7–10

- Clean and polish brass, silver (tie in plastic bags or plastic wrap or foil).
- Sharpen knives.
- Wash and wrap the china you rarely use.
- Wash glasses and stemware and turn upside down.
- Wash punch and salad bowls and stretch plastic wrap over them.
- Arrange to borrow or rent any extras you'll need. Consider disposable foil ovenware for cooking once-a-year dishes.
- Lay in paper and plastic dishes, glasses.
- Use up freezer foods to make room for holiday dishes.
- Save cartons, etc., to store frozen or refrigerated do-aheads (toss them out after the holidays!).
- Pick a day to go tree-chopping if that's your custom. Be sure to call the tree farm in advance.
- Order turkey (or other special foods).

Dec. 11–15

- Check table linens; launder, iron if necessary; hang tablecloths in closet to prevent wrinkling.
- Shop for canned goods, frozen foods to go in freezer, cranberries; wine, bottled beverages, mixers.
- Order any baked goods, pies, rolls that require special order.
- Finish Christmas shopping.
- Wrap gifts.

 TIP *Any time you need to tie a package tightly, wet the cord. (It stretches when wet, then shrinks a little as it dries.)*

- Hang wreaths, etc.
- Buy any other ornaments; inspect Christmas lights and bulbs. Discard cracked bulbs, frayed cords.

- Consider a toddler-proof tree using festive red and green rubber bands instead of wire hooks looped through your ornament tops.
- Do-aheaders make cranberry sauce (keeps in the refrigerator), pie pastries, and any other dishes that freeze.

Dec. 16–18

- Now for other do-aheads in the amounts you'll need for recipes: cutting, slicing, chopping, grinding nuts, dried and candied fruits. Shredding coconut; chopping parsley; grating rinds; squeezing juices. Refrigerate or freeze until you cook.
- Get major house cleanup done. Brief the family on what's expected of them in the way of preparation.
- Clean and press any clothes you plan to wear.
- Buy packaged ice cubes now or start making extra trays of cubes to store in freezer. (Don't use water to release cubes: keep them dry or they'll stick together.)

 TIP *Put cubes into several plastic bags, small enough so each will provide the right amount for your ice bucket.*

- Remove some bric-a-brac to make way for holiday decorations and party accessories.

Dec. 19–20

- Pick up turkey, start it thawing on refrigerator shelf.
- Buy all vegetables except the tender fresh ones.

Dec. 21–24

- Do any precooking you can. Set out candles, paper napkins, coasters. Be sure there are ashtrays around; also wastebaskets with plastic liners.

Set up bar. If you're having mixed drinks, make a batch.

TIP *For a big party, turn the washing machine into a soda cooler, protecting the tub with towels or plastic. Stash cans in ice in it. When the party is over, let the ice melt and spin the water away.*

- If you're serving buffet, and can do so, arrange the table now. Stick moist towelettes in an unobtrusive basket on the buffet if you're serving gooey food or having children at the party.
- Arrange any decorations not yet in place.
- Check the coat closet. Enough hangers? Can you move stuff out to make more space? Make a place for boots and umbrellas.
- Put up the Christmas tree and trim it. Last of all, arrange the presents around it. Set out a big cardboard box to receive discarded wrappings as gifts are opened.

Dec. 25—morning

- Check the bathroom: fresh soap? enough toilet tissue, towels? If you're using the bedroom as parking space for guests' belongings, have you cleared space there?
- Finish setting the table. Do any further cooking and kitchen work possible. Parboil vegetables, wash and store salad makings, etc.
- Get out the hors d'oeuvre.
- Check the kitchen: is everything conveniently set out for serving? Use trays and rolling carts as much as you can—they expedite both serving and clearing.

NOTES

. . . .

. . . .

. . . .

MEMOS TO YOURSELF AND ANYONE ELSE WHO HELPS WITH HOLIDAY
PREPARATIONS

Phone Numbers   Other Notes on Special Chores, Guests' Needs, etc.

....

....

....

....

....

....

....

....

....

....

....

....

....

....

....

HOUSEHOLD CEMENT RESIDUE

See Master Stain Removal Section (Adhesives).

HUMIDIFIERS

Clean the reservoir twice a season, say manufacturers. But if you live in a hard-water area or are concerned with bacterial and mold growth, clean at two-week intervals. Use with excessively hard water can produce a fine film of dust on room surfaces, which normal dusting will not remove.

Unplug the unit before cleaning or filling. Scrub the reservoir with a solution of 1 tablespoon chlorine bleach to 1 pint water or 2 tablespoons white vinegar to ½ gallon water. Rinse thoroughly to avoid bleach or vinegar odor after the unit is turned on. Do not use chlorine bleach solution to clean pads. Never use detergent. Detergent film can reduce humidification output.

Some humidifiers come with tablets or liquids the manufacturer suggests adding to the water to deter mold and slime buildup. Check the use-and-care manual for exact directions.

If odors are a problem, try adding 1 tablespoon of borax to 1 gallon of water to the unit.

TROUBLE SHOOTER

Humidifier Troubleshooters

No Air, No Mist: Too much water in the tank; remove some.
Properly secure tank top. Free the float for proper operation.
Air Blowing, but No Mist: Water scale buildup on float; not enough water in the tank or too much water in the tank; tank accidently washed with detergent. Rinse and see cleaning instructions.
Odors: Caused by detergent cleaning or bacterial buildup. Clean and refill tank. See cleaning instructions.

HYDROGEN PEROXIDE

The hydrogen peroxide indicated in this book is the 3-percent solution sold as an antiseptic and not the strong peroxide solution sold as a hair bleach.

It is safe for use on all fibers, but be sure to test dyed fabrics for colorfastness.

Store it in a cool dark place and discard it when it no longer bubbles.

The Pacific Northwest Extension Service advises that all-fabric bleach can substitute for hydrogen peroxide, but is slower-acting, and very thorough rinsing is needed to remove it from fabric.

Neither peroxide nor all-fabric bleach should be stored in metal containers, or used with metal objects. Metal can speed up the action of the bleach enough to damage fabric, and you may produce additional stains on fabrics if you have metal in contact with bleach or hydrogen peroxide.

HYPOCHLORITE   This is a term indicating the presence of hydrochloric acid. Its inclusion in the ingredients list of a bleach identifies the product as chlorine bleach.

ICE CREAM STAINS See Carpet Stain Removal Guide; Master Stain Removal Section (Dairy).

INK STAINS See Grout Stain Removal Guide; Vinyl Flooring Troubleshooters; Wood Floor Troubleshooters; Master Stain Removal Section. For ball point or India ink see Carpet Stain Removal Guide.

INSECTICIDES See Pesticides.

INSULATED OUTERWEAR The outdoors is more and more inviting in winter weather with the array of lightweight but warm outerwear now available—whether it is downfilled, insulated with needlepunch or with fiberfill, including the new fiberfill products like 3M's Thinsulate or Du Pont's Thermolite.

See Down, Fiberfill, and Needlepunch for care information on these insulating materials.

IODINE STAINS See Grout Stain Removal Guide; Master Stain Removal Section.

IRON Iron is found in the home in cook- and bakeware, plumbing pipes, some appliances, and plumbing fixtures. It is a strong, hard, rigid metal that rusts easily.

To clean, see Cookware Mini Manual (Cast Iron), Rust, and Wrought Iron.

IRON RUST STAINS See Master Stain Removal Section.

IRONING See Mini Manual on next page.

Ironing

When do you iron?

Same time you do laundry? Then remove the clothes to be ironed from the dryer before the dry cycle is complete. It's easier to iron wrinkles from clothes that are slightly damp.

Later? Then place damp clothes in a plastic bag and store in the freezer for up to two days without mildewing.

Just stack dry clothes that need pressing. Then, when you are ready to iron, sprinkle them with warm water and store in a plastic bag for thirty minutes to allow for an even spread of moisture.

TEMPERATURES

Use a low heat setting for fabrics of unknown fiber content.

Iron fabrics needing the lowest heat setting first: low, man-made fabric; medium, silk, wool; high, cotton, linen.

Heat setting for a blend should be the one recommended for the most delicate fiber in the blend.

IRONING STRATEGIES

Use a back and forth motion, ironing fabric lengthwise with the weave to avoid stretching.

Iron the smallest and thickest areas (collars, cuffs, facings) first, on both sides. Iron the inside first and then the outside. Hems should be ironed on the inside to prevent puckering.

A flower mister is perfect for moistening heavily wrinkled garments as you iron.

Need just a little moisture? Keep an ice cube in a handkerchief or light cloth napkin to dab on small dry areas.

Don't bother with your regular ironing board when you have just a touch-up to do. Use your sleeve board, if you have one.

A sleeve board is perfect not just for sleeves, but for making short work of baby things, too.

Stand on a rubber mat while ironing.

Iron whenever you have a favorite TV show.

Do not use starch on fabrics rinsed in fabric softener. (Causes iron to stick.)

To prevent shine, iron dark fabric, acetate, rayon, linen, and some wool on the wrong side. (Do not dampen woolens before ironing.) If ironing must be done on the right side, protect the fabric by using a pressing cloth.

Hang or fold clothes immediately to prevent the need to re-iron.

PLEATS

Pleats are ironed right side out from the hem to the waistline.

When you work with unpressed pleats, you may want to pin them to the ironing board along the waistline and the hemline, and steam them just to set the shape, never resting the iron on the fabric. Let the pleats dry before removing the pins.

Add extra moisture to pleats, creases, and tucks to aid in pressing.

To iron pressed pleats, pin them right side out to the board along waistline and hemline, using brown paper strips under the folds. Place a press cloth between the pleats and the iron. Then press. Repeat the procedure with the garment wrong side out for a sharp, lasting crease.

Never set the iron on the pins, or you will wind up with pin marks.

PRESSING

Pressing differs from ironing in that you lower and lift the iron, achieving greater control—smoothing cloth without stretching it, shaping delicate fabrics. You generally press from the wrong side and use a press cloth or a soleplate cover.

For a sharper crease in knit slacks, dampen them with a cloth wrung out from a solution of one-third white vinegar and two-thirds water. Place a brown paper bag over the crease and press.

Answers to Some Pressing Problems

When pressing a garment with a bias cut, go with the straight grain of the fabric. Never press sharp creases into bias-cut items.

Napped fabrics, pile fabrics, laces, and sheers are all pressed on the wrong side with a steam iron, with the material face down on a terry towel. Materials with raised surface designs are handled the same way, but with a dry iron. Embroidered and quilted fabrics benefit from a towel padding and wrong-side pressing, too.

Other ironing and pressing tips may be found under fabric and fiber listings.

CUT DOWN ON IRONING

With the advent of durable press, some people consigned their irons and ironing boards to the attic or the nearest thrift shop, and many others have developed tactics to avoid ironing.

You really can avoid wrinkles in durable press fabrics if you follow directions for washing and drying. In the washer: Avoid wringing and spinning while warm. If hand washing: Rinse in cold water and just squeeze gently.

True no-iron results can be obtained only by tumble-drying. Tumble clothes with a damp towel in the dryer for a few minutes at the durable press setting. Remove clothes from the dryer immediately, and hang on hangers right away. (One expert says that the one important feature machine dryers lack is a robot arm to remove dry clothes quickly!)

- Keep some hangers in the laundry room, ready for just-dry clothes.
- Do you really care if your towels, underwear, pajamas, or sheets are ironed? If not, skip this work. One shortcut: Iron only the top third of the sheet.
- You may not have to press your woolen sweater if you just sandwich the still damp/nearly dry garment between two towels and smooth it firmly with a rolling pin.
- Give some articles a quickie press by hanging them in a steamy bathroom.
- Try a wrinkle-remover spray on lightly creased clothes.
- Make your ironing last:
  Be sure ironed items are entirely dry before putting them away.
  When you iron large items like tablecloths or long skirts, avoid mussing the ironed areas. Pull a card table or chair or two close to the board to receive the lengths you've ironed.
- Keep hangers near the ironing board, so you'll hang up freshly ironed clothes right away.

IRONS   Today's technology has advanced dramatically since our ancestors heated irons over a bed of hot coals. Those antique irons that remain have been lovingly given jobs as doorstops and bookends. No matter if your iron is one of the more traditional steam/drys or the newer cordless, self-clean, or thermostatically-controlled models, it needs care if it is to have a long life and give your fabrics the best possible treatment.

Your iron is lighter than Grandma's. Don't feel that you must therefore bear down hard as you iron. It's controlled, even heat (not pressure) that produces smooth results.

Care

Always turn the iron controls to the off position and unplug after using. (Even if your iron has the automatic shut-off feature.) If possible, fill the iron with distilled water. It contains no mineral, dust, or alkali particles that clog the steam vent holes. Black & Decker cautions against using water processed through a home water-softening system. Either purchase distilled water or use a demineralizer.

Empty all water from the iron while it is still hot. This keeps the soleplate from becoming pitted. If your iron has a self-clean feature, empty some or all of the water using that feature to flush out any lint or mineral deposits in the steam vents.

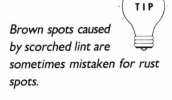

Brown spots caused by scorched lint are sometimes mistaken for rust spots.

When ironing, avoid touching the cord with the heated iron, and be sure the appliance is cool if you wrap the cord around it.

When the iron is cool, store in an upright position to prevent any excess moisture from dripping out of the iron onto the soleplate.

Cleaning

The soleplate can be cleaned with a paste of very mild scouring powder and water. Rub it on the cool iron with a damp cloth, then wipe off. Do not use a metal scouring pad. Flush any remaining cleaner from the vent holes with the steam control, the self-clean feature, or extra steam.

Then set the temperature to a low setting, run the iron over waxed paper and finally over a dry cloth.

The soleplate may also be cleaned by rubbing it with a mixture of equal parts of white vinegar and salt, heated in an aluminum pan. Use as a polish.

Commercial soleplate cleaners are available at service centers and hardware stores.

Clean a clogged spray nozzle with the point of a fine sewing needle.

Clean the reservoir by flushing the water out after each use. Some manufacturers recommend against using commercial steam iron cleaners or vinegar solutions, as they may damage the interior of the iron.

Troubleshooters

Scratches: If in the soleplate, rub very fine waterproof sandpaper over the scratches until the soleplate feels smooth. If on a badly scratched surface, use a dry, green Scotch-Brite Brand Scouring Pad. The polished appearance will be gone, replaced by a smooth satinlike finish. After polishing, clean the soleplate with denatured alcohol.

No Steam: If steam fails, tap the soleplate on the ironing board once or twice to start steam action.

Water Drips: Allow the iron to preheat one or two minutes before ironing. If dripping continues try a higher heat setting.

Spitting: Caused by clogged vent holes. See care and cleaning sections, above.

Synthetic Fabric Residue: Heat the iron, then iron over an old, all-cotton rag. After removing as much of the synthetic material as you can, cool the iron and clean as directed in the cleaning section, above.

IVORY   Ivory is a hard white substance derived from the tusks of elephants and walrus, often found in decorative objects, piano keys, and billiard balls. Ivory will yellow with age and do so more quickly if kept away from the light.

To clean, dust often. Wash with mild soapy water applied with a clean cloth wrung damp. Rinse with a damp cloth and dry. Ivory may also be cleaned with a cloth dampened with denatured alcohol. Leave piano keyboards open and art objects displayed to deter yellowing. For more information, see Pianos.

J

JACQUARDS   Brocades and damasks are typical jacquards—figured fabrics with detailed designs woven into the material. These materials from a jacquard loom may be wool, silk, cotton, even polyester. See Linens (Table) for ironing technique, and other fiber listings for general care directions.

JEANS   Jeans in today's market most likely feature the original yokeback, rivets, and wide belt loops, even when their design omits the low rise, patch rear pocket, and tight fit on which true fans insist.

But they now come in corduroy, chino, canvas, drill, khaki cloth, and even silk and other luxury fabrics—all a far cry from the 100 percent cotton denim that long ago made them a favorite of cowboys and laborers.

The only safe way to care for designer jeans is to follow labels, since their fashionable tight fit and special color treatment can otherwise cause you special problems.

For care information on cotton denim, or cotton blends, see Denim.

K

KETCHUP STAINS See Carpet Stain Removal Guide; Master Stain Removal Section (Tomato).

KETTLES, ALUMINUM To remove discoloration, bring the kettle to boil with 2 teaspoons cream of tartar to 1 quart boiling water. To remove lime scale, fill the kettle half and half with boiling water and white vinegar. Let the mixture stand in the kettle overnight. In the morning, scrub the inside with a steel wool pad, wash in detergent and water, and rinse thoroughly.

KITCHEN/BATH CLEANUP See Mini Manual on next page.

KNITS (Hand) Handknits like coats, wall hangings, beaded sweaters and silk are obvious candidates for dry cleaning. But you can wash most hand-made items, from baby mittens to afghans, using lukewarm-to-warm water, mild detergents and gentle washing action. (Soak in the suds, and squeeze; don't twist and wring.) Then rinse thoroughly.

To prevent stretchy knits from drying out of shape, you must block them. First, before washing, measure the item and record its dimensions, or spread it on brown paper and trace its shape.

After rinsing, roll the item in a towel to remove excess moisture, then lay flat to dry, bunching it or spreading it on the paper pattern, or other drying surface.

See Blankets, Gloves, Hosiery, Sweaters for more tips.

Kitchen/Bath Cleanup

This is a super-quick morning routine adapted to quarters where it pays to use just one to two products for everything! If you have a large house, you may prefer the routine in the Weekly Go-Round charted on page 16.

You need just a liquid or spray all-purpose cleaner and a glass cleaner, a couple of sponges, and/or some paper towels. That's all, for all kitchen and bath surfaces except floors and wood cabinets. And if you don't have an all-purpose cleaner handy, then just one of the glass cleaners that contain ammonia or vinegar will do for everything. *Note:* Do not use all-purpose cleaners on glass or mirrors.

1. In the kitchen apply liquid or spray cleaner to counters, tables—all surfaces where you eat or prepare food. That includes range top and sink.

Let the cleaner sit while you tend to the bathroom.

2. In the bathroom, apply cleaner to all surfaces—toilet seat and rim, vanitory, sink, and shower/tub.

Use glass cleaner on mirrors and chrome.

Add a few ounces of liquid bowl cleaner to the toilet each day, at a time when it will not be used for an hour or so. If you add a sanitizer-deodorizer to the toilet tank you can skip this. You will need to deal with the toilet bowl itself only on a weekly basis.

Empty the waste basket.

3. Return to the kitchen and wipe clean all the surfaces where you applied cleaner. Damp rinse with a sponge or paper towel. Polish dry if you have the time. Refrigerator fronts, ovens, and backsplashes can be left for the once-a-week cleaning, unless they are truly loaded with fingerprints, spatters, or grease.

Empty kitchen garbage.

If there is time, vacuum or damp-mop the floor. (Sweeping only spreads the dirt around.)

4. Go back to the bathroom. Repeat the wipe/rinse/dry process and you're done!

A thin sponge in soap dishes will reduce scum residue.

A weekly coat of kitchen/appliance wax will ease daily cleanup.

A plastic tablecloth or clear Plexiglas top to cover special tablecloths and cherished wood dining tables will make cleanup easier.

Add a handful of bubble bath or water softener to bath water to prevent "bathtub ring."

To be certain doors on medicine cabinets slide, coat the tracks with a light film of petroleum jelly. It helps protect against moisture corrosion on metal shower rods, too.

For the weekly cleaning checklist for these rooms, see the Weekly Go-Round, page 16. For grimy dirt, stains, and other problems, see the individual appliance, surface, or plumbing fixture listings.

KNITWEAR
(Machine)

Synthetic Knits, especially double knits, are usually machine-washable and dryable. Treat them as durable press.

Machine-wash, using warm water and a detergent.

Machine-dry at the medium setting.

Knits can also be hand washed, gently, in warm water, with a detergent. Rinse in cold water. Drip dry. Do not twist or wring.

See Sweaters, for sweater instructions.

Fabric softener in the final rinse wards off static electricity in synthetics.

Cotton Double or Single Knits: No problem with washing these, if the fabric has been finished to resist shrinkage. Note that cotton knits without a stabilizing finish should be shaped and air dried on a flat surface.

Wool Knits: Wool and worsted knits react best to dry cleaning. But single-knit jerseys and washable sweaters may be machine-washed using a delicate setting, and unless the label directs to tumble or machine-dry, block them to shape on a flat surface, and leave to air-dry.

Blended Knits: Knitted polyester/cotton blends may be hand- or machine-washed. Wool blends should never be washed unless the label recommends washing. Otherwise, follow the care label or tailor your cleaning method to the fiber that dominates the blend.

Delicate Knits: Use slow or gentle agitation for a few minutes, or alternate brief periods of agitation with soaking time. If care labels permit tumble-drying, use the regular or permanent press cycle. Select the delicate temperature setting, if available.

To press, use the temperature setting suggested by the fiber content of the knit. Wool requires steam-pressing and other knits may also profit from it.

Firm double knits may be hung on shaped hangers, but they will keep their shape better if folded carefully and placed in a drawer for long storage periods.

TROUBLE SHOOTER

Forestall stretching and snagging by putting knits in a mesh bag before they go into the washer.

TIP

For safe seasonal storage, place single knits flat to avoid excess stretching.

TIME SAVER

Want a "quickie" press? Just hang your knit near a steaming shower.

TIP

Knits need a "rest" between wearings as this permits them to regain their original shape.

LABELS   If you clean a garment as the label instructs you and it shrinks or changes color or is damaged in some other way, the manufacturer may be responsible.

Take the garment to the store where you bought it and explain what happened. The store will almost surely deal with your complaint. But if it doesn't, ask for the name and address of the manufacturer and write to them. At the same time, send a copy of your letter to the Federal Trade Commission, Correspondence Branch, Washington, D.C. 20580. The FTC strongly encourages this, because while it doesn't have the resources to solve individual problems, it uses such consumer complaints as a basis for taking action against companies that repeatedly violate the law.

Very few articles of clothing are exempt from the FTC care labeling rule. Only fur, leather, suede, and apparel that doesn't cover or protect the body, like footwear, gloves, hats, ties, belts, do not come under this rule.

The manufacturer is required to list only one safe method for care, even if there are other safe methods, and need not warn you if other methods are unsafe.

The manufacturer need not tell you the fiber content on the permanent care label. Though this information is required, it may be on a temporary tag.

Dry Cleaning: When the label says "Dry-clean," you can use any normal dry-cleaning method, including coin-operated machines. But if it says "Professionally dry-clean, short cycle, tumble warm," you must go to a dry cleaner equipped to follow the recommended process.

Laundering: If no temperature is given, you can use any temperature. Hot means up to 150° F (66° C). Warm means 90° F (32° C) to 110° F (43° C) or hand comfortable. Cold means up to 85° F (30° C) or initial water from a cold tap.

If there is no bleaching information, any bleach is safe unless the label warns against it. If it says nothing about ironing, ironing is not needed.

LACE   Old lace can be very fragile. Contemporary laces manufactured from synthetic fibers can be machine-care items. Fiber content dictates care.

But if you are working with small, delicate items, there are two precautions you can take when you wash them. Use a mesh bag to keep them from snagging. Or shake them in a jar partly filled with warm, soapy water, rinse in the same jar, and dry flat on a terry towel. Rustproof pins can hold them in shape.

When you iron lace or embroideries, always work from the wrong side, with the articles face down on a terry towel, using the temperature specified for the particular fiber content.

LACQUER STAINS   See Master Stain Removal Section.

LACQUERED FURNITURE   See Wood Finishes.

LACQUERED METALS   See various metals.

LAMBSWOOL   Lambswool comes from the first shearing of a lamb and shows up in fabrics with a soft, luxurious hand, in apparel such as sport coats or sweaters. See Wool for care suggestions.

You will also find lambswool dusters on the market, prized because their natural oils trap dust. They don't scratch and may be washed.

LAMINATED AND BONDED FABRICS

In bonded fabrics, an adhesive joins two layers of material, very often a lining and a face fabric, making a reversible fabric.

In a laminated fabric, fabric and foam are joined, or an outer fabric and a lining sandwich a layer of urethane foam. Double laminates are popular for winter sportswear, while single laminates are lighter in weight and may be used for rainwear, etc.

In the hands of reliable manufacturers, bonding/laminating methods produce apparel that is easy to keep and a joy to wear. The garments may be designed by the manufacturer to be either washed or dry-cleaned. They rarely require ironing. But if you do press laminated fabrics, use a steam iron at a low setting on the right side, with a press cloth. Never let the iron touch the foam.

LAMINATED PLASTICS

See Plastics (Laminated).

LAMPSHADES

Dust lampshades weekly with the dusting brush attachment of a vacuum cleaner.

Washable shades of plastic or fiberglass can be wiped clean with a damp cloth. Washable fabric shades that have colorfast trim and are sewn onto the frame (not glued) can be cleaned by dipping the shade in a tub filled with warm water and a mild detergent. Rinse and dry. (Do not dry silk in direct sunlight.) Dry as quickly as possible, to avoid rusting the frame and staining the fabric. (Try using an electric fan or portable hairdryer set on low.)

Nonwashable shades, handpainted shades, and shades that are glued to the frame can be cleaned professionally or with a dough cleaner of the type used to clean nonwashable wall covering. Dough cleaner may be purchased at hardware and paint stores, or use the recipe under Dough Cleaner.

LAUNDRY

See Mini Manual on next page.

Laundry

A MINI MANUAL

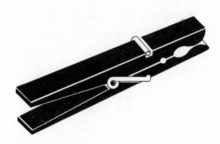

The washer is a remarkable machine, engineered to think through a series of processes to produce fresh, clean laundry.

However, it cannot sense what we are putting into it. That's our job.

GET READY: SORT . . .

Make 4 Piles

Whites	Solid Pastels	Medium &	Dark Colors
White backgrounds	Pastel backgrounds	Bright Colors	
Pastel designs			

These piles make separate loads.

Pull Out Other Troublemakers

Are there lint-givers and lint-lovers?. . . . . Separate them
Like corduroy and towels?

Are some items stained or heavily soiled? . . . . Pretreat them
Use a presoak (e.g., Axion) or
prewash (e.g., Shout) laundry product.

Are a lot heavily soiled? . . . . .Wash in separate load

Are some greasy? . . . . Wash separate from polyesters

And finally . . .   EMPTY POCKETS!
                          ZIP ZIPPERS!
                       BUCKLE BUCKLES!
                         HOOK HOOKS!
                       BRUSH OUT CUFFS!
                      TIE SASHES & BELTS!
                      MEND RIPS & TEARS!
                      TURN DARK SOCKS
                          INSIDE OUT!

GET SET . . .

SELECT WATER TEMPERATURE

For washing—HOT! The hottest safe for your fabric

For rinsing—COLD/WARM! Hot water creates wrinkles; cold doesn't.

USE THE PROPER WATER TEMPERATURE

Temperature	Use for	Comments
HOT: 130° F/54° C	1. Sturdy whites 2. Colorfast items 3. Diapers 4. Heavily soiled permanent press fabrics	Does the quickest and best job of cleaning and sanitizing but is not suitable for all items
WARM: 90°–100° F/ 32°–38° C	1. Moderately soiled clothes 2. Colored fabrics that are not colorfast 3. Silks, woolens, permanent press, nylon, acrylic, and other man-made fiber fabrics and blends	Minimizes wrinkling permanent press fabrics and reduces shrinkage of knits. With warm instead of hot water, there is less chance of washing out color or damaging fabric finishes.
COLD: Up to 80° F/ 27° C approximately	1. Extrasensitive colors 2. Very lightly soiled clothes 3. Items that are not shrink-resistant	Minimizes wrinkling and fading of colors but does not clean as well as warm or hot water.

From *The How to Clean Handbook,* © The Procter & Gamble Company, with permission

SELECT DETERGENT

Your wash product package tells you what you need for an average load of laundry, moderately dirty.

Very dirty wash? Use more.
Bigger load? Use more.
Harder water? Use more.
Cold water? Use more.
Gentle agitation? Use more.

GO!

Put some water in the washer first, then add detergent.

Now load, arranging items evenly around the agitator. *Don't cram.* That both reduces cleaning action and produces excessive wrinkles in permanent press items. *Strategy:* Mix large and small items in a load, if you can. You'll get better washing action.

PICK YOUR THREE SETTINGS

A. WASHING ACTION

For *sturdy items*, use regular/normal.

For *delicates*, use slow/gentle.

B. RINSE CYCLE

Rinse in cold/warm water to minimize shrinking and wrinkling.

If extra rinsing is needed, set to the last rinse cycle.

Synthetics and permanent press items washed in a wringer-type washer should be wrung out by hand to avoid excessive pressure on fabric.

 TIP *To sweeten wash and remove perspiration odors, add ½ cup of baking soda to the rinse cycle.*

C. SPIN CYCLE

Use regular spin for sturdy or absorbent fabrics.
Use slow spin for delicate, synthetics and permanent press to reduce wrinkles and fabric damage.
One-speed washers use a shorter spin time, reducing the amount of pressure.

If you think you should be getting better results than you're achieving with the steps we've just described, see Laundry Troubleshooters.

DRYING TIPS

Machine-Drying or Tumbling
- Don't overload. That increases drying time—and wrinkles!
- Separate heavy and light items, so they'll dry more evenly.
- You can shorten drying time by doing loads consecutively in a warm dryer.
- Remove permanent press as soon as dryer stops. This reduces wrinkling.

- Overdrying can cause shrinking, and excessive wear.
- Never machine-dry fiberglass, foam, plastics, or rubber.
- Freshen pillows, draperies, etc., with the air-fluff feature (unheated air flow).
- And finally . . . clean lint filter when you're through!

Line-Drying

- Be sure the clothesline and clothespins are clean.
- Smooth items as you hang them.
- Dry colors in the shade.
- Distribute weight of heavy items to avoid stretching the line.
- Outdoor drying will give you more even results with heavy items.
- Place a handkerchief between clothespins and delicate fabrics.
- Shake clothes to remove wrinkles before hanging.
- When you dry colored clothes outdoors, turn them inside out to prevent fading.

Flat-Drying
(especially necessary for wools and some knits)

- Dry away from direct heat.
- Dry items on a clean absorbent surface (towel).
- Turn item over midpoint in the drying time.
- Drying screens can be purchased to speed up drying by increasing air flow.

Keep a little brush in the laundry room to brush out pockets before washing.

When you sort clean wash, use boxes—each box for a different closet or a different room (or a different kid).

TIPS FOR HAND LAUNDRY

In all honesty, *any* fabric that can be washed by hand can be washed in a machine, except fiberglass. But there are times when hand laundry is most convenient.

Sort by color, pretreat heavy soil and stains, and choose the right detergent.

Light-duty laundry liquids do not provide whitening agents to keep fabrics at their whitest and brightest. They do provide the most protection against color bleeding, since they are neutral. But they don't cope with really soiled items—and the delicate washables we tend to do by hand aren't always just lightly soiled.

Soaps work well in soft water but may leave a soap curd deposit on fabric if combined with hard water.

Granular detergents should be dissolved in warm water before adding washables.

Three-Step Procedure for Laundering by Hand

1. Keep handling and agitation to a minimum, especially when washing wool, silk, acetate, and loosely woven knits. Squeeze gently, *never* wring or twist.

If colors are unstable, do not soak for more than five minutes and wash separately.

2. Rinse items at least twice to remove all soiled water and suds.

3. Flat dry items that may stretch or need to be shaped. Hang sturdy items on a rust-free hanger or rack to dry.

TROUBLESHOOTERS

You have followed pretty standard washing procedures, and lo! your laundry doesn't come out as you hoped and expected. Here are remedies.

Wrinkles in Durable Press Fabrics

1. Be sure you use warm wash and a slower or shorter spin speed, and a cold rinse. Remove articles promptly from dryer; hang or fold.
2. Don't overload.
3. To remove wrinkles from overdried clothes, put them back in the dryer, and set the control for fifteen to twenty minutes on permanent press of timed cycle. Heat and cool-down period will cope with the wrinkles.

Buildup of Body Soil

If this happens despite regular laundering, it has three principal causes: (1) you use too little detergent; (2) your wash water is not hot enough; (3) you're treating synthetic fabrics too delicately.

1. Increase the amount of detergent and/or use an all-fabric bleach.

2. Wash in the hottest water safe for your fabric.

3. Are you hand washing synthetics with a light-duty detergent or treating them with short, gentle, cool washes? Try hot water, at least 130° F (54° C), using a permanent press cycle, with a cool-down to lower the water temperature before the first spin. Also increase the amount of detergent and/or use an all-fabric bleach.

To Prevent in Future: Launder frequently and in a washer with water at least 100° F (38° C) with a laundry detergent.

For extremely discolored synthetics that cannot be bleached with a chlorine bleach, soak in a product containing enzymes. Or treat with a color remover by soaking according to package directions. Then wash in washer.

Gray Laundry

1. Use more detergent and/or use an all-fabric bleach.

OR

2. Increase your wash water temperature.

OR

3. When you sort, separate heavily soiled items from lightly soiled ones. Use more detergent, the hottest water safe for the fabric, and a bleach safe for the fabric.

If you spot a transfer of color in the wash, don't dry the items affected. Rewash immediately with detergent and a bleach safe for the fabric. Otherwise, the damage may be permanent.

Streaks on Wash

Undissolved detergent, or a residue from a nonphosphate granular detergent used in hard water is a likely culprit. Add detergent to the washer first, then add the clothes—and then start the washer to avoid undissolved detergent. Or dissolve the detergent in warm water before slipping it into the wash.

To treat streaks caused by a mineral residue, add one cup of white vinegar to one gallon of warm water. Use a plastic container. Soak item and rinse.

To Prevent in Future: Use hottest water safe for the fabric; don't overload the washer. Or use a liquid laundry detergent or a nonprecip-itating water softener with a nonphosphate granular detergent.

TIP *As a precaution when washing fabrics with colors that may run, immerse them in white vinegar before washing. The color will then remain fast.*

Lint on Laundry

Lint is the result of poor sorting, of overloading or too little detergent to hold the lint in solution during the wash time, or failure to clean the lint filter. (Towels are also a major source!)

Tips for Preventing Lint:

- Use fabric softener in washer or dryer to reduce static attraction of lint to synthetics.
- Throw a yard of nylon netting into your dryer with the wet clothes—dark net for dark clothes, white for light ones.
- Remove items from the dryer while they are still slightly damp.

TIP *When you clean the lint trap of your dryer (say the bird lovers), put that nice soft fuzz along with odd pieces of string and yarn in a small container and fasten to a tree or fence post for the birds to use for nesting material.*

To Fix an Article with Severe Lint Deposition: Hand-pat the dried item with transparent or masking tape. Rewash with detergent and use fabric softener in the final rinse. Dryer dry.

If it's a synthetic fabric that's been overdried, rewash, using a fabric softener in the washer or dryer or a detergent containing softener in the wash. Remove such an item from the dryer while slightly damp.

Blue Stains

If the culprit is a detergent or a granular laundry aid that didn't dissolve, add 1 cup white vinegar to 1 quart of water. Use a plastic container. Soak item for one hour; rinse.

If the fabric softener is at fault, rub stains with laundry bar soap; wash.

To Prevent: First put in the detergent or laundry aid, start the washer to add water, then add the clothes, and if you're using a fabric softener, dilute it before adding to the wash or rinse cycle, or to the dispenser.

Greasy, Oily Stains

To Remedy:

1. Treat with prewash stain remover or a liquid laundry detergent. Also increase the amount of detergent.

2. Increase water temperature.

3. Rub fabric softener stains with laundry bar soap; wash.

Preventive Tips:

1. Use enough detergent and the hottest water the fabric can stand.

2. Don't pour undiluted liquid fabric softener directly on fabric. Dilute rinse cycle fabric softener before adding to the final rinse.

3. If you use a dryer-added type: (a) add a few bath towels to the dryer when you have a small load; (b) be sure you use the appropriate dryer cycle, i.e. permanent press cycle with polyester/cotton blends, etc.; (c) reduce dryer temperature. Check dryer instruction booklet to be sure dryer is operating properly.

Shrinking

Many fabrics can shrink when laundered, and you should allow for this when purchasing such goods. Some hints:

- Remove knits from the dryer, especially cottons, while they are slightly damp. Stretch back into shape and lay flat to finish drying.
- When laundering woolen items, keep agitation at a minimum in both wash and rinse cycles. Use slow agitation or soak methods of washing and rinsing.

TIP *By the way, regular spinning does not contribute to shrinkage and will speed up drying.*

Stiff, Harsh Fabrics

Line-drying may be the cause.

If you machine-dry, hard water and your powdered detergent may be leaving a residue. Switch to a liquid detergent, or use a nonprecipitating water softener with a nonphosphate granular detergent.

To treat, add one cup of white vinegar to one gallon of warm water. Use a plastic container for the purpose. Soak item and rinse.

Yellowed Antiques

There is little you can do. Your cleaner may be able to help by adding brighteners in a dry cleaning process.

Yellowing Fabric

Chlorine bleach stains on silk, wool, or spandex are probably permanent. But if your victims are wash-and-wear cottons, linens, or rayons, the

Water Quality Association suggests dipping them in moderately hot water containing two tablespoons of an acid-type color remover, or sodium hydrosulfite. Then wash in soap and water.

Overexposure to light can cause discoloration (a breakdown of fluorescents in the fabrics). It is usually impossible to correct this.

Manganese stains: Try laundering in hot water with detergent and a rust remover, placing stained fabric over a container of boiling water and squeezing the juice from a lemon on it, or treating with oxalic acid. (See Oxalic acid.)

These stains will not respond to either soaps or detergents, and those with alkaline builders may make the stains worse.

If you have a recurring problem caused by water quality, buy demineralized bottled water or get water-softening equipment.

LAUNDRY AIDS

Bleach: These chemical agents brighten, whiten, remove soil and stains, and sanitize laundry. If used incorrectly, bleach can permanently damage fabric. Bleach is an assistant for detergents, *not* a replacement.

Chlorine Bleach (identified by the word *chlorine* or *hypochlorite* on the bottle) should be diluted with at least 4 parts water and added *after* the washer is full and washing. Chlorine bleach can damage animal fibers (silk and wool), some dyes, and spandex. Do not use on these fabrics.

Oxygen: *All-Fabric Bleach* is available in liquid or granular form. Safe for all fabrics. To be most effective, it must be used regularly.

Bluing is rarely used today. Contemporary laundry products contain brighteners to make wash appear whiter.

Borax is a water conditioner that controls alkalinity and odors. It aids in soil release and stain removal—especially baby food, milk, and formula.

Enzyme Products are available either as presoaks, or added to some detergents. They are good for removal of protein stains and ground-in dirt. (They virtually "eat up" these stains.) They are safe for all fabrics, and aid in restoring whiteness to yellowed or grayed fabrics. (See Presoak below.)

Fabric Softeners eliminate static-cling from durable press, nylon, polyester and acrylic fabrics. They also help to minimize wrinkling and make items soft. There are three basic softeners on the market.

1. Rinse-added—added to the final rinse.

2. Wash-added—added with or in the detergent.

3. Dryer-added—added when tumble drying.
   See Fabric Softeners for more information.

Phosphates inactivate water hardness minerals. They not only act as water softeners, but aid in soil removal as well. Some areas have banned detergents containing phosphates because of environmental reasons. Even if your area has not banned phosphates, read the detergent package to determine if it contains phosphate. Most detergents still contain phosphates, but the level has been reduced, and reduced phosphate detergents can be ineffective in areas of very hard water or when removing heavy concentrates of soil. See heavy-duty detergents in Master Product List.

Presoak Products offer pretreatment for heavily soiled and stained fabrics. Presoaks contain enzymes and in some cases bluing and oxygen (all-fabric) bleach. (See Enzyme Products above.)

Prewash Spray, Liquid, and Stick. These products pretreat stains and stubborn soils, and are especially useful for greasy soil on collars and cuffs. They are also effective for greasy soil on permanent press. Apply and allow to sit for a few minutes before adding item to wash load.

LEATHER, SUEDE, AND "SPLIT" LEATHER

Smooth leather may be cleaned with a damp cloth and mild soap (not detergent). Spread the garment, wipe with soaped cloth, wipe off soap, and pat dry.

Do not use home cleaning fluids, solvents or grease cleaners, shoe creams or saddle soap. Many manufacturers process leathers to stay supple indefinitely, and some use a finish that is damaged by anything except the damp cloth/soap cleaning. Stains and general cleaning should be handled by a professional dry cleaner specializing in leather.

When a leather garment gets wet, air dry it away from heat, on a wood or covered hanger. Do not hang on a hook.

Wrinkles? Just leave the garment in a damp room overnight. Pressing is generally inadvisable, but if you wish to press an item, set iron on lowest setting. (Do not use steam.) Use heavy wrapping paper as a press cloth, working on right side of garment one panel at a time with a light, quick hand to avoid overheating and shine.

Storage: Keep dust-free with a cloth cover in a reasonably cool, well-ventilated closet. Never use plastic bags: leather must breathe!

Suede and "Split" Leather

Suede is the animal skin turned inside out and buffed to a soft velvety nap. "Split" leather is a cowhide and can be recognized by its rough "brushed" nap.

Cleaning: Suede should stay clean if you brush it regularly with a terry towel to keep dust from settling in the nap. If new suede garments shed loose dust, remove it with a terry towel. Of course heavily soiled suede should be professionally dry-cleaned. Do not use home dry cleaners and sprays.

Spots, Stains: Remove with a soft gum eraser, emery board, or a chalk cleaner.

If suede gets wet or rain-spotted, dry away from heat. When it is dry, brush with a terry towel to restore original appearance.

For Leather Gloves, Shoes, Upholstery, see these listings.

MONEY SAVER

Repair torn hems of leather garments with glue. Thin spots can be reinforced with "iron-on" mending tape.

LEMON JUICE   Lemon juice is a mild acid, used much like vinegar, as a bleach, deodorizer, and cleaner.

LEMON OIL   This is referred to in this book as a commercial cleaning product used for furniture polishing.

LIGHTS   Dust with a dry or damp cloth or vacuum cleaner tool.

To give them a thorough washing, use the products that work on windows and mirrors: commercial solutions, some with aerosol sprays; solutions of water combined with light-duty detergent, ammonia, vinegar, or denatured alcohol. (Never use soap—it smears.)

Unplug the cord when you wash a light fixture, or turn off the switch. Never wash fixtures when the power is turned on. Always let bulb cool and always remove bulb, tube, or diffuser before you wash it. Then rinse, dry, and replace.

LINEN   Linens can be laundered or dry-cleaned, depending on the dye, finish, and construction of the item. But wash linen if you can. It is extremely strong, and it gains in strength when wet, so it can endure frequent laundering and becomes softer and more lustrous with use and laundering.

It is bleachable with chlorine bleach. But test fabric for color-fastness, and don't overbleach, since this weakens the fiber.

Linens withstand high washing and ironing temperatures unless they are resin-treated. Be careful with wrinkle-resistant linens, as shrinkage can occur if they are laundered in hot water.

TIP

For dull finish, iron on the wrong side. To develop sheen, iron on the right side.

Dampen linen lightly and evenly before ironing. You can use a hot iron, but adjust the temperature to suit your fabric. Lightweight linens don't require as hot an iron as the heavier ones. Do not press to sharpen creases.

Both linen and linen-look fabrics are likely to be sized, and if you do dry-clean them, they can be resized.

LINENS (Table)

To launder: Launder frequently so you don't accumulate oily food stains, and treat stains as soon as they occur. (See Master Stain Removal Section for methods.)

Fiber content should determine your laundry procedure.

To iron: Again, observe the rules for the fabric with which you are dealing. Go lightly on folds—you don't want to iron creases into tablecloths. Press lace tablecloths between two sheets. Iron jacquards first on the wrong side (to bring up the pattern), then on the right (to bring out the sheen).

Professional laundries are well-equipped to handle tablecloths.

To store: To avoid last-minute pressing, roll table linens on tubes, or hang on hangers. If you do store them flat, fold them gently, with nothing stacked on top. Don't wrap in tissue paper since tissue may contain acids that will cause spots on linen.

Avoid plastic bags. They do not allow for evaporation. And avoid hot, damp areas, which encourage mildew stains.

TIP

To keep table linens from creasing, hang them over a wire coat hanger covered with a paper towel roll you have slit, then taped to the bar.

LINGERIE

Most home economists agree that machine-washing on the delicate cycle is an adequate way to handle lingerie in general. This is not just because machine-washing is easy, but because when you wash by hand you're more likely to use water that's not hot enough, and less likely to achieve the thorough rinsing a machine can give you. Over time, then, your lingerie may acquire a dingy look.

However, most people wash lingerie by hand, and some items clearly demand hand care. Use plenty of detergent, especially on soiled areas—bra and slip straps, underarm areas, etc. For underarm stains, rub in a light-duty liquid detergent. Don't skimp on washing product, as these items are more heavily soiled than they look. And be sure your wash water is hot enough. To remove body oils, water at 90° F (32° C) to 110° F (43° C) is necessary.

Note: In case you use chlorine bleach for hand laundering white items, dilute it before adding it to the detergent solution. Noxious fumes can result from mixing chlorine bleach and liquid detergents full strength!

TIP

Roll small items like panties, girdles, and T-shirts. They take up less room, and this arrangement makes inventory easier to take.

LINOLEUM   Linoleum should be cleaned according to vinyl flooring recommendations with the addition of an application of wax for shine only. Note that it can be adversely affected by ammonia, alkalis, chlorine bleaches. See Vinyl Flooring.

LINSEED OIL (Boiled)   This is an ingredient in some polishes, like lemon oil and Danish oil. It is also recommended for treating wood surfaces. It is toxic and flammable. *Never* boil it yourself. Boiled linseed oil is available at hardware stores.

LIPSTICK STAINS   See Carpet Stain Removal Guide; Grout Stain Removal Guide; Vinyl Flooring Stain Removal Guide; Master Stain Removal Section.

LIQUOR STAINS   See Master Stain Removal Section (Alcohol).

LUCITE   See Plastics.

LYE (Caustic Soda)   Lye is the strong alkali in many oven cleaners and drain cleaners. It is poisonous and toxic as well as caustic. Don't breathe fumes. Avoid contact with skin and eyes. Don't get on chromium or aluminum—or your hands. Store out of reach of children. You may prefer to use less dangerous substances (e.g., ammonia solutions for ovens, washing soda for drains).

MADRAS

Authentic Indian madras is distinguished by its bold plaid designs woven from yarns dyed with native vegetable colorings. These dyes bleed when washed; use cool water for Indian madras and wash items separately.

Many Madras shirt fanciers immerse them in white vinegar before washing, to deter color loss.

MAKEUP STAINS

See Carpet Stain Removal Guide; Master Stain Removal Section (Cosmetics).

MANGANESE STAINS ON LAUNDRY

See Laundry Troubleshooters.

MAN-MADE FIBERS (And Fabrics)

For most of human history we have made our clothes from silk and wool (animal products) or from cotton and linen (plants).

We now have a choice between the apparel and household goods produced with animal and plant fibers and a vast array of goods made with manufactured fibers. The man-made fibers, in particular, have produced great variety in the marketplace.

They cater to our new tastes—and we are very demanding. We want fabrics that require virtually no care. We also insist on textiles that will (or won't) stretch, that will (or won't) absorb water, that will keep us warm (or cool), that will drape, or stay stiff, etc. Our wants have created markets for fabrics that combine natural fibers with man-mades and man-mades with other man-mades, and it is not uncommon to find textiles combining several different fibers.

In buying or caring for any fabric, the only sure way to avoid bewilderment is to pay attention to the label required by the

Federal Trade Commission. Forty years ago, when the consumer started buying the new blends, responding to stories and advertisements describing them as "wool-like," "silk-like," etc., the Federal Fiber Identification Act was passed to help purchasers know what they were buying.

So each family of man-made fibers has a generic name—rayon, acetate, nylon, polyester, etc.—just as each manufactured fiber has its own definition, its own unique chemical formula or construction. At the same time as the FTC started establishing these definitions, it also required that the fiber components in a blend be listed in decreasing order: e.g., 65/35 polyester/cotton or 55/45 polyester/wool.

As a very general guide to manufactured fibers, first note that there are two main kinds of manufactured fibers.

1. Rayon, acetate, and triacetate are cellulosic fibers. Rayon is composed largely of regenerated cellulose, while the fiber-forming substance in the acetates is cellulose acetate.

Since cellulose is the fibrous substance in all forms of plant life, you might expect fabrics in this group to behave like the naturals, and rayon is like them in its capacity to absorb moisture, while acetate and triacetate are more like other man-mades, with low absorbency.

2. Synthetic fibers, from coal, gas, sulphur, and other nonfibrous materials make up the rest of the fibers in use.

In most of these, the fiber-forming substance is a long-chain synthetic polymer, with entirely different formulas for each fiber: This is the case with acrylic fibers, anidex, modacrylics, olefin, polyester, saran, spandex, vinal, vinyon. In aramid and nylon, the fiber-forming substance is a long-chain polyamide, again with two different formulas.

Metallic fiber, another man-made product, is composed of metal, plastic-coated metal, metal-coated plastic, or a core completely covered by metal.

Glass is of course the fiber-forming substance in glass fibers, natural or synthetic rubber in rubber fibers.

These synthetic fibers do not absorb water. They're fast-drying, don't shrink; they're hypoallergenic, mothproof, and mildew-proof. While the smooth, nonporous surfaces of synthetic fibers keep dirt and grime from becoming imbedded, oily stains are a problem to remove. They also collect static electricity. But they are the greatest boons to those who hate ironing.

For care information, see the listings for the various fibers.

MARBLE

Man-made marble is practically indestructible. Just wipe fresh spills with a damp cloth, take a household cleanser to dried-on stains. You shouldn't use a synthetic marble countertop as a cutting board (it scratches), but you can remove minor scratches, knife cuts or burns with an abrasive cleanser or fine sandpaper. A hot pot should not scar the surface. It also won't chip.

Genuine marble, on the other hand, is porous and alkaline, and to preserve its glorious color and sheen, you must give it the same sort of care you give fine wood.

It is really not all that difficult to clean. It may be washed with a clean soft cloth and warm water, with a twice-a-year wash with warm water and a mild detergent to remove any ingrained dirt.

If you wish, use a non–yellowing wax to shield it from dirt.

To avoid problems with any beautiful marble surface, remember just two principles:

1. Oil stains marble.

2. Acid "etches" the stone. That means fruit juice, milk, vegetables, etc. Use coasters. Wipe up spills.

Also protect marble from hot dishes, and bric-a-brac or rough-bottomed dishes that can scratch the surface. (Hot plates, felt protectors, place mats, please.)

Stain Removal

Stains are the bugaboo of the proud owner of marble furnishings and floors, because they seep down into the pores of the stone.

Do consider using the services of a marble dealer if you have some exceptionally fine marble. Also take a look at the products designed to clean and polish this stone.

The most common treatment for marble, to remove deep-seated grime and dirt, is a poultice made with common laundry bleach, or a 6 percent hair-bleaching solution of hydrogen peroxide. You can buy a poultice for this purpose. Or you can make one.

In the basic recipe, you combine a strong liquid cleaner (bleach or peroxide) with an absorbent (like untreated white flour, white tissue or paper towels, white powdered chalk, talc, fuller's earth, etc.), making a paste the consistency of oatmeal or cake icing. You figure on making one pound of paste per square foot of surface to be treated.

To apply, moisten the marble with the same liquid you used for making the paste. Apply the poultice paste with a wood or plastic spatula to a uniform thickness of ½ inch. Be sure the poultice is in full contact with the stone—there should be no air pockets. Then tape plastic wrap with masking tape over the poulticed area, and let it sit for forty-eight hours.

Just before you remove it, dampen it with clean, cool water to control dust. Use the same sort of spatula to remove it; then rinse the cleaned area with more water; blot or wipe off excess water and allow the work to dry. If dirt shows after the area is thoroughly dry, a second poultice application is necessary.

Choosing the cleaning liquid to use: Many stains respond to the bleach or peroxide solution just described, but there are special poultices recommended for other situations.

Pinkish-brown organic stains caused by food, leaves, flowers, tea, coffee, bird and animal droppings, and tobacco may disappear when the offending substance is removed. If not, treat with a poultice with a liquid base of hydrogen peroxide in a 6 percent hair-bleaching solution.

Similar stains caused by urine take a strong chlorine bleach-based poultice.

Dark oil stains caused by butter, milk, cream, salad oils, cosmetics, mustard, etc., are treated with an acetone poultice.

Rust stains (orange-brown) often take the shape of the item producing the stain. First remove the cause or causes—the source of moisture, the flower pots, metal furniture, etc. Clean and paint these last with a clear coating such as varnish, shellac, or a plastic spray-on/brush-on coating so they'll quit staining. Superficial stains may then be removed by thorough scrubbing, seated stains by using commercial naval jelly or other rust remover, following manufacturer instructions. If this fails, try scouring powder followed by a second application of naval jelly. (As a last resort, get your marble dealer to help with a poultice using either sodium hydrosulfite or sodium hypochlorite as the base.)

With fire or smoke damage, first try one of the smoke removers many marble dealers carry. Or scrub off surface dirt with a detergent and a fiber brush. If deep-seated dirt and stains remain, make a poultice with an alkaline cleaner (like baking soda) and water. Let it stand twenty-four hours before removing.

Etch marks caused by acids like wines, beer, fruit juices, vinegar, tomato products, mustard, carbonated beverages, ink, and salad dressing should first be washed with clear water. If a stain remains, poultice the area following either the general poultice method or the method described for your particular stain.

Polishing

When you apply a poultice to a marble with a polished finish, there is a possibility that you will lose some of its gloss. If this happens, wet the surface with clear water and sprinkle on marble-polishing powder (from a hardware or lapidary store or your

To prevent urine stains in the bathroom, periodically sprinkle a powder cleanser containing chlorine bleach around the toilet, dampen it and let it stand overnight.

When using these cleaning methods, wear rubber gloves and eye protection, ventilate the area, use wooden or plastic spatulas to apply, and remove poultices to prevent scratches. Don't combine liquids containing ammonia and bleach (you'll produce toxic fumes) and don't use sandpaper or cleaners containing grit or abrasives on polished marble unless they are specially recommended.

marble dealer). If etch marks persist, consult your local marble dealer.

The Marble Institute of America, 33505 State Street, Farmington, MI 48024, publishes an inexpensive booklet answering homeowners' questions about the care of marble, granite, slate, limestone, and other decorative stone popular in home building and furnishings.

MARKING PEN STAINS   See Carpet Stain Removal Guide.

MASCARA STAINS   See Carpet Stain Removal Guide; Master Stain Removal Section (Cosmetics, Grease).

MATTRESSES   Air your mattresses routinely, periodically turning them to alternate sides and ends for even wear, and vacuuming them occasionally.

Odors. To cope with odors, use a disinfecting spray or sprinkle with baking soda, letting it stand briefly, then vacuuming off.

Neutralize urine odors by dampening the spot and sprinkling borax over it. Rub in, then let dry and vacuum or brush to remove the borax.

See Waterbeds for waterbed mattresses.

MAYONNAISE STAINS   See Carpet Stain Removal Guide; Master Stain Removal Section (Grease).

MEAT JUICE STAINS   See Master Stain Removal Section.

MELAMINE   Melamine is found most often as plastic dinnerware. It may also be a component in countertops and in control knobs on appliances. To clean, see Plastics (Thermoset).

MERCERIZING Mercerizing is a strong alkali treatment that gives cotton yarns or fabric greater strength, luster, absorbency, and dyeability. It requires no special care.

MERCUROCHROME STAINS See Carpet Stain Removal Guide; Grout Stain Removal Guide; Vinyl Flooring Stain Removal Guide; Master Stain Removal Section (Iodine).

MERINO This wool fiber, obtained from the Merino brand of sheep, is very fine in diameter and used to produce the finest of wool and worsted clothes. Sometimes it is mixed with cotton, wool, or silk. It may also be found in seat covers, mattress pads, etc., where it is sometimes processed to permit machine-washing.
For care, see Wool.

MERTHIOLATE STAINS See Carpet Stain Removal Guide; Grout Stain Removal Guide; Master Stain Removal Section (Iodine).

METALLIC FABRICS Glittering beachwear may withstand ravages from salt water, or the chlorinated water in swimming pools, while other articles containing Lurex cannot even be washed (much less bleached).
Attention to the care label is all-important.
When metallic content is small, you will probably use the laundry method recommended for the predominant fiber (cotton, wool, etc.), always bearing in mind that metallic yarns may be heat-sensitive. Iron with a cool iron, unless otherwise instructed by the manufacturer. If you need to disinfect, use a small amount of chlorine bleach.

MICARTA See Plastic Laminates.

MICE See Rats.

MICROWAVE OVENS Microwave cooking is cool cooking, so foods don't burn on oven walls. But food spatters, and if left in the oven cavity, will eventually spoil and possibly contaminate what you are currently cooking. Very soiled ovens could also result in slower cooking.

To clean the oven cavity, wipe the walls with a paper towel dampened with warm water after each use. Once a week, clean the walls with detergent and warm water, rinse, and dry. For hard-to-remove soil, boil a cup or dish of water in the microwave. The steam will loosen the food particles. Wipe them away with a nylon pad or sponge. Never use abrasive cleaners.

Wipe door seals (gasket) after each use with detergent and water. Grease and soil buildup on the door gasket lessens the tightness of the seal and may allow some radiation leakage.

If your oven has a ceramic floor, scrub with a nylon pad and baking soda and water.

Never operate the microwave when it is empty.

Foods left in the microwave for an extended period of time may cause odors. To remove, boil ¾ cup of water mixed with ¼ cup of lemon juice in the oven cavity.

MILDEW Mildew is a thin growth—black, white, or bluish-green in color—that is produced by molds. It is most likely to show up in damp, warm weather on surfaces in poorly aired and poorly lighted areas.

Mildew discolors fabrics and may cause them to rot and fall apart. Natural fibers (silk, wool, cotton, linen, and rayon) are most vulnerable. But soil on synthetics can supply enough food to encourage mildew growth on these normally mildew-resistant materials.

To Remove Mildew

Brush off surface growth. Do this outdoors so spores won't scatter in the house.

Vacuum to draw out more mold. Use the upholstery attachment, empty the bag outdoors, and throw it out immediately.

Finally, sun and air articles outdoors if you can. Sun and air are the best preventives and the best cures for mildew.

If Mold Remains

On Washable Fabrics: Launder with soap or a detergent and water. Rinse and dry in the sun.

If stain remains, moisten with lemon juice and salt, and spread in the sun to bleach. Then rinse thoroughly. Or use another bleach, first testing fabric for colorfastness. Soak the stain in an oxygen bleach solution (1 to 2 tablespoons powder with 1 pint of water) or sprinkle the dry powder on the dampened stain. Let stand thirty minutes or longer, then rinse. Stubborn stains, says the U.S. Department of Agriculture, may need overnight soaking in the bleach solution, with the solution at or near the boiling point when it is applied. Just be sure the fabric will withstand this treatment.

Or, if your fabric withstands chlorine bleach, mix 2 tablespoons of liquid chlorine bleach with 1 quart of warm water and sponge the stain or soak the stained area in the solution. Allow the bleach to stay on the fabric five to fifteen minutes, then rinse. You can stop bleaching action with an additional soaking in weak vinegar (2 tablespoons to a cup of water).

On Nonwashable Fabrics: Dry-clean, identifying the stain to your dry cleaner.

On Mattresses and Upholstery: After removing surface mold and vacuuming to get at mold that may have penetrated the article, do everything possible to dry out the item. Sun and air. Or use an electric heater with a fan to carry away the moist air.

You can also sponge lightly with thick suds of soap or detergent, wipe with a clean, barely damp cloth, taking care not to get the filling wet. Or wipe the furniture with a cloth moistened with diluted alcohol (1 cup denatured alcohol to 1 cup water). Then dry thoroughly.

On Rugs and Carpets: Sponge with thick suds or use a rug shampoo. Wipe off suds with a cloth dampened in clear water, and dry thoroughly, in the sun if possible.

If you cannot remove the carpet for treatment, you may be able to rent a vacuum capable of removing water from the carpet and padding. You may need to lift a portion of the carpet to get at the underlayment. It is essential to get the flooring as well as the padding and the carpet dry, or the problem will just grow worse.

On Leather Goods: Wipe with a cloth moistened with diluted alcohol (1 cup denatured alcohol to 1 cup water). Dry in airy place. If mildew remains, use thick suds made from a mild soap or detergent, saddle soap or a soap containing a germicide or fungicide. Then wipe with a damp cloth and dry in a current of air. Polish shoes and luggage with a good wax dressing.

There are sprays to cope with the fungus that often affects shoes (available at shoe and department stores).

On Wood: Increase air circulation and heat to dry out mildewed wood.

Scrub mildewed woodwork with a mild alkali, such as washing soda or trisodium phosphate (8 to 10 tablespoons to a gallon of water), or with a quaternary disinfectant or pentachlorophenate. (At paint and hardware stores and janitors' supply houses.) Rinse wood well with water. Dry thoroughly, then apply a mildew-resistant paint.

On Paper and Books: If the paper is damp, first dry it in an airy place. Spread book pages fanwise to air. If books are very damp, sprinkle cornstarch or talcum powder between the leaves, letting it remain for several hours. Then brush off. You can also use your microwave oven to dry papers and books.

TROUBLE SHOOTER

If molds have penetrated an article, send it to a reliable disinfecting and fumigating service. See "Exterminating and Fumigating" or "Pest Control" in the Yellow Pages.

CAUTION

Don't use mildew-resistant paints on windowsills, playpens, beds, or toys. They are injurious if they reach the mouths of small children.

If your problem is wallpaper, heat the room for hours or even days to dry plaster as well as paper. (Just note that plaster will crack if you try to dry it too fast.)

Washable paper may be wiped gently with a cloth wrung out of thick soapsuds, then with clear water. Wet as little as possible, and don't scrub. Finally pat with a soft, dry cloth. If stain remains, bleach with a solution of household bleach, then sponge with a damp cloth wrung out of clear water. A commercial ink eradicator may work on a small stain.

To Get Rid of Musty Odors

In Basements: Sprinkle chlorinated lime (commonly called chloride of lime or bleaching powder) over the floor and let it stay until all mustiness disappears. Then sweep it up.

On cement floors, tiled walls, and floors: Scrub with a chlorine bleach solution ($1/2$ to 1 cup of liquid household bleach to a gallon of water). Rinse with clear water and wipe dry. Keep windows open till walls and floors are thoroughly dry. (*Precaution:* Work quickly and carefully on plastic and asphalt tile to avoid spotting the surface.)

Aerosol sprays for cleaning and sanitizing bathroom walls are also available.

Useful Preventives

Thorough cleaning is your first, best preventive action.

When putting articles away for storage, first wash or clean them, omit starch (on which molds may feed), and consider using paradichlorobenzene spray in cans or using paradichlorobenzene crystals. Paraformaldehyde is another mildew inhibitor.

You can treat fabrics with water-repellent sprays. There are also fungicide products on the market and some germidical and mothproofing sprays that protect against mildew.

Do not inhale the spray from these chemicals. They are poisonous. Paradichlorobenzene also damages some plastics (buttons, ornaments, plastic hangers). Read warnings carefully.

CAUTION

You may also consider the use of chemicals that absorb moisture, like silica gel, activated alumina, anhydrous calcium sulfate, or a product called Molecular Sieves (from scientific supply houses or industrial chemical suppliers) to use with stored items. Or control moisture in your house with air conditioning, fans, dehumidifiers, or an electric light in the closet.

In areas where mildew is prevalent, you may be able to get further advice from your state or county Cooperative Extension Service. This section on mildew is largely derived from the U.S. Department of Agriculture's inexpensive bulletin, "How to Prevent and Remove Mildew (Home Methods)." Your Extension Service may offer it for sale, or you can procure it from the Cornell University, Department of Design and Environmental Analysis, New York State College of Human Ecology, Ithaca, New York 14850.

MILDEW STAINS   See Carpet Troubleshooters, Grout Stain Removal Guide; Wall-Covering Troubleshooters; Master Stain Removal Section.

MILK STAINS   See Carpet Stain Removal Guide; Master Stain Removal Section (Dairy).

MILLIPEDES   See Centipedes.

MINI-VACUUM   See Vacuum.

MIRRORS   The challenge is to wash the face of the mirror while keeping the backing dry.

Your best bet may be commercial liquid glass cleaner, the spray-on kind, but sprayed onto a cloth, not on the mirror, so you have greater control. Or use water with a little vinegar or ammonia, applied with a cloth. Dry with a lint-free cloth or chamois.

You can have damaged mirrors resilvered. Consult a furniture restorer (or hardware store).

MIXERS AND CORDLESS BEATERS

Wash beaters and attachments in hot water and detergent or place them in the silverware basket of the dishwasher. Wipe the mixer with a damp cloth after each use. Do not immerse power unit. Remove difficult food spots with a sponge dampened with a nonabrasive liquid cleaner. Rinse with a damp cloth or paper towel and dry.

When storing the mixer, do not wrap the electrical cord around it. Remove the cord and store it folded into loops.

MODACRYLIC

Your wig or your fake fur is likely to be modacrylic in its composition. Also your paint rollers, your stuffed toys, and perhaps also your awnings, blankets, flame-resistant draperies, etc.

In general, you will be directed to dry-clean upholstery and to use a fur-cleaning or dry-cleaning process for deep-pile garments.

But for washables, proceed as follows:

1. Machine-wash in warm water and add a fabric softener during the final rinse cycle.

2. If dryer is used, use low setting and remove articles as soon as tumbling cycle has stopped.

3. If ironing is required, use low setting. Never use a hot iron.

MOHAIR

Mohair comes from the Angora goat or rabbit. For laundry procedures on mohair washables, see Sweaters, Wool.

MOIRÉ

This watered effect may be either temporarily or permanently ironed on fabric, often acetate or silk taffeta. See care labels.

MOLD　　See Mildew; Master Stain Removal Section (Mildew).

MOTHS AND CARPET BEETLES

There are seven major ways of coping with the moth menace.

1. Buy woolens or wool blends pretreated by the manufacturer with a moth-resistant finish.

2. Spray your woolens yourself. You can buy oil-solution insecticides in ready-to-use pressurized containers that deliver a coarse spray, or you may buy a liquid insecticide to apply with a household hand sprayer. When you do this, hang the clothing or blankets on a clothesline. Spray lightly to get their surfaces uniformly moist. If there's a white deposit when they dry, brush it off. (A heavy deposit requires dry cleaning, which removes the insecticide and leaves the article unprotected.) Dry articles before you wear or store them.

You might also spray wool or mohair draperies, also mattresses, pillows, or upholstered furniture. But note that the chemicals only help prevent infestation—they don't kill the pests already inside the stuffing. So you must take such infested articles to a reputable pest-control firm for fumigation.

Do not spray rugs and carpets (get professional advice and treatment) or furs. (Use commercial storage for furs or store them in tight containers with moth crystals, flakes, or balls.)

3. Store with pesticides—moth crystals, flakes, or balls in tightly sealed boxes or closets.

4. Seal mothproofed areas carefully, including even cracks in the closet ceiling, walls or floor. Protection is lost if the closet door is opened frequently.

Naphthalene flakes or balls kill adult moths. Paradichlorobenzene crystals kill both the moth and the eggs, and they have less odor than naphthalene. However, paradichlorobenzene tends to dissolve plastic, so do not use plastic hangers or plastic garment bags.

CAUTION

Pesticides are safe and effective when correctly used, but dangerous when misused. Store them properly. Dispose of them safely. Read labels carefully. Keep out of the reach of children. Launder or dry-clean any infants' sweaters or blankets you have treated before you return them to use. Don't breathe in pesticide sprays or dust. Don't swallow or splash on yourself. Note that oil-solution insecticides are flammable, can stain some fabrics, can dissolve asphalt and soften and discolor some linoleums and plastic materials.

TIP

If fresh air doesn't re-move mothball odor soon enough to suit you, hang your clothes in the bathroom, fill the tub with hot water and one quart of white vinegar, close the door and leave the clothes for a few hours.

CAUTION

Don't let moth balls, nuggets, and flakes touch fabric directly. And don't mix different kinds of mothproofers Drop moth-proofers into socks, tie at the top, hang in garment bags and closets, or place among your packages.

TIP

If you hate the smell, try mixing cloves or cinnamon sticks with your mothproofer.

Use 1 pound of the crystals, flakes, or balls for each 100 cubic feet of space, placing them in a shallow container on a shelf or suspended from a clothes rod or hook in a thin cloth bag or perforated container.

Often you will also protect woolen clothes simply by wrapping the freshly cleaned items in paper or sealing them in a cardboard box. Cedar chests are good, too, because of their tight construc-tion. But be sure the woolens are free of larvae before you put them away, and use moth crystals, flakes, or balls after your cedar chest is two years old.

5. Clean. You can rid woolen clothing, blankets and unupholstered furnishings of insects and their eggs and larvae by brushing and sunning them, or by having them dry-cleaned.

Vacuuming also disposes of eggs, larvae, and adult insects most efficiently, so long as you also dispose of the bag promptly and carefully. Pay special attention to hard-to-reach spots.

6. Treat surfaces where insects crawl—along the edges of wall-to-wall carpeting and the rest of the hard-to-clean places. Use coarse sprays. Aerosols don't give lasting protection to surfaces.

7. Use a reputable pest-control firm, says the U.S. Department of Agriculture, if you have a serious infestation.

MUCUS STAINS   See Master Stain Removal Section (Urine).

MUD STAINS   See Carpet Stain Removal Guide; Master Stain Removal Section.

MURIATIC ACID
(Hydrochloric Acid)
This is used to remove difficult stains from brick. It is both poisonous and caustic, and should be used only by professionals.

MUSTARD STAINS
See Carpet Stain Removal Guide; Master Stain Removal Section.

MUSTY ODORS
See Mildew.

NAILPOLISH REMOVER   See Acetone.

NAILPOLISH STAINS   See Carpet Stain Removal Guide; Grout Stain Removal Guide; Vinyl Flooring Stain Removal Guide; Master Stain Removal Section.

NATURAL FIBERS   Our four widely used natural fibers are silk and wool, both animal products (protein), and cotton and linen, both fibers occurring in plants (cellulose).

Characteristically, they all absorb moisture, soil, and stains, but are easy to clean. They may shrink or lose shape when they're washed, and they are slow-drying. They require pressing and, with the exception of wool, they cannot be heat-shaped (to achieve permanent creases, etc.).

But they are all comfortable to wear. Cotton and linen, the cellulosic fibers, are durable and easy to care for. The animal fibers, wool and silk, resist wrinkling and resume their shape if you let them air and rest.

Of course, today's finishes can give them resistance to shrinkage, wrinkling, stains, and insect damage, and they are now often blended, sometimes with each other, often with man-made fibers as well.

NEAT'S-FOOT OIL   Neat's-foot oil, from shoe repair shops or hardware stores, is a leather conditioner. It is not a cleaner (use it after cleaning the leather item). And it is not a polish (it soaks in, leaving a dull finish).

NEEDLEPUNCH OUTERWEAR   Needlepunch is a web of man-made fibers (usually polyester) providing an insulating interlining for cold-weather clothes. It's lightweight, nonallergenic, and both machine-washable and dry-cleanable. Care depends on the outer fabric.

NOMEX   See Aramid.

NONSTICK FINISHES ON COOKWARE   See Cookware Mini Manual.

NYLON   Textiles made from this manufactured fiber are easy to clean.

Use warm water for heavily soiled and white or colorfast articles. Prespot soiled areas with liquid detergent. You may use chlorine bleach (but test colors for bleach-fastness).

Wash your white nylon items only with other whites.

Do not dry white nylon in the sun: prolonged exposure can cause yellowing.

Most nylon builds up static cling, so use fabric softeners to reduce static electricity.

Rinse in cold water.

Use moderate heat in the dryer, removing items as soon as the dryer stops.

Use a warm (not hot) iron or steam iron.

Just tumble-dry knitted nylon items: they need no ironing.

> **TIP**
>
> *Nylon fibers pick up color from any colored items in your wash water, including white items that have been washed with other colors.*

ODORS   Throughout the book we suggest methods to remove or eliminate odors under different subject headings. If you have a particular problem you may want to check under Carpets, Drains, Refrigerators, etc.

There are two ways to attack odors: mask them or eliminate them. The odor is attacked at the source either by taking out the garbage, emptying the kitty litter or by neutralizing the odor with some of the newer "scent free" commercial deodorizers and electronic air purifiers, which mix molecules of odor with those of another.

Odor Tips

Bathrooms: Turn on vent fan or open a window.

Use a solid, continuous air freshener.

Deodorize bath fabrics (curtains, mats) with spray.

Spray hamper with a nonstaining fabric deodorizer.

Allow towels to dry before placing in hamper.

Kitchen: Dispel cooking odors by boiling 3 tablespoons of white vinegar in 1 cup of water.

Disposers: Grind up the peel of a lemon or orange.

Sprinkle 3 tablespoons of borax in the drain and let stand fifteen minutes. Flush with water.

Oven-Cleaner Odor: After cleaning the oven, place orange peels in the oven and bake for fifteen minutes at 300° F (or 177° C).

Refrigerators: Keep an open jar of vanilla beans on the door shelf.

After washing the refrigerator add a dash of lemon extract to the rinse water.

Lunch Boxes: Dampen a piece of bread with white vinegar and leave it in the box overnight.

Kitty Litter: Sprinkle baking soda or borax in the litter box.

Perspiration: For odor on clothes after laundering, soak garments in warm water containing ¾ tablespoons salt for each quart of warm water for an hour or more. Rinse well before drying.

OIL STAINS See Carpet Stain Removal Guide; Wall-Covering Troubleshooters; Wood Floor Troubleshooters; Master Stain Removal Section (Grease).

OLEFIN Olefin fibers are uniquely able to draw body moisture from the skin up through the fabric to its outer surface, so they are frequently found in disposable diapers, knitted sportswear, underwear, and pantyhose. Their largest single use is in outdoor carpets.

To care for olefin products:

TIP

A stain on your olefin carpet? Just blot it away with an absorbent tissue.

1. Machine wash in lukewarm water and add a fabric softener to the final rinse cycle.

2. If machine-drying, use a very low setting. Remove items from dryer immediately after tumbling cycle. Avoid commercial or laundromat gas-fired dryers.

3. Never iron anything of 100 percent olefin. If touch-up ironing is required for olefin blends, use the lowest possible temperature setting.

ORGANDY This is a thin, transparent, stiff cotton fabric used in dresses, trimmings and curtains. If it is chemically treated (Swiss organdy), the crisp finish will last through repeated launderings. If not, it loses crispness in laundering and will require re-starching. Just press organdy to cope with mussing.

ORGANZA   See Sheers.

OVEN CLEANING   Standard

The only option available for cleaning a standard oven is manual labor. But if you always wash the broiler pan and wipe out the inside of the oven with liquid dish detergent and water after each use, the cleaning job won't build up to strenuous proportions.

For spots of burned-on soil, apply a cloth saturated in ammonia over the spots for thirty minutes. Wipe clean with detergent and water.

To loosen soil buildup, leave a dish of ammonia in the oven overnight.

Scrape off large spillovers with a single-edge razor blade. Safety holders for these blades are available in hardware and paint supply stores. The razor edge will not harm the porcelain enamel oven lining.

TROUBLE SHOOTER

To prevent spillovers, place ½ paper straw in fruit pies to release steam and juice.

The whole oven will need the application of a commercial oven cleaner. These cleaners are formulated to attack stubborn stains and spatters. Follow the manufacturer's instructions carefully. Misuse of oven cleaners can etch porcelain enamel.

Be careful when using cleaners in aerosol form near the open flame of a gas range.

Do not spray oven cleaner into a hot (over 200° F /93° C) oven. This will cause the cleaner to become a corrosive agent.

Continuous

With a continuous cleaning (catalytic) system you eliminate most soils during the cooking process, and the higher the oven temperature and the longer the cooking time, the better the cleaning will be.

Occasionally, wipe the entire oven interior with a nylon pad dipped in clear water. Wipe dry and set oven to 475° F (246° C) for two hours.

Never use metal soap pads, steel wool, or abrasive cleaning powders.

Never use a commercial oven cleaner.

Protect the bottom of the oven from spillovers with a cookie sheet, foil, or oven liner. Take care not to cover the vent holes at the bottom of gas ovens. Keep protective liners away from the heating elements in electric ranges.

For very large spillovers, blot up the excess spill while the oven is still slightly warm. When the oven has completely cooled, spray with an all-purpose cleaner (Fantastik, 409). Work the cleaner into the surface with a nylon brush or net pad. Let the cleaner remain for thirty minutes. Scrub the softened soil and rinse with cold water. Do not allow water to run down into base of oven. Set oven to 475° F (246° C) for two hours.

Self-Cleaning

This system literally burns away oven soil at very high temperatures (850° F/454° C to 1000° F/538° C). At the end of the cleaning cycle nothing is left but a residue of white ash. Even though the oven does most of the work for you, there are still a few points to keep in mind.

To reduce smoke during the cleaning process, wipe oven interior with a damp cloth or sponge before setting the clean cycle.

If you clean racks and drip pans in the oven, they will eventually take on a blue tinge. If you wish to avoid this, the stainless racks and pans should be washed by hand.

The exterior portions of the oven frame and door should be wiped clean before setting the clean cycle. High cleaning temperatures will bake on soil outside of the oven and make cleaning the exterior of the range much harder.

Wipe up the white ash residue after the cleaning process. If

TIP

Form a foil tent to place over roasts or turkey to eliminate oven splatters and the bother of basting. Crimp foil onto long sides of pan to hold in place.

TIP

Foil is also a work-saver when placed on the rack beneath a pie or casserole to keep the oven bottom clean. The sheet should be only one inch longer than the dish for proper heat circulation.

the oven is not completely clean, set the cleaning time for a longer period.

Never use a commercial oven cleaner. The high heat of the clean cycle combined with the chemicals in the cleaner can etch the porcelain enamel finish on the oven lining.

OXALIC ACID   This is a strong acid used for bleaching and an invaluable aid in removing ink and rust stains from fabric.

To prepare an oxalic acid solution, mix 8 ounces of oxalic acid crystals (from the hardware store) with 1 gallon of water, using a plastic pail in which to dip the stained article. Dip several times, squeezing the fabric gently between dippings. Rinse thoroughly in fresh water and wash in soap and soft water.

Oxalic acid is poisonous and a skin and eye irritant. Do not breathe vapors. Use rubber gloves. Rinse the container well after dipping. Do not dispose of oxalic acid solutions in porcelain sinks, washbowls, or tubs. Dilute the solution with extra water, pour it into the toilet, flushing immediately several times.

OXYGEN BLEACH   See Bleaches, Laundry Aids.

PAINT

Wait at least thirty days before washing a newly applied coat of flat paint.

Interior paints may be water base (latex), oil base (alkyd), or enamel (varnish/resin base). Paint finishes may be gloss, semigloss, or flat. In general, the higher the gloss, the more washable the paint.

Washable paints are cleaned with a mild all-purpose cleaner. Avoid abrasives. Gloss or enamel finishes can take more frequent and vigorous cleanings than flat finishes.

To Wash: Use a commercial cleaner or make your own soap jelly. (See recipe under Soap Jelly.)

Change water often to avoid washing clean areas with dirty water.

Nonwashable Paint: Purchase a commercial "eraser" from your hardware or paint store, or use our dough cleaner recipe. See Dough Cleaner.

For more information, see Walls and Ceilings, Woodwork.

Use 2 buckets. One for the cleaner and one for rinsing. Wash from the bottom up to avoid "clean streaks."

PAINT BRUSHES

See Brushes and Brooms.

PAINT STAINS (Latex)

See Carpet Stain Removal Guide.

PAINT STAINS (Oil)

See Carpet Stain Removal Guide; Vinyl Flooring Stain Removal Guide; Master Stain Removal Section (Grease).

PAINT STAINS (Water-based)

See Carpet Stain Removal Guide; Master Stain Removal Section.

PAINTINGS AND PRINTS

Unless you are an expert, just dust your oil paintings carefully with clean absorbent cotton or a soft brush.

You can protect prints by framing them correctly—sealing the frame to keep out dust and air, using mats to keep the prints from touching the glass. Both mats and the board sealing the back of the frame should be of all-rag board content. Seal the back with gummed linen tape: Scotch tape and masking tape should not be used.

Oil paintings should not be hung next to air conditioning or heating vents, nor on damp walls. In fact, dampness can harm most pictures, and watercolors and prints should also be protected from sunlight.

If a print buckles inside its frame, let it alone. It will often correct itself.

Using double-face tape will keep pictures straight.

TIP

To hammer the nail instead of your fingers: Hold it with the teeth of a comb. Another trick is to hold the nail in place with a bobby pin.

PANTRY PESTS

These unwelcome houseguests include bean and rice weevils, a variety of beetles and Indian meal moths. Some are specific feeders (i.e., they eat only whole grains and hard cereal products or only rice or only beans). But most will eat practically anything in the pantry, including dried foods like milk, dog food, fruit, dried and cured meats, candy, nuts, chocolate and cocoa, spices—even drugs. You treat them all alike.

To Disinvite Them

Store your dry foods in metal, glass, or heavy plastic containers with tight, insect-proof lids. (Most flexible plastics, cardboard, cellophane, metal foils, and cloths won't keep them out.)

Vacuum pantry shelves. (It's the best way to pull crumbs from corners.)

To Treat Infested Foods

You can sterilize the food in an oven at 140° F (60° C) for thirty minutes. (Spread contents of large containers on flat cookie sheets or pie pans to insure adequate penetration of heat.)

Freezing at 0° F (− 18° C) for three to four days will also kill insects.

Put dried fruit in a small cheesecloth bag in the freezer or dip it in boiling water for six seconds (then dry thoroughly before storing again).

Once treated, food can be sifted out and consumed. (These insects are harmless to animal and man if eaten. Actually, they add a bit of protein!)

To Fight Infestation

Apply insecticide to the clean surfaces of your cupboards, using paintbrush, paint roller, or spray can. Be sure you get into all drawers, cracks, and crevices. Aerosol sprays are not recommended because they do not leave enough insecticide residue. A diazinon or chlorpyrifos spray should be effective.

Then do *not* wash the treated surface. Let it dry and then cover with paper or other material to keep food containers from coming in contact with any insecticide residue.

When using liquid insecticides, empty all cupboards. Move all food and utensils from the area (or cover them). Don't treat food in packages. Keep insecticide off tables, countertops, sinks, cooking utensils, and silverware. Wait till shelves dry before replacing contents.

Appropriate insecticides include compounds of methoxychlor, malathion, propoxur or diazinon.

PARAFFIN STAINS   See Master Stain Removal Section.

PATENT LEATHER   See Handbags, Shoes.

PEACH STAINS   See Master Stain Removal Section (Fruit).

PEAR STAINS   See Master Stain Removal Section (Fruit).

PEN (MARKING) STAINS   See Carpet Stain Removal Guide; Master Stain Removal Section (Ink).

PENCIL MARKS   Remove with soft eraser.

PERFUME STAINS   See Master Stain Removal Section.

PERMANENT PRESS   This describes garments or other items treated to retain a smooth appearance, shape, and creases or pleats in laundering. They require no ironing, particularly if they are tumble dried. Also referred to as durable press.

PEROXIDE   See Hydrogen Peroxide.

PERSPIRATION STAINS   See Master Stain Removal Section.

PESTICIDES   There are many multipurpose or all-purpose mixtures on the market, as well as special-purpose products. They break down into two traditional groups.

TIP

"For years I fought with white flies on my favorite plant. Then I tossed a flea collar into the pot and I haven't seen a white fly for months."

1. Space sprays and foggers control flying insects, killing them on contact. This group includes some highly toxic products along with the pyrethrins (from dried, powdered chrysanthemum flowers), favored because they act fast and because of their low toxicity to humans and pets.

In case of illness, call a Poison Control Center or physician for instruction. Then take the victim and the pesticide container (or at least a copy of the label) to the nearest clinic or hospital.

2. Residual insecticides (sprays, paint-on emulsions, baits, and dusts) are intended for crawlers like cockroaches and ants, which can seldom be sprayed or dusted.

Bait trays are a popular residual product, because they are odorless and child-resistant, and there is no danger of contaminating food preparation areas with them, as with sprays and foggers, etc.

Another method of pest control is termed Integrated Pest Management. This can be less hazardous to pets—and people—because the product affects the metabolic rate of pests, halting their ability to take energy from their food; or it acts as a birth-control agent, sterilizing the insect or preventing eggs from hatching. Many experts anticipate continuing development of such products because of their safety factors, and because they may combine fast initial action with longer pest-free periods. No one foresees methods offering permanent control.

Check containers for advice on any restrictions. Oil-based solutions should not be used on asphalt or vinyl tile floors. Some insecticides should not be used on rugs or tapestries, etc.

All Pesticides Are Poisons

Store pesticides where children and pets cannot possibly reach them.

Keep products in their original containers so you cannot mistake them for something else.

Do not get insecticides on food—or anything that comes in contact with food, even food-preparation counters.

Never smoke, drink, or chew gum while you are handling pesticides.

Insecticides need time to work. Many are slow-acting, and you should wait twenty-four hours (to several days) to see if they are doing the job for you.

For Help: Every state has an Extension Service that advises consumers on home pests and pesticides.

All pesticides must be registered by the U.S. Environmental Protection Agency, and all of us who use pesticides use them lawfully only if we follow label directions.

PET FOOD STAINS   See Carpet Stain Removal Guide.

PETROLEUM JELLY   Well known under the brand name Vaseline, this is a lubricant with many household uses, from shining patent leather to eliminating squeaky faucets to warding off rust on iron.

PEWTER   Pewter is largely care-free.

Use a mild soap to wash items in everyday use, then rinse and dry immediately with a clean, soft towel. Polish by rubbing in one direction. (Machine-washing is not recommended.)

You may want to use a commercial polish to remove spots, stains, and minor scratches, rubbing it gently over the piece, then removing the polish and buffing with a soft cloth.

Antique pewter gets its unique dark sheen from its lead content. If you use a commercial cleaner, be sure it's specially made for pewter.

To clean heavily tarnished pewter, use a paste of whiting and boiled linseed oil. Dip a small piece of 0000 steel wool into the paste, then rub the pewter piece in one direction to remove tarnish. Then polish. Make only as much paste as you need for immediate use. You can store the ingredients separately; do not try to save the paste. (Do not boil the linseed oil; you purchase it boiled.)

The standard polish for a dull finish of your own making is a paste of boiled linseed oil and rottenstone, applied with a soft cloth to rub it over the pewter. (Again, in one direction.) And again, make only enough for immediate use.

Brittania alloy and white metal are sometimes confused with pewter. They are of the same general family and should receive the same care.

> **TIP**
>
> *Don't use pewter for storage. Some foods stain or pit pewter if allowed to remain on it for a long period. Party dips, eggs, salad dressings, oils, salt, and fruit juices should be removed immediately. And don't store a pewter bowl or vase so it rubs against another hard object or it will be scratched.*
>
> *Never use pewter for cooking or put it in the oven, or near the burner, or in a microwave.*

PIANOS   *Professional Care:* Steinway & Sons say their concert grands are tuned before every concert, and they recommend that pianos in the home be professionally tuned at least three (preferably four) times a year.

Do-It-Yourself Care: Remove finger marks and dust with a clean, soft, lintless cloth, such as cheesecloth, very lightly dampened with water. Wring it out well and shake it to remove excess moisture. Then make a pad of the cloth and rub the finish in the same direction as the grain of the wood, using long, straight strokes.

If any water droplets remain on the piano, remove them with a dry pad of cheesecloth, stroking as you did before.

Do not use furniture polish on the piano case. And Steinway warns that no cloth or polish will remove marks left by heavy vases, clocks, picture frames, etc., unwisely placed on your piano.

The keys may be cleaned with a clean, soft cloth dipped in a mild, white soap solution, wiping them one by one lengthwise. But don't let moisture run down the sides of the keys. It's best to use a separate cloth and soap solution for the black keys.

Do not use cleaning fluids, lacquer thinner, alcohol, benzine, or other solvents on the keys.

As for the interior, hire a professional to do periodic cleaning, or to come to your aid if you drop a pencil or other foreign objects into the interior. If you're just worried about dust, you might turn your vacuum cleaner on exhaust and blow accumulated dust into the room. (Then vacuum the room!)

If you go away in winter, the piano should cool gradually when the heat is turned off and warm up gradually, too.

Select a dry, clear day to close the piano.

Bunch perfectly dry newspapers into balls the size of your fist, and place these inside the piano, on the strings, under the top cover.

Now close the top and also the fallboard over the keys.

Place blankets on top of the piano; tie them fast with strings.

PILE FABRICS

Long-pile fabrics are widely used for fake fur coats, small rugs, cushions, and the like. For care information, see Furs, Synthetic.

Short-pile fabrics include velvet, velveteen, corduroy, velour (plush and velour are often used interchangeably), and terry (in which the pile is uncut).

Fabrics like these must be steamed rather than pressed. If you use a steam iron, hold it about ½ inch above the ironing board, steaming the item right side up. Then brush gently with a soft brush while the fabric is still damp. Let dry without further handling.

If you press on the wrong side, place the garment wrong side out on a turkish towel, a piece of self fabric or a needle board, and steam lightly. Brush and let dry.

Stretch terry, stretch velour: Your main special concern is retaining the original shape. If the stretch is horizontal, use padded hangers. If it's vertical, store your garment flat. If the fabric does stretch, you may find that washing and drying or steaming will return it to its original shape, and some synthetic fabrics regain their shape on the hanger or in the drawer.

PILLING   Those little fuzz balls that form on the surface of soft yarn fabrics represent a wear problem that cannot be completely prevented. Pilling is common on some synthetic and permanent press fabrics. It also occurs on cotton and wool fabrics, but the fuzz balls fall off in wear. The polyester fibers are very strong and prevent the pill from falling off.

To prevent, turn garment inside out when washing. Use a fabric softener in the washer or dryer to lubricate the fibers.

Watch out for abrasion from other items in the wash load. Wash alone or with fewer items.

To remove, brush with wire clothes brush, suede brush, or pumice stone. There are also various gadgets and appliances available to scrape or shave off pills. When pills attract lint, use a lint brush or roller with masking or transparent tape.

Some people treat pilling by stretching the fabric to make the balls stand out, then carefully clipping or shaving them away with scissors or a razor blade. Clipping is the only remedy for pills on the surface of rugs and carpets.

PILLOWS

Fluff pillows daily. You may also freshen those with down, feather, or polyester fiberfill in the dryer. Use low heat for ten minutes to remove humidity and keep them resilient.

To wash washable pillows, machine-wash using short/delicate wash and warm water. Do no more than two at a time, pushing them down if necessary to keep them submerged. (Stop the machine, of course, before you do this.) Most important, rinse in warm water three times to remove all detergent, then dry in the dryer at low heat or pin them on the line if weather permits. Be sure to get them entirely dry or you will encourage mold. For further information on care of down, see Quilts.

Kapok pillows will become lumpy if laundered. Do not attempt machine-drying.

To dry special items like rubber and foam rubber, line dry or machine-dry on air-fluff (no heat). Foam rubber in a heated dryer creates a fire hazard.

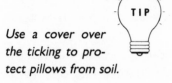

Several clean tennis balls in the dryer help to fluff feather pillows.

Use a cover over the ticking to protect pillows from soil.

PINE RESIN/TREE SAP STAINS

See Master Stain Removal Section.

PIQUÉ

True piqué has a woven-in design that will not flatten out, even if you iron it. There are embossed fabrics imitating piqué that should not be ironed.

PLASTIC COOKWARE

See Cookware (Plastic).

PLASTIC-COATED FABRICS AND WEBBING

Wipe off with a detergent solution or all-purpose household cleaner. A soft brush works on webbing or textured plastics.

PLASTICS

Although the varieties of plastic ware seem endless, there are just two types: thermoset plastic, such as melamine, and thermoplastic, such as acrylic and vinyl.

Thermoset plastics, set into a permanent shape by heat and pressure, are heat-resistant and durable, but not impervious to scratches, marring, or discoloration. Most thermoset items are dishwasher-safe but should be kept away from very high heat.

To reduce or remove stains, soak in a solution of chlorine bleach and water or dishwasher detergent and water. Some stains can be scrubbed out with a paste of baking soda. Avoid harsh, abrasive powdered cleansers.

Thermoset plastics include melamine (Melmac) and phenolic (Bakelite). These "rigid" plastics are found in the home as heat-resistant dinnerware and pot handles.

Thermoplastics are generally molded and can be softened by heat. Some are dishwasher-safe, but in the top rack only. Most can be cleaned with a liquid all-purpose cleaner, rinsed, and dried. Avoid harsh, abrasive cleansers, and solvents containing nailpolish remover, cleaning fluid, and the like.

Alcohol is a good cleaner for acrylic sheets (like Lucite)— ordinary rubbing alcohol (or the stronger 99 percent isopropynol alcohol). Do not use products containing ammonia on acrylics.

Thermoplastics include acrylic (Lucite and plexiglas), nylon, polyethylene, polystyrene, polyurethane, polyvinyl chloride (PVC), and vinyl. These "soft" plastics are found in the home as housing for small appliances, disposable dinnerware, table tops, and refrigerator liners.

TIP

Dip-It should remove most coffee, tea, and food stains from melamine dinnerware.

PLASTICS, LAMINATED (Formica, Textolite, Micarta)

These show up most often as countertops, tops for dining and coffee tables, and on children's bedroom and recreation area furniture. They are resistant to alkalis and acids and have a moderate resistance to stains and heat (up to 270° F/132° C). Protect your counters with cutting boards, trivets, or hot pads when preparing food.

To clean, use detergent and water or a general household cleaner in liquid or spray form. Avoid abrasive, gritty cleansers.

A coat of kitchen wax, after cleaning, will offer extra soil-repellence and make cleaning easier.

Stains: Although laminated plastics resist most stains, items like mustard, grape juice, and tea bags can cause problems. To remove stains, sprinkle baking soda on a soft, damp cloth and rub lightly. For more difficult stains dampen the stained area with water and sprinkle with a cleanser containing bleach. Let stand about ten minutes and rinse off (do not rub) with clear water. (Standing for more than fifteen minutes may bleach out the color of the plastic.)

PLEATS See Ironing.

PLEXIGLAS See Plastics.

PLISSÉ See Seersucker.

PLUM STAINS See Master Stain Removal Section (Fruit).

POLLUTED WATER See Water (Polluted).

POLYESTER It was polyester fiber that first introduced the world to wash and wear in blends with cotton.

Polyester presents very few care problems. But it may pill when abraded. And while polyesters resist water-borne stains, they attract oil-borne stains. (They absorb body oils.)

Pretreat all stains before washing, especially greasy ones, by rubbing in undiluted liquid detergent or applying a spray-type pretreatment product.

If stains remain, apply dry-cleaning solvent as directed on container, then rub in undiluted liquid detergent; wash.

Machine-wash in warm water and add a fabric softener to the final rinse cycle.

Machine-dry at a low temperature, removing articles as soon as the tumbling cycle is completed.

If ironing is desired, use a steam iron or a moderately warm iron.

Most polyester items can also be dry-cleaned. However, the Man-Made Fiber Producers Association warns that pigment prints on polyester double knits do not withstand dry cleaning well.

POLYVINYL CHLORIDE (PVC)

Polyvinyl chloride is a flexible to rigid plastic used in dishwasher liners and racks, outdoor furniture, etc. To clean, see Plastics (Thermoplastic).

PORCELAIN ENAMEL

See Enamel.

PORCELAIN ENAMEL COOKWARE

See Cookware (Porcelain Enamel).

PRESOAK

See Laundry Mini Manual, Laundry Aids, Pretreating.

PRESSING

See Ironing.

PRESSURE COOKERS

Pressure cookers are cleaned according to the type of metal they are made of.

It is especially important to wipe the inside of the lid after each use and wash the rubber gasket with detergent and water. Rinse and dry.

Troubleshooters

For Steam Leaks: Refit or replace the rubber gasket. Check the gauge and safety valve, they may be clogged. Clean or replace.

If the Lid Sticks: Rub edges of the cooker lid and pot with cooking oil or unsalted fat.

PRETREATING

Pretreating is often recommended in this book as a useful method of coping with unusually dirty items in the laundry basket or as a preliminary step in handling spots and stains on washable fabrics.

You'll find a number of products formulated to work on the main problems.

• Extra-dirty laundry yields to soaking with all-purpose detergents containing enzymes or special presoak products.

• Dirty collars and cuffs or other small stained areas are easier to handle with the direct application of a heavy-duty detergent, a bar soap, or a special pretreatment product.

• Spots and stains are best pretreated with special products containing enzymes or oxygen bleach.

See Laundry Aids. Sample products are listed in the Master Product List.

PSOCIDS

See Book Lice.

PUMICE

This is an abrasive stone, available on the market in stone form (to buff dead skin off heels and elbows, etc.) or as a powder (at paint and hardware stores) to assist in scouring or polishing, or as an ingredient in scouring powders. Pumice stone is handy to remove pills on fabric.

PVC

See Polyvinyl Chloride.

QUARRY TILE   See Tile Floors.

QUILTED FABRICS   Most quilted blankets, bedspreads, robes, etc., designed for wear around the house are washable, unless they're made of velvet or satin or the like. If you need to press a quilted item, test an inconspicuous spot (especially if the face fabric is nylon, taffeta, ciré, etc.) Use a dry iron on a low setting with a press cloth, and as little pressure as possible, since you don't want to lose the attractive loft in the design.

For care of outerwear, see Down, Fiberfill, and Needlepunch.

QUILTS AND COMFORTERS   Cotton and polyester battings are common in quilts. So is down filling. Cover fabrics may determine the correct care, and if your care tags don't give you complete instructions, check the fabric listings in the ABCs.

To Wash

Polyester shell fabrics and polyester fiberfill may be machine-washed in warm water on the gentle or delicate cycle with mild detergent. Rinse repeatedly if necessary to remove all residue. Spin dry on the delicate setting.

Sturdy cotton quilts can be similarly machine-washed, but hand washing is desirable for delicate cottons.

General method for cotton/polyester quilts: Fill a large sink or tub with tepid water and ¼ cup of mild detergent. Accordion-fold the quilt to make it easier to handle before you place it in the bottom. Soak fifteen to thirty minutes. Drain the tub and refill with cool water. Repeat this rinsing process as often as necessary to remove all residue. Be careful—a wet quilt is heavy and if you agitate it too much, you may damage it.

To Dry

Smaller quilted items can be partially machine-dried, retrieved from the dryer while slightly damp, then smoothed into shape, folded, and finished by flat-drying.

To flat-dry a comforter or quilt when you're through rinsing it, first blot it dry with towels to remove as much moisture as you can that way. Then spread it out flat where air can circulate around it. To finish the drying process, drape it over several clothes lines to distribute the weight.

Machine tumbling on low or delicate heat or on "air" only can puff up your quilt.

You can also generally dry-clean comforters and quilts. But air out a polyester-filled quilt after dry-cleaning, to let any dry-cleaning fumes disperse.

Down quilts are washable, of course, but they are slow drying and hard to handle, and you may elect to dry-clean them. Don't, however, alternate methods: dry cleaning solvents may remove oil from the feathers, making them too brittle to machine-wash. Cleaners who specialize in down also replace feathers and down. For tips on the care of down, see Down Coats and Vests.

To Iron

If you want to iron quilted items, select the setting for the type of the shell fabric being pressed, and use a light hand, to avoid flattening the batting. If you have corduroy or velveteen or velvet on one side, protect the pile when pressing. See Corduroy, Pile Fabrics, Velvet.

RADIATORS AND HEAT REGISTERS

Dust radiators and heat registers often, especially during the heating season. (Dust acts as insulation and wastes heat.) Remove covers and grillwork, use the dusting brush and crevice tool on your vacuum cleaner. Wash radiators when the heating system is off, with a solution of detergent and warm water. Rinse and dry.

RADIO CASSETTE PLAYER

See Audio.

RAMIE (China Grass)

Ramie is a bast fiber that comes from a tropical plant. (Linen is also a bast fiber—from the stem of the flax plant.) Ramie fibers are durable (Egyptian mummy cases were made of ramie), resistant to mildew and alkalis (but not to acid), and can withstand high ironing temperatures.

Once chiefly used in table linens, ramie has been coming onto the market in knit goods in which it is combined with cotton and other fibers. You may launder or dry-clean ramie items, depending on the construction, finishing processes and dyes employed. Its lack of resilience makes ramie garments subject to wrinkling and may prevent even a sweater from retaining its shape. You can bleach white ramie fabrics; darks may present a problem. You are advised to follow care-label procedures most carefully with all ramie items.

RANGES

Whether your unit is gas or electric, the exterior parts of the range should be wiped clean every day. Spills and spatters need immediate attention. One minute of wiping could save thirty minutes of more strenuous cleaning later. Pay attention to the back panel and drip pans (collectors of grease and grime). If you have a ceramic, smooth-top range, see Cooktops.

Porcelain, baked enamel, or stainless range surfaces can be cleaned with a detergent and water solution, rinsed, and dried. You can also use a grease-cutting spray or liquid all-purpose cleaner. To remove baked-on or stubborn soil, allow the cleaner to soak into the spots for a minute or two, then rub gently with a plastic or nylon scrub pad.

Surface Cooking Units: For gas burners, remove the grates and drip bowls, soak them in a pan of hot, soapy water and $1/2$ cup of chlorine bleach. If scrubbing is necessary, soak in a solution of liquid all-purpose cleaner for fifteen minutes, then rub with a nylon or plastic scrub pad, rinse, and dry. Very stubborn, caked-on soil can be removed by covering the soiled pieces with an ammonia-soaked cloth for an hour or two, then scrub with soapy water, rinse, and dry.

Clean out burner holes with a thin wire or metal paper clip. Some ranges have drip pans molded into the surface, but the top lifts up. If this is the case, remember to lift the range top once a week and wipe out the inside.

For electric elements, the heating element is self-cleaning. Food soils will burn off during the cooking process. Electric elements are not immersible. If you have excessive food spills, turn the unit to high and burn clean. Unplug or tilt-up cooking elements to reach drip bowls and clean the bowls as suggested for gas burners, above.

Control Knobs: These can be pulled off, washed in warm sudsy water, rinsed and dried. Be careful to remove, clean, and replace only *one* knob at a time to avoid mixing up the controls and the knobs.

Switches: Push-button switches can be cleaned with a cotton-tipped swab, lightly dampened with ammonia or glass cleaner.

Broiler Pans and Grills: Remove the pan and grill while still warm from broiling and pour off grease. Rinse with very hot water. Pour dish detergent onto the pan and cover with wet paper towels. When pan has cooled, wash with a nylon scrub pad and

TIP

Drip pans or bowls may be made of aluminum, and excessive scrubbing and powder cleansers may scratch or dull the finish. If the top portion of the burner assembly is removable, this can be soaked with the grates and drip bowls.

hot soapy water, rinse, and dry. Do not use foil to cover grid when broiling. This keeps fat from draining to pan below and may cause a fire. However, you can line the bottom portion of the pan with foil to make cleanup easier.

Oven Racks: Remove racks and scrub clean with detergent and hot water, or a coating of oven cleaner. *Caution:* follow manufacturer's directions. Racks can be cleaned at the same time self-cleaning oven is on clean, but they may discolor.

See Oven Cleaning.

Range Troubleshooters

If your range quits working, first check the general troubleshooting guide under Appliance Troubleshooters.

If you own an electric range and one of the surface units or the oven will not heat, try pushing the terminals of the heating units firmly into the receptacles. The timer may be set at off or automatic. Reset the timer control to the manual position.

If the oven heats improperly, the thermostat may be set wrong or it is out of adjustment. In the latter case, check the temperature of the oven with a meat thermometer and compare the reading with the temperature the oven is set for. Then readjust the thermostat—oven temperature control knob to reflect the difference in degrees.

If you own a gas range, and the burners do not stay lit, check for drafts that could put out the flame, or a dirt buildup in the burner holes. Clean holes with a thin wire or metal paper clip. If oven fails to light, clean the burner and try again.

TROUBLE SHOOTER

Some ovens, if out of adjustment, will maintain the set temperature at high heat but not at lower heats. So after readjusting be sure to check with the thermometer again. More often ovens do not maintain temperature because the door is opened too often during baking, allowing heat to escape.

RASPBERRY STAIN   See Master Stain Removal Section (Fruit).

RATS AND MICE   Your best bet is to keep these pests out.

Block common routes of entry, like openings in the foundation of your house, even small holes around pipes and windows. (A mouse needs only a dime-sized hole to slip into a building.) Screen wire, sheet metal, and putty or cement are commonly used to plug up entryways.

Keep garbage cans covered and empty them regularly.

Store food in tight containers or closed cupboards.

To eliminate rats and mice, you have a choice of using poison baits or traps.

Traps come in different sizes for rats and mice. Set a number of them. Bacon rind, cheese, or peanut butter make food bait. Use fresh bait every day and fasten it firmly to the trigger.

Use strategy in placing baits and traps. Rats and mice run inside and under things and alongside walls. So place a trap against a wall, with the trigger as close as you can get it.

You may also want to keep baits and traps in and under things so kids and pets can't reach them. Hide bait and trap in a length of pipe, or house your bait and trap inside a poison bait station— like a box with a door cut in one side.

You will also find ready-made bait stations in most pesticide departments.

If you are really plagued with rats or mice, engage an exterminator (see Yellow Page directory).

RATTAN   See Wicker.

RAYON   Rayon is the oldest of the man-made fibers. It comes in staple fibers and in filament yarns.

It is highly absorbent, soft, and comfortable and makes up into garments and other items that drape well. It is nonpilling and static-free, and when solution-dyed, it is colorfast to sun, washing, and perspiration. It's often used with polyester to produce durable press blends.

Read care labels on rayon to be sure of the correct handling. Rayon fabrics may wrinkle and shrink in washing.

If there is no caution against washing, proceed as follows.

Machine- or hand wash in warm water. If hand washing, gently squeeze suds through the fabric and rinse in lukewarm water. Do not wring or twist, as rayon is weaker when wet. Just smooth or shake out and place on a nonrust hanger to dry.

Do not use chlorine bleach on wrinkle-resistant rayons unless the label says it's safe.

Gentle agitation should be used in machine-washing.

Rayon needs ironing unless it is specially finished. Press while damp on the wrong side with your iron set at moderate. Use a press cloth if you must finish on the right side.

Dry cleaning is recommended for some rayon garments because of their construction and trim.

RED WINE STAINS   See Carpet Stain Removal Guide; Master Stain Removal Section (Wine).

REED   See Wicker.

REFLECTIVE INSULATION (Linings)   Draperies and curtain liners may be treated with a metallic coating to keep heat in *or* to reflect the sun's rays away.

Some of this surface finish may come off in cleaning, but the loss may not significantly cut the warmth realized with such insulation.

Follow the manufacturer's care instructions.

REFRIGERATOR / FREEZER   With the advent of frost-free refrigeration the refrigerator/freezer stays trouble-free with a minimum of work.

To insure good performance, use the manufacturer's recom-

*To unstick postage
stamps put them in
the freezer for fifteen
minutes.*

mended temperature settings. Don't overload: this forces the unit to run longer and harder than it should. While you have your vacuum out for weekly cleaning, suction dust from the condenser (just behind the base grille).

Cleaning Tips

Unplug the refrigerator/freezer before cleaning.

Exterior: Sponge with warm water and detergent, or a liquid or spray all-purpose cleaner. Avoid abrasives and harsh cleaners.

Rinse and wipe dry.

Apply a coat of kitchen appliance wax (Jubilee, Star brite) to repel or reduce soil and sticky fingerprints.

Vacuum the back of the refrigerator every four to six months, more often if there are pets in the house.

Shelves, Crispers, Ice Trays, Gaskets, and Removable Parts: Wash these with a mild detergent and warm water. Rinse and dry.

Interior and Door Liner: Wash with a solution of 2 tablespoons of baking soda to 1 quart water or warm water and detergent. Rinse and dry thoroughly, to reduce the time and effort the system will expend to remove excess moisture.

Defrost Pan: Remove the grille at the base of the refrigerator and slide out the defrost pan. Empty the pan if necessary and wash with a mild detergent and water.

Air Condenser (behind the base grille):

Static Condenser (on rear of unit, on older equipment): Vacuum this part every two months, weekly if you have pets.

Floor Under the Refrigerator: Pull the unit forward, protect the floor with a mat if the box does not have rollers. If there is an automatic ice maker, take care not to move the unit farther than the water line allows. Vacuum and wash floor as you would the rest of the kitchen floor. When returning the unit to its place, leave air space behind the refrigerator/freezer and do not kink the ice-maker water supply line.

MONEY SAVER

*Lipsticks won't get
gooey if stored in
the refrigerator. Nail polish
kept on ice is less likely to
lose its color and viscosity.
You can get a sharper point
on eye and lip pencils if you
refrigerate them before sharpening. Iced cologne is especially refreshing and
astringents and toners also
feel better when they come
from the refrigerator.*

Refrigerator/Freezer Odors

Cause of Odors: Odors develop when food is improperly packaged or left to spoil. Store food in moisture-proof, vapor-proof foil, paper, or containers. Do not reuse disposable packaging, and thoroughly wash reusable containers.

Odors may also be caused by stale water in the drip or drain pan located at the base of the refrigerator or develop when the unit is off and the door is closed for a period of time.

Odor Prevention: Absorb odors by placing an open box of baking soda or a solid air freshener in both the refrigerator and freezer sections.

To Remove Odors: Wash the refrigerator with a solution of 1 cup white vinegar to 1 gallon of warm water. Rinse and dry.

In Extreme Cases: To remove odors caused by moisture, possibly embedded in the insulation or plastic lining, use the following method. (It is advised only for frost-free models or after manual defrost units are defrosted and the interior is completely dry.)

1. Disconnect the refrigerator from the outlet.

2. Clean the refrigerator with a solution of 2 tablespoons of baking soda to 1 quart water. Rinse and dry.

3. Place activated charcoal, kitty litter, or silica gel on paper plates inside the refrigerator. Put a hair dryer set on high in the completely dry, unplugged refrigerator to apply heated forced-air circulation.

4. Leave the door open and turn the hair dryer on. Check every fifteen minutes or so for odors. If you believe all the odor-causing moisture has been dispelled, remove the hair dryer and absorbent material and reconnect the refrigerator.

Defrosting Manual and Self-Defrosting Freezers and Frozen Food Compartments

The freezer should be defrosted when the frost buildup reaches a thickness of a quarter of an inch. Upright freezers need to be

TROUBLE SHOOTER

If refrigerator racks tend to stick, wipe on a light coat of petroleum jelly (Vaseline) to make them glide more easily.

TIP

A full freezer stays cold and uses less energy. If yours has empty areas, fill them with containers of water.

defrosted about every six months and chest freezers every twelve months.

To Defrost:

1. Unplug or turn the control knob to the off or defrost setting.

2. Remove the ice trays and the frozen foods. Wrap foods in newspapers, place in cardboard cartons or ice chests, and insulate with blankets.

3. Place a roasting pan and terry toweling on the top shelf of the refrigerator section to catch melting ice from the bottom of the frozen food compartment if necessary.

4. Put a pan of hot water inside the freezer to speed up the defrosting; leave the door open. Change the water when it gets cold. Do not use the ice trays for hot water containers. The hot water will cause ice cubes to stick to the trays later.

5. Let the ice melt by itself. Do not use sharp objects to remove it. Knives and ice picks may damage the cooling unit. Avoid using fans or hair dryers to speed up defrosting. Combining these with water from melting ice invites severe electric shock.

Note: Many chest and upright freezers are equipped with siphon hoses or drains to remove melted ice water.

While the Ice Is Melting:

1. Remove food from the refrigerator section. Throw away un-used leftovers and food that has spoiled.

2. Clean the refrigerator section according to directions in the preceding refrigerator cleaning section.

After Defrosting Is Complete:

1. Empty the pans of water and soak up any remaining moisture.

2. Wash the freezer inside and out with a solution of mild detergent and warm water or 2 tablespoons baking soda to 1 quart warm water. The baking soda both cleans and deodorizes.

3. Rinse and dry.

4. Plug in or reset the controls and re-store the frozen foods.

5. Wash the ice trays using warm (not hot) water; fill and place them in the freezer.

REGISTERS   See Radiators.

RESILIENT FLOORING   See Vinyl Flooring.

RINGS FROM STAIN REMOVAL   See Master Stain Removal Section (Nine Good Techniques).

ROACHES   See Cockroaches.

ROTTENSTONE   This is a soft abrasive powder, available at paint stores, used to polish soft metals and remove white spots from furniture. Usually mixed with oils for such jobs.

ROVANNA   See Saran.

RUBBER   Pre-Columbian Indians used latex (a milky plant secretion) for balls, shoes, and waterproof fabrics. It became known as rubber when its use as an eraser was discovered in 1770.

Today's manufactured rubber fiber may be either natural or synthetic.

Remove wet rubber gloves without tearing them by lifting the cuff and blowing into the palm. Air pressure loosens the fingers.

Rubber is heat-sensitive, will deteriorate at high drying temperatures, and may be softened by perspiration and body oils.

Frequent washing best promotes the wear life of rubber fiber items. Where you have no instructions from the manufacturer, wash with warm or cold water. Avoid heat and exposure to direct sunlight. If bleach is used, go easy on it. Do not dry-clean.

Never attempt to machine-dry any article containing rubber. It is a fire hazard in a heated dryer.

Dry on the air-fluff (no heat) setting. If you're dealing with lingerie or other clothing that has just elastic bands, don't worry. The amount of rubber is insufficient to cause spontaneous combustion. But stay with air-fluff drying for bras, bathing suits, etc. with foam rubber content.

Do not use solvent-based cleaners on rubber articles. Soap, water, and ammonia are the best cleaning agents, whether you're dealing with rubber gloves, combs, shower curtains, boots, mats, or other items. Air dry rubber items after washing, don't put them away wet, or let rubber layers cling to each other. (Separate shower curtains so they hang free, blow into your rubber gloves and dust a little talc into them to keep them from sticking.)

RUBBER CEMENT STAINS   See Master Stain Removal Section (Adhesives).

RUBBER SILICONE (GROUT)   See Grout.

RUBBER TILE   See Asphalt/Rubber.

RUGS   Rugs should lie absolutely flat on the floor with pads under them to protect both floors and rugs. Don't place rugs over carpeting, since this causes extra wear. And most particularly, warns the Arkansas Cooperative Extension Service, don't use small broadloom pieces over larger rugs in heavy traffic areas since the underside of broadloom is rough.

Grandma may have beaten or shaken her rugs, but experts advise against this, now that vacuum cleaners are available.

Antique rugs should have professional care.

For care of ordinary rugs, see Carpet Care Mini Manual.

RUST

In any hardware store, you will find a variety of products to prevent the formation of rust on iron and steel; also rust removers.

If rust occurs on your iron cookware, use steel wool to remove it, then wash, rinse, and reseason.

For light rust stains on porcelain, brown rings around faucets, and rust spots on faucets and window glass, try lemon juice or white vinegar, followed by thorough rinsing. For more stubborn stains, use a commercial rust remover or a weak solution of oxalic acid (1 teaspoon oxalic acid in 1 cup of hot water), with a first rinse with ammonia solution, a second with water. Oxalic acid is poisonous: see precautions under Oxalic acid.

Fair warning: Once an article has started to rust, the spread is difficult to control. You must be sure to remove it all, or it will continue to form, even under a layer of paint, and your cleaned surface must be entirely rust-free, dry, and clean before you apply sealer.

For rust stains on fabric, see Master Stain Removal Section. (Those little brown spots on old fabrics are rust spots that came about because of iron particles in your water.)

For rust stains on floors, see Vinyl Flooring Stain Removal Guide.

TIP

If you collect antique iron utensils and have rust problems with them, after "derusting" them, use stove blacking to restore their color, then a film of petroleum jelly to prevent further rusting.

SALAD DRESSING STAINS

See Master Stain Removal Section (Oily).

SANDWICH GRILL

See Waffle Irons.

SANITIZERS

See Disinfectants.

SARAN

Saran fiber, a practical choice for flame-resistant curtains and draperies, is machine-washable in water at a warm setting, or may be dry-cleaned.

SATIN

This is a lustrous fabric made from almost any fiber or combination of fibers, and fiber content determines correct care. To avoid marring its lustrous surface, use a moderately warm, dry iron and press on a smooth, solid surface where you can be sure to prevent unwanted impressions.

SCISSORS AND SHEARS

Wipe them with a clean cloth before and after each use. Oil them occasionally. Use a drop of sewing machine oil on the open blades near the joint, make a series of cutting motions until the oil works its way to the screw. Put them away for a day or two, then wipe off any excess oil before using them again.

Take them to a repair shop (hardware shop or fabric store) for sharpening or adjusting.

Note to sewers: don't use your sewing scissors on paper or materials other than fabric.

SCORCH MARKS See Master Stain Removal Section.

SCORPIONS To discourage scorpions from entering the house, spray a barrier strip of pesticide around the foundation.

Effective sprays for outside use contain malathion, propoxur, or diazinon. For inside use, the Oklahoma State University Extension Service suggests aerosol or ready-to-use sprays containing 0.5 percent diazinon, or 1 percent Baygon, or Bendiocarb (Ficam) 1 percent dust. However, these pesticides are often formulated for use by pest control experts, and you may be advised to get professional help if you must spray under the house or in the attic.

Not all scorpions are poisonous, but you may want to see a doctor if you are stung.

SEERSUCKER True seersucker has a permanent woven-in puckered design that you may iron or not, as you wish. There are fabrics resembling seersucker, with a plissé design, consisting of puckers chemically produced. Do not iron; heed the care label.

SEPTIC TANKS Inspect the septic tank once a year. Measure the level of scum (floating layer of soil) with a piece of white terry cloth wrapped around the bottom of a long stick or broom handle. There should be at least three inches of scum-free area between the bottom of the depth of the scum and the bottom portion of the outlet T (midpoint in the tank). Next, measure the sludge level. Tie another clean piece of white terry cloth to the stick and pass the stick through the T outlet to the bottom of the tank. The top of the sludge level should be twelve inches or more from the bottom of the T outlet. If sludge and scum levels are too thick, the system will have to be pumped out professionally. Check your Yellow Pages or your local Board of Health for the names of septic system service contractors.

Note: Special additives will not eliminate the need for cleaning the system. General household cleaning products will not harm nor interfere with the system. Do not allow paper products, disposable diapers, kitty litter, and so forth to flow into the septic tank. Look for and purchase toilet tissue declared safe for septic tanks.

According to Washington State University Cooperative Extension Service, drainfields "suffer most frequently from neglect of the septic tank." Septic-tank neglect can result in the costly relocation of a drainfield.

A few tips: Don't enter an empty or partially-filled septic tank. Interior gases are explosive. Wet spots or odors in the drainfield indicate a faulty system—have it checked by a professional. Practice water conservation to extend the life of your drainfield. Don't allow drainspouts or water drains to empty into the septic system.

To avoid clogging, backups, corrosion, and odors, pour 1 cup of baking soda down toilets on a weekly basis.

SEWING MACHINES

A cleaning and oiling regimen is vital to long life for your machine.

Remove the lint and dust that collects around the bobbin and feed dog. If not removed, soil will pack down and clog the machine. Clean with the brush the manufacturer provided or a slightly stiff bristle artist's brush. Hard-to-reach lint and fabric threads can be removed with a pin or a very small pair of tweezers. Clean often: either every time you begin a sewing project or just after you finish one.

Oil moving parts with an oil recommended specifically for sewing machines. In general, they should be oiled after approximately eight hours of sewing, more often if the machine is stored in very damp (basement) or very warm (attic) places. One or two drops of oil is all that is necessary. Wipe off excess oil. Oil is a natural magnet for dust and lint. Check your use-and-care booklet before attempting to oil the electric motor. Self-oiling can damage the new machines that are preoiled and sealed in the factory.

If you don't have a use-and-care manual, write to the manufacturer, specifying style and model number.

A pipe cleaner is useful to clean the lint that collects around the needle and inside your sewing machine.

SHADES   See Window Shades.

SHEEPSKIN   Sheepskin is a general term for tanned hide with the wool still intact on the pelt or leather. Variations have also been classified as Shearling or Sherpa. For care, see Leather (Suede).

Shearling is the soft natural short wool pile backed with sheepskin, used in powder puffs, slippers, rugs, and coats.

SHEERS AND LACE   Many sheers and laces are now available in synthetics or blends for which machine care is recommended. Follow instructions for the fiber content involved.

You can protect small or delicate items by enclosing them in a mesh bag.

If you choose to hand wash sheers and laces, treat them gently, soaking out the soil rather than rubbing it out.

Items that might stretch or lose their shape should be dried flat, on a towel or plain clean paper (not newspaper) away from direct heat.

Pressing: If you lack manufacturer instructions, test the iron temperature on a fabric sample. Some sheers pucker when pressed with steam. As for lace, press face down on a towel to avoid flattening the raised design.

Note: Many sheers and laces may be sized, to give the fabric body. When a liquid is spilled on such fabrics, rings may appear. These may disappear with washing or dry cleaning, but some are difficult for even a dry cleaner to remove. For information about stiffening agents, see Sizing and Starch.

SHOE POLISH STAINS   See Carpet Stain Removal Guide; Master Stain Removal Section.

SHOES AND BOOTS   To precondition, get a professional polish, or do the job yourself with a coat of paste wax the same color as the shoe. Buff vigorously with a soft cloth (old socks are great), then brush to a high shine with a clean, dry shoe brush.

While shoes are still brand-new, you might also invest in gridded, composition half-soles. Your shoemaker can apply them. They help to hold the shape of the shoe and cushion the sole for greater comfort, too. Another wear-saver is the tap your shoemaker can affix to the toes of your shoes (preferably the composition variety rather than metal, so you don't scratch the floors.)

Special Problems

Scuff marks: Cream polish keeps leather soft and pliable, and also camouflages marks. Black scuff marks often come off if you use cleaning fluid or white vinegar on a clean cloth.

Salt: It can corrode leather if it's not washed off right away. Sponge such stains away with warm sudsy water to which a spoonful of vinegar has been added, cleaning heels and soles as well as uppers. Rinse with clear water. Stuff toes with paper and dry away from heat for at least 12 hours.

Patent Leather: It wipes clean with a soft cloth dampened with white vinegar. You can shine it with Liquid Glass Cleaner, Pledge, or a patent cleaner.

Metallic Leathers: Spray with acrylic fixative (from an art-supply store) to keep the finish intact. Use a neutral color cream polish on scuff marks.

Leather Boots: Stick with good quality transparent paste wax on boots. Colored polish can alter color, no matter how well it seems to match.

Leather boots can be sponged clean with mild soap and lukewarm water. Do not saturate them, and let them dry thoroughly before rewaxing.

Rewax boots often and always when they are fully dried out after foul-weather accidents.

TIP

Product Use: Wax protects and polishes, creams clean and soften leather, and foams and liquids cover scuffs particularly well. To clean leather, for example, use a cream to lift the dirt, then follow with a wax to protect and polish.

CAUTION

Shoes last longer if you don't wear the same ones day after day. Moisture builds up when you don't give them a day to air out, encouraging bacterial growth and material rot of the linings.

Waterproofing Boots and Shoes: Well-polished boots and shoes tend to shed rain, and there are silicone sprays you can buy for both. But note that silicone will stain light colors and suede, and don't use heavy oils like neat's foot or mink oil because they dull the finish and make boots and shoes impossible to shine.

Spray the sole line and seams of dark colored leather boots to increase waterproofing.

Fabric Sports Shoes: Most sneakers can be put through the mild temperature, gentle action cycle of the washing machine with a bit of detergent, and then set to dry away from heat.

Leather sneakers should be washed by hand.

Other Fabric Shoes: Some really delicate shoes (silk, satin, lamé, faille) are truly difficult to clean. Keep them as clean as possible. Tree them (they are unusually crease-prone). And take them to a dry cleaner when they're soiled.

But other fabric shoes respond well to an initial spray with a dirt-repellent like Scotchgard. They can then be carefully cleaned with soap and water, shampooed with upholstery cleaner, or given one of the detergent shampoos for fabric shoes (Kiwi Sneaker Shampoo, Esquire Fabric Cleaner).

Take note of the shoe's construction. If you have a shoe with washable fabric cemented to the sole, the answer is thick, dry suds. Make them in a deep bowl by whisking a tablespoon of liquid detergent with $1/4$ cup warm water until the suds stand in soft peaks like well-beaten egg whites. Stuff the shoe tightly with an old towel (or paper towels) so the suds won't leak through to the sole. Then apply the suds—*only* the suds. A nail brush makes a handy applicator. Use it to rinse off the suds, too, first rinsing and shaking it almost dry. Repeat rinsing as often as necessary to remove all the suds. Let the shoe dry away from any source of heat.

Children's Scuffed Shoes may call for a three-step process:

1. Remove loose dirt by brushing with a dry brush, then wipe with a cloth, dampened slightly if necessary, to remove dried-on

dirt. Let the shoes dry away from any source of heat.

2. Apply foam polish the same color as the shoe. It will help to even out the color in the scuff. Let dry.

3. Finally, apply paste wax and shine vigorously.

Suede: Suede brushes clean the nap and keep it nappy, but use them gently. An art-gum eraser removes light dirt. Use a nail file or fine-grade sandpaper on small spots. Liquid suede cleaner can discolor shoes: use it sparingly and only when you must.

SHOWER CURTAINS, PLASTIC

Light to medium curtains can be washed in the washing machine on the gentle or delicate cycle. Use warm water and detergent. Remove before the final spin cycle, shake out moisture or towel dry. Rehang immediately.

Very heavy curtains may need to be spread out and wiped clean with detergent and water. After washing, rinse in the tub or hose off on an outside clothesline.

To avoid mildew and excessive soap-scum buildup, pull out full on shower curtain rod after each use, until dry. For more information, see mildew.

To clean the shower curtain hangers, put them in a sock, knot the open end and toss them into the washer with the curtains.

TIP

Vinegar added to rinse water helps to reduce annoying static.

SHRINK RESISTANT FINISHES

Be guided by the labels: shrinkage of 3 percent in a garment means that it may no longer fit after washing. Two percent is considered acceptable in wovens, says Iowa State Extension Service, and 5 percent in knits, because these can be stretched back to fit.

SILICONE

Silicone is an "inorganic" plastic, neither plastic nor metal. It is highly heat- and water-resistant and widely used for waterproofing and coatings for nonstick finishes.

SILK   Silk fabrics range in weight from sheer organzas and chiffons to rich, heavy satins and brocades. It is the only natural filament yarn and, according to the Silk Institute, it has been woven into at least 200 different textiles.

Although silk is the thinnest of fibers, it is also the strongest. So silk garments keep their shape and last for years—hundreds of years, in fact. If you go to Saint Peter's Church in Rome, look at "Charlemagne's coronation robe." While experts doubt that it was worn on that historic occasion, they say it goes back to 1500. Many museums display silks of great antiquity.

Care

If you would prolong the life of your favorite silks, here are useful do not's.

- Do not hang on wire hangers. Rust may stain the silk.
- Do not wear pins. They can leave permanent holes.
- Do not expose to the sun, strong lighting, or dry heat for long periods of time. These fade or yellow silk.
- Do not hang in plastic bags. Silk is an organic fiber that needs to breathe.
- Do not wear silk clothes that are too tight. The fabric will stretch and weaken, causing pulls and sagging.
- Do not apply deodorants, body lotions, colognes or perfumes while wearing silks. Apply deodorant, let dry, then dress. Note that silk is weakened by perspiration.
- Do not allow stains to linger. Take immediate action. Rinse washable silks in lukewarm or cold water. Send nonwashables to the dry cleaner.

To Wash or Dry-Clean?

Most labels say, "Dry-clean only."

Luxury silk fabrics like chiffon, georgette, taffeta, satin, and charmeuse clearly demand dry cleaning. So do garments with elaborate trim or intricate construction.

Some silks that would otherwise be washable are not treated to prevent shrinkage, and ironing may or may not restore the length you need. Washing may fade dark or bright colors or prints. Hand washing is preferred to machine-washing.

Washing the Washables

More and more washable silks have come on the market, including some pure silks as well as silk/cotton and silk/polyester blends guaranteed to machine-wash. Follow care labels when washing these.

But the three cardinal rules are:

1. Wash by hand.

2. Wash separately.

3. Wash with gentle care. (Silk loses strength when wet.)

Colorfastness: Check this the first time you wash a garment. Wet an inconspicuous corner. Blot the wet area between paper towels with strong pressure. If color bleeds onto the towels, your garment is not colorfast. Dry-clean it.

Washing: Silks should be washed in lukewarm or cool water with a synthetic detergent such as Woolite or mild soap such as Ivory Flakes.

Wash gently. Do not wring or rub. Do not soak in water for a long time, as this may cause fading.

The Silk Institute advises that pale-color silks that have yellowed can be rejuvenated: "Add 3 tablespoons of white vinegar to a basin of cool water and wash gently."

Do not use chlorine bleach. All-fabric (oxygen) bleach may be used on white silks.

TROUBLE SHOOTER

To protect against color loss add a tablespoon of white vinegar to the wash water. This helps with many washable fabrics.

Rinsing: Rinse gently but thoroughly in lukewarm or cold water. Do not wring. Let water flow through the fabric until all soap is out. Too much detergent makes rinsing difficult.

Drying: Wrap in a towel to remove excess water. Then hang on a padded hanger until ready to iron. (Avoid rust marks: do not use a wire hanger.)

Drying

Do not put any silks or silk blends in the dryer—excessive heat can cause silks to disintegrate.

You must never iron silk dry, so do not dry completely. If you want to keep a garment damp until you have time for ironing, try storing it in the refrigerator, wrapped in a towel or plastic bag. To speed up drying time, hang it in front of an electric fan until it is only slightly damp and ready for ironing.

If the garment is not damp enough, hang it in the bathroom while you shower. (But don't get water drops on it, since that may cause water spotting.)

Some silks need little or no ironing if hung on padded plastic hangers after they've been rolled in towels to remove excess water. Hang the garment straight and smooth out the seams.

Ironing and Pressing

Iron at low temperature or with a steam iron. Temperature is usually marked for silk, between 250° F (121° C) and 300° F (148° C). Temperatures over 330° F (160° C) will disintegrate silk garments. Do not use a steamer to remove wrinkles, for the same reason.

Always press silk on the wrong side. Finish seams, collars and hems on the right side with a pressing cloth to protect the fabric from the iron.

SILVER   Silver improves with age. Constant use creates a lovely soft patina made up of tiny surface lines.

Most silver, both sterling and silverplate, is dishwasher-safe, if you allow enough space between pieces to avoid scratches. Remove silver from the dishwasher before the dry cycle begins, say most silver companies. Buff dry with a clean soft dish towel, as steam drying can leave spots.

Hand Washing

You should wash silver promptly after meals and may therefore want to do it by hand. Dry with a soft cloth. Avoid draining on rubber mats: contact with rubber promotes tarnish. In fact, if you so much as let rubber bands lie on silver, it can be so deeply etched that the damage will require a silversmith's attention.

The foods that affect silver include salt, olives, salad dressing, mustard, eggs, vinegar, and fruit juices: keep them in other containers. And if you admire flowers and fruit in a favorite silver vase or bowl, use a plastic or glass liner.

Never let knives with hollow handles soak in hot water for a long period. This can cause the handles to loosen.

CAUTION

Do not use polishing dips or solutions if your silver has design contrast added by the manufacturer. These products remove intentional oxidation of the silver.

CAUTION

Removing Tarnish

You can't avoid tarnish entirely. It is the natural result of exposure to chemicals such as sulphur compounds in the air.

There are many good commercial cleaning preparations, including a tarnish-preventive polish. Use a sponge or a soft cloth; rub briskly and always in the same direction. Use plastic gloves. They won't mark silver as rubber will. Rinse with warm water and polish dry with a soft cloth, making sure no polish remains, since it will just cause the piece to tarnish faster.

You can cut down on the number of times you polish silver if you use 3M's tarnish-preventing strips with pieces in storage. Or use camphor cakes: camphor fumes keep silver from tarnishing, and the fewer times you polish it the longer it will last.

Use a cotton-tipped applicator to clean crevices, and silver polish on a string to polish between tines.

Storage

Between uses, keep silver in a silver chest, or bag of tarnish-resistant cloth or a drawer similarly cloth-lined.

For extended periods, protect silver from moisture by wrapping in waxed paper. Keep in a clean, dry area. Never store near heat registers where it is exposed to heated air.

SILVERFISH AND FIREBRATS

Silverfish are shiny, pearl gray, or silver; firebrats a mottled tan. Both are about half an inch long, with antennae on the head and three long filaments protruding at the tail. They feed on paper (books, wallpaper), rayon fabrics, and starched clothing.

Vacuum all cracks and crevices, then spray in areas where you see these pests. They like warm, damp places, such as closets, shelves, and areas under sinks and steam pipes.

Propoxur, malathion, and diazinon are effective insecticide agents. You may find dusts more desirable to use than spray.

SINKS AND TUBS

Sinks and tubs should be wiped clean after each use. No matter what the surface, a sponge wrung in hot, soapy water, or liquid or spray all-purpose disinfectant cleaner will do. Rinse with clear water.

Avoid harsh, abrasive scouring powders. They scratch the surface and the scratches become dirt traps. Mild stains and film may be removed with baking soda and a nylon scrub pad.

To remove soap scum and hard water stains:

TIP

A small amount of lemon oil applied to the inside of a glass shower door, according to Merry Maids cleaners, will reduce the water and soap scum that often builds up on the door.

1. Apply a nonprecipitating water softener (Calgon) to a damp sponge and rub.

2. Wipe stained areas with a sponge soaked in white vinegar.

3. Use a commercial product (Lime-A-Way, Tile-X) according to label directions.

Rust and Mineral Stains: The simplest way to remove is to soak the stain with white vinegar or lemon juice. If the sink or tub is very old and encrusted, you may need to apply an oxalic acid paste. Use one part oxalic acid, 10 parts water, thicken with cornmeal. Oxalic acid is a poison. Use caution and wear gloves. Apply the paste to stained areas. Let sit for a few minutes, then rinse. Do not allow the acid to touch chrome plumbing fixtures.

Commercial rust removers (dr. rust) are available at grocery and hardware stores.

TIP

A water softener added at bath time will eliminate bathtub ring.

SIZING

This is one of the routine finishes given to many fabrics to increase their weight, stiffness, and smoothness. (Sheers like marquisette and organdy, mosquito netting, etc., are so treated. Denim and linen fabrics are frequently sized.)

Beware of items with excessive sizing, which you can recognize by rubbing two layers of cloth together, or by scraping the surface with your fingernail or a knife to see if particles flake off.

If you lose sizing, spray-on products like Easy-On, Faultless, Miracle White, and Niagara restore body. You may also add liquid starches during a final rinse. Solid starch requires cooking, but it is inexpensive. (For more information, see Starch.)

Stiffening agents are not likely to be removed by solvents. In any case, your dry cleaner can restore sizing.

SLATE AND STONE FLOORS

Natural stone and slate, like any surfaces, should be dusted or vacuumed first to remove any fine particles of dirt that may scratch them or make the cleaning job harder.

Slate and stone may be scrubbed clean with an all-purpose liquid cleaner and warm water or detergent and water. Use a soft scrub brush or lint-free cloth to clean the floor. Sponges tend to shred on rougher parts of the slate and grout and will leave a residue. Slate and stone are porous. Stains and spots are difficult to remove. If you have stains, try a more vigorous scrubbing with a stiffer brush. Rinse the floor thoroughly two or three times to insure all traces of cleaner are removed.

To protect slate or other natural stone, seal it with a clear sealer available at hardware stores and stone dealers. Stone sealers may eventually darken the original color and will add a slight shine. Make sure the floor is absolutely dry before applying sealer. In some cases, it is best to wait a day or two after cleaning.

SLATE FURNISHINGS

While much of the "slate" we see in contemporary furnishings is artificial, true slate is featured in accessory pieces. Just wash and dry it when it needs cleaning. Don't wax if it is used for a hot dish server.

Polish it with boiled linseed oil (purchase, don't boil your own). Briskly rub a small amount with a soft cloth on clean slate. Wipe off excess oil and buff with a clean soft cloth.

SLEEPING BAGS

Cleaning a sleeping bag can be a troublesome business, and the ruination of the bag if handled incorrectly. Some people like to say that when a sleeping bag gets too dirty the best thing to do is buy a new one. That is not the only answer.

The bag's insulating material determines the best cleaning method. Is it down or a synthetic filler?

Down

Use soap (Ivory Flakes) and water softener. Never use detergent because detergents strip natural oils from the feathers. Machine-dry on low or no heat. Too much heat can burn off the natural oils.

Clean down bags about once a year, not just for sanitary reasons, but to maintain the insulating loft of the filler.

Hand Washing: This is the best method, according to Dr. Leona K. Windley of the Utah State University Extension Service, and we are giving her instructions, with her permission.

To handle, dissolve water softener and soap in a clean bathtub with enough lukewarm water to cover the bag. (Use lukewarm water, never hot.)

Press the bag into the soapy water, starting at the foot and working to the head of the bag, thus letting air escape from inside. Be gentle or the weight of the down will tear the baffles and ruin the bag. Gently knead and turn to push the soapy water through the bag. Let the bag soak for an hour. Then scrub off the surface dirt with a sponge or soft brush. Drain the tub and hand-press water and soap from the bag.

Refill the tub with warm water, water softener, and soap. Knead again to work the solution through the bag. Drain and rinse again until the water is clear of soap and again remove water by hand-pressing. Let the bag drain in the tub for half an hour. Don't wring or twist the water out!

Gently roll the bag into a laundry basket, and lay it outside on a mesh surface like a chaise longue. The weight from the water will tear the baffles if you hang it on a line.

Machine-Washing and Drying (using a commercial washer and dryer): Some sleeping bags of exceptionally strong exterior construction and good strong fabric may be recommended for machine-washing.

Use the gentle cycle and warm water (not hot), water softener, and soap (not detergent). Rinse twice to remove all soap. Tumble dry in a large commercial dryer on low heat, no heat, or air, with a clean sneaker without shoe laces. The weight of the sneaker helps to fluff the down, and the rubber builds up static electricity to renew the loft.

Dry two to four hours, making sure the down gets completely dry. *Note:* If the sleeping bag fails to loft properly, you probably haven't rinsed out all the soap. In this case, rinse and re-dry.

Outdoor Drying: After a day of drying outdoors, turn the bag inside out. Complete drying may take three to five days. Occasionally pull apart the down filling. Make sure the down dries completely or it will mildew.

Even if you completely dry your bag outdoors, you should put it through a no-heat cycle to fluff the down to its original loft.

Dry Cleaning: Because dry-cleaning solvents are toxic, the U.S.

Bureau of Standards warns against dry cleaning as too risky. Dry-cleaning solvents can also strip away down's natural oils. Your cleaner should use one of the milder ones. In any case, if you have your bag dry-cleaned, air bag outside for at least a week to remove all traces of the chemical solvent.

Synthetic Filler

Machine-Washing: This is the easiest way to clean a synthetic sleeping bag. Use a front-loading commercial washer in a laundromat. Before washing the bag, zip it closed and safety-pin the filling to the outer nylon shell if there are large areas of filler without quilting. Make sure you have sharp pins or you can snag the outer shell.

Set the machine for the gentle cycle. Dissolve a mild detergent in lukewarm water (never hot water). Check the water temperature while the machine is filling. If it's too hot for your hand, it's too hot for the bag. Add fabric softener to the rinse cycle. It coats the fibers and reduces static electricity so your bag will have more loft.

Tumble dry, using a large commercial dryer on the no-heat setting.

Hand Washing: This is a gentler method. The procedure is about the same as for down, using a tub half-filled with warm water—not above 140° F (60° C)—and a mild detergent or soap and water softener. After soaking, and rinsing out all the soap, rinse in warm water and fabric softener, so your bag will have more loft.

If you prefer, you can dry it in a large commercial dryer set for low or no heat. But a synthetic bag will also dry in an hour or less in open air.

Dry cleaning is not generally recommended. If you do have your bag dry-cleaned, air it outside for at least a week to remove any traces of the chemical solvent.

TIP

A little petroleum jelly will lubricate the metal zippers on your sleeping bag and help prevent rust from rain and dampness.

SLIPCOVERS (UPHOLSTERY)   Fabric content determines the correct cleaning method for slip-covers. Washable ones respond to the following procedure.

Vacuum or shake out dust. Soak covers for five to ten minutes in a solution of cold water, laundry detergent, and an all-fabric (oxygen) bleach. Agitate for five minutes on the delicate cycle of your washer. Spin dry until slightly damp. Replace the covers on your furniture while they are still moist—they will dry to fit.

SMOKE DETECTORS   To test, simply blow smoke into the detector—an extinguished, but still smoking match will do. To stop the alarm, blow the smoke out. (Some detectors have a test button. Consult your manual.) Test twice a year.

Clean a detector at least once a year, vacuuming the chamber or dusting with a cloth, unless your manual suggests other procedures. The cover may be washed with mild soap and water, but dry thoroughly before reassembling.

Change the battery in battery-operated units once a year—faithfully. Some detectors signal when the battery is running low. If you know you won't replace batteries, get an AC-powered unit instead. The bulbs in photoelectric types normally need replacing every three to five years.

SNEAKERS.   See Shoes.

SOAP   Soap remains a favorite in many households for personal grooming, baby care, hand washing, use on delicate fabrics, etc. But synthetic detergents have displaced it as the major household cleanser, because they perform successfully in both hard and soft water. Soap, on the other hand, is likely to form curds ("bathtub ring") in hard water that has not been softened.

Soap, you will notice, is recommended for some stain removal procedures, and for use in washing when you do not want to strip a material of its oil content.

See Master Product List for brand name examples.

SOAP JELLY   The Cooperative Extension Service of South Dakota State University offers this recipe for cleaning washable paint.

Dissolve 1 cup soap flakes in 4 cups boiling water. Allow the solution to cool to a jellylike texture. When cool, dip a clean cloth in the jelly and gently clean the soiled surface. Wipe away jelly and soil with a damp cloth and let dry. For greasy surfaces, mix 1 tablespoon household ammonia in the solution before cooling.

SODA COMPOUNDS   The two most common soda compounds (aside from sodium chloride, or regular salt) are bicarbonate of soda (or baking soda) and carbonate of soda (or washing soda). See Baking Soda, Washing Soda.

SODIUM PERBORATE BLEACH   See Bleaches.

SOFT DRINK STAINS   See Carpet Stain Removal Guide; Master Stain Removal Section (Beverages).

SOFTENERS   See Fabric Softeners, Water Quality.

SOIL RELEASE FINISHES   These are applied to 100 percent polyester or blends of polyester and cotton or polyester and rayon. They improve a fabric's ability to release oily soil and help to keep soil from redepositing itself during laundering. In addition, soil-release-finished fabrics are more comfortable and less prone to static clinging.

SOLVENTS

Water alone, or in combination with cleaning agents, is the most widely used solvent, efficiently dissolving and flushing away many kinds of dirt.

For oily dirt, some of the best agents are spirit solvents. They are found in all-purpose cleaners, sanitizers, drain cleaners, waxes and polishes for furniture and floors, and floor-wax removers. Paint thinners, turpentine, and kerosene are all spirit solvents.

Spirit solvents are flammable. Keep them away from heat, sparks, and open flames. If you spill some on your clothing, don't wear it near a heat source.

Be careful how you dispose of empty solvent containers because even a small amount of solvent in a container can ignite and cause an explosion if left in a warm place or sunlight.

Do not use spirit-solvent floor wax on asphalt or rubber tile, because it softens the flooring. Some floor waxes are water-emulsion waxes, which damage wood and cork. You can distinguish them from spirit-solvent waxes by the label statement "Keep from freezing."

Dry-cleaning solvents are the principal ingredients in many products sold for spot removal. (Common brand names: Carbona, K2r.) They are all poisonous, most are flammable, and a danger to skin and eyes.

The cautions on the labels protect your health and may save your life. Keep these solvents away from children and pets. Work in a well-ventilated area. Don't smoke or use flammable solvents in a room with an open flame or gas pilot light, or where there may be electrical equipment. Don't pour solvent into a bowl, and make sure the fumes blow away from you. Fumes are especially toxic to anyone who has been drinking.

Never use dry-cleaning solvent in a washing machine, and don't put articles with damp solvent spots in a dryer.

Flammable solvents are usually harmful or fatal if swallowed. The rule is: do not induce vomiting. Call a physician immediately.

SPACE HEATERS   See Heaters.

SPANDEX   This is the man-made elastomeric fiber of choice where stretch is desired. Our dancewear, swimwear, and foundation garments owe their two-way stretch and smooth fit to spandex, as do many slacks and men's suits. It also makes one-way stretch items less restrictive, like two-piece swim suits.

Spandex is lightweight and also very strong, but although it has excellent stretch and recovery, you should avoid constant over-stretching.

When combined with polyester, spandex is unaffected by chlorinated water, but in some other fiber combinations, it may be yellowed by chlorine bleach. Spandex may also yellow with age or exposure to light.

To Clean: Hand- or machine-wash spandex items in lukewarm water. About three minutes is enough to get them clean. Unless the label directs otherwise, use all-fabric bleach in preference to chlorine bleach. Rinse thoroughly, and then drip dry or tumble dry at a cool setting.

To Iron: Spandex fabrics require little or no pressing. But you can use a steam or dry iron at a low temperature, pressing with a back and forth motion. A press cloth helps to reduce shine and to keep the fabric from stretching during pressing. Ernestine Porter of the University of Idaho suggests covering a table with a thick terry cloth, which will give you a larger surface and help prevent stretching.

SPIDERS   Spiders are shy, rarely bite, and are beneficial, in that they feed on other insects (including other spiders). There are only two kinds of poisonous spiders—the black widows, found throughout the country, and the brown recluse spiders, mostly in the middle of the country and the Southeast. You are unlikely to encounter either one, and only those allergic to insect venoms need fear other spider bites.

So you may choose to take a live-and-let-live attitude to the spider.

If you want to eliminate spiders, good housekeeping is your first line of attack—brushing down webs, regular dusting in corners, around windows, under the furniture, vacuuming to gather up the eggsacs (be sure to dispose of the cleaner bag contents).

Aerosols (with pyrethrum, resmethrin or propoxur) kill spiders if the spray contacts them. You might hang insecticide strips in little-used rooms, following package directions.

SPONGES

Sponge mops should be thoroughly rinsed before storage to prolong the life of the sponge. Cellulose sponge mops tend to hold odors and dry slowly. So dry them thoroughly in an open area after rinsing.

Squeezing synthetic sponges improves their absorbency by opening up additional cells. All sponges, whether natural or synthetic, should be squeezed (never wrung).

SPOONING STAINS AWAY

To loosen a stain on a sturdy fabric, work it with the back of a smooth stainless steel spoon.

Place the stained fabric on a hard surface protected with foil, without any absorbent material underneath it, and add the correct stain remover.

Then, holding the spoon with your thumb in the bowl and a side edge of the spoon on the fabric, move the spoon back and forth on the fabric about 1/4 inch in each direction. Make short strokes and don't press down so hard that you damage the fabric.

STAIN REPELLENT FINISHES

These finishes are water-repellent (silicones). Or they may be both water-repellent and oil-repellent.

Trade names include Scotchgard, Spotshed, and Zepel.

If you happen to stain treated fabrics, blot or wipe off the staining materials immediately. Follow directions on the care label; thorough rinsing is important to maintain the finish.

STAINLESS STEEL

This is a durable material produced by combining steel, chromium, and nickel. It is used for cook- and bakeware, utensils and flatware, and some washer and dryer tubs. It can also be found in sinks, ranges, and countertops, as well as oven and microwave oven interiors.

To Clean: It is easy to care for, and dishwasher-safe. Wash with a solution of detergent and hot water, rinse, and polish dry. For burned-on food add 2 tablespoons of baking soda to a quart of water, bring to a boil, remove from heat and let stand. For stainless that is not used in food preparation, pick a liquid glass cleaner or all-purpose liquid household cleaner. Try a commercial stainless steel cleaner to remove discoloration.

Do not let flames lick up the sides of a cookpot. Stainless steel is a poor conductor of heat and can develop a bluish tinge in areas where it is overheated. Such discoloration is virtually impossible to remove. For more information, see Cookware (Stainless Steel).

TIP

Spots on stainless-steel kitchen equipment can be removed by rubbing spots with a cloth dampened with white vinegar.

STARCH

The development of easy-care fabrics has reduced the need for starch. However, you may still want it on your laundry shelf. Starch restores crispness and body to fabric, and adds a fresh, smooth appearance to items that need ironing. Starch can also aid in soil-removal. Soils cling to the starch rather than fabric fibers and are removed more easily the next time the item is washed. Aerosol spray starch is most convenient and best suited for cottons and other natural fibers. Dry starches are economical but more work and are best suited for large wash loads or large items like Grandma's linen tablecloth.

Starching Hints

Aerosol Sprays: Hold container six to twelve inches from fabric. Spray smoothly, using a back and forth motion. Use one spray for light to medium finish. Use a double spray for a heavy finish.

Dry Starch in Sink or Wash Tub: Do not crowd items to be starched. Dampen fabric for better penetration of starch. Dip fabric up and down, squeeze starch solution through item. Wring fabric and damp-dry for pressing.

Dry Starch in Washer: This gives an even starch distribution and is practical for starching a large quantity of bulky items. Follow package instructions for amount of starch and water temperature. Fill machine tub with water. If filling only part way, reduce amount of starch accordingly. Add starch solution and distribute by running washer about one minute. Add items and agitate one to two minutes. Prolonged spinning will result in loss of starch.

TIP

Do not starch items that have recently been washed with fabric softener. This combination will cause the iron to stick. If this happens, your only solution is to rewash.

STATIC

Static is a nuisance and sometimes a hazard, as well. Besides making socks stick to trousers and slips ride up, it is dangerous in operating rooms and around computers. It is a dustmaker, inviting soil and lint to cling to fabrics, furniture, and equipment.

Antistatic finishes ameliorate such problems. You will find them on many carpets, draperies, upholstery, and other fabrics containing man-made fibers such as nylon and polyester. To care for such fabrics, see care labels.

Fabric softeners are also helpful in controlling static. For details on their use, see Fabric Softeners.

If you must control static around computer equipment, a humidifier offers some protection, as do various antistatic devices and covers on market. An *antistatic spray* is handy also.

STEAM IRON

See Irons.

STEEL WOOL
Steel wool is marketed as long shavings of steel formed into pads or balls, used as abrasives for scouring, smoothing, and polishing. There are eight grades of steel wool to cope with various cleaning and polishing tasks.

The following guidelines are offered by the American Steel Wool Company.

#0000	Super Fine	For rubbing varnish smooth
# 000	Extra Fine	To create a slightly dull finish
# 00	Very Fine	To clean copper and brass
# 0	Fine	To scour cookware and remove rust
# 1	Medium	To buff floors
# 2	Medium-Coarse	To remove wax and dirt
# 3	Coarse	For abrasive cleaning
# 4	Extra Coarse	For heavy abrasive cleaning

STEREO CASSETTE PLAYERS
See Audio Equipment.

STORAGE STRATEGIES
See Mini Manual on next page.

STOVE
See Ranges.

STRETCH FABRICS
Expanding with movement, then springing back to shape, these are popular for every kind of wearing apparel from foundation garments to sportswear. Additionally they offer superior wrinkle resistance and they drape so beautifully that they are well adapted for use in home furnishings items.

Specific care depends on an item's fiber content and construction. There is no true alternative to reading the care labels.

In general, you can restore stretching by steaming, washing, or dry cleaning even when a garment has stretched on a hanger. But it's wise to store stretch items flat to help them retain their shape.

Storage Strategies

A MINI MANUAL

If you have "a place for everything and everything in its place," you are probably listening to a symphony, or looking at a soap opera—and not bent over this page.

You have also thrown out or given away tons of stuff. Souvenir sellers and bargain merchants have you marked down as one tough customer, as have the people now in business to organize your closets for you.

SOME DISORGANIZATION PAYS OFF

When kitchen planners assembled homemakers some years back to divine just what new, special storage units they wanted, some women voted for drawers especially sectioned for lids and some for cabinets designed to handle trays and so forth, but they were unanimous in wanting some unplanned space—a closet, or drawer, even just a box—where they could throw things when company came, or in fact any time when they had no immediate time for cleanup. And they were delighted to find that others felt the same way they did about the merits of some disorganization! So, somewhere in your storage plans develop one handy catchall.

PLAN ORGANIZED STORAGE

Clutter is your biggest enemy. Remember that the more stuff you keep, the more time you'll spend not only cleaning it, but moving it to get at other cleaning. Decide how much you can tolerate, and throw out or give away the rest of the stuff that makes closets bulge and rooms look as if a storm just blew through.

Spend a few moments at your hardware or department store "closet shop" section to see the terrific new ideas in closet, wall, and shelf organizers.

Now then, make it easy to put stuff away and retrieve it in good condition without straining your back, bopping yourself on the head, or going into gymnastics to get ahold of it.

DISCOVER YOUR "EASY REACH" AREAS

From Mid-thigh to Shoulder Reach: Keep (1) things most often used, like coffee pots and seasonings. (2) Things to get quickly, like bandages. (3) Medium-weight items.

From Shoulder Reach Up: Keep (1) lesser-used articles, like guest towels and extra blankets. (2) Lightweight items, like cereals and toilet tissue. (3) Medium-weight items no bigger than your grasp, like glass pitchers.

From Mid-thigh to Toes: Keep heavier items, such as unabridged dictionaries, stacks of company-only dinner plates and little-used portable appliances.

HAVE STUFF WHERE YOU WANT IT
WHEN YOU WANT IT

- Try pairs: broom and dustpan, hammer and nails, scissors with thread and buttons. Keep them together.
- Store bed linens in the bedroom.
- If kids play in the kitchen, make drawer or cabinet space there for their toys.
- Put storage cabinets and tables on wheels and roll out your supplies to the spot where you use them.
- Use baskets and buckets as portable totes for movable storage.

FIND STUFF WITHOUT HUNTING

- Park your rings on a cup hook near the sink while you do grimy work.
- Know your management style. Is it better for you to keep all top sheets in one pile and bottom sheets in another? Or are sets of tops, bottoms, and pillowcases handier?
- If you can see it, you can find it. Organize deep shelves with tall items to the back, or like items on the same shelf. Step-shelf organizers or lazy Susans or turntables may do the trick for you.

LOOK FOR MORE STORAGE SPACE

- Store extra blankets and pads between the mattress and box spring.
- Storage walls in bedrooms and family rooms not only provide generous storage but create sound barriers between rooms.
- To prevent pile-ups, add stacked shelves to regular shelves to create more levels.
- Take advantage of unused spaces, nooks, and crannies. Skinny spaces, for example, are handy spots for tray or table-pad storage.

KEEP CLOTHES AND LINENS LOOKING THEIR BEST

- Don't cram things into closets or jam them into drawers. This only makes for more work later, like mending and ironing.
- Hang silks on padded hangers. Stuff sleeves with tissue paper, to avoid creasing them.
- Store whites in blue tissue paper to avoid yellowing.
- Most knits should be stored flat, neatly folded, to preserve their shape. Some stable knit dresses are exceptions, and may be stored on padded hangers.
- Slacks and tablecloths will stay crease-free if placed over a hanger padded with a cardboard tube from a roll of paper towels.
- A tie wardrobe will keep its press if hung over a curtain rod bracketed on the inside of a closet door. For extra protection, cover the rod with felt.
- Shoe trees preserve the shape of your shoes, and cardboard tubes will hold boots upright.

HARD-TO-STORE ITEMS

- Store placemats on shelves or in drawers using a heavy cardboard file folder for each set of mats. (Select one set without disturbing another!) Or use a clipboard to hang mats wrinkle-free.
- Small items, like craft and sewing materials, won't scatter or get lost if kept in empty prescription bottles. Childproof caps protect them from curious little helpers, too.

GET THE CHILDREN TO HELP

- Encourage them to put things away by keeping their shelves, clothes rods, etc., at reachable heights.

- Supply them with tote boxes to help them organize their gear. Paste on picture cutouts to help nonreaders identify the right boxes.
- Laundry or shopping bags on wall hooks fill quickly with scattered toys.

STORE SAFELY

- Store fabric items clean. Insects will eat any textile with food stains on it.
- Protect clothes stored in the basement by packing them in plastic trash cans to keep out dampness and mold.
- When putting clothes away for the season, safeguard them with dust bags. Leave the bottom of the bags open so garments can breathe. (Polyethylene bags may emit a gas that will affect some dyes.)
- Dry climates and plastic bag storage don't mix. It's a combination that produces dust-attracting static electricity.
- A tightly sealed bag in moist climates may seal in moisture and invite mildew.
- You can safely use naphthalene flakes or balls to kill or deter moths. Use caution with paradichlorobenzene crystals. They tend to dissolve plastic garment bags and hangers.

IN BOX—OUT BOX

Take a tip from the business world. Set out two large boxes or cartons labeled "In Box" and "Out Box" to route your clutter to its proper place.

Let the Out Box be your catchall for the temporary storage of items to be "filed" later.

Make the In Box your junk box. This centrally located container is the spot where all must go to claim their precious misplaced clutter.

SUEDE, SYNTHETIC

Synthetic suedes are available in a wide price range. The woven synthetic suedes and knit fabrics with a napped or sanded surface resembling suede are relatively inexpensive. The nonwoven synthetic suedes (e.g., Ultrasuede), which most realistically simulate this luxury leather, are expensive.

In general, nonwoven suede launders beautifully, by hand or machine, just so long as the linings and trims permit washing. These fabrics are also wrinkle-free, colorfast, won't water-spot, stiffen, shrink, pill, fray, or crock (color doesn't rub off).

To Machine-Wash: Use the durable/permanent press cycle on the washer and dryer. Otherwise use warm wash, cold rinse, slow or short spin.

Select a mild detergent without bluing agents (e.g., Ivory Snow, Woolite). Do not bleach, and wash alone to avoid staining from other fabrics.

To Hand Wash: Squeeze gently, do not wring or twist. Hang to dry.

To Machine-dry: Do not use dryer fabric softener sheets when machine-drying synthetic suede garments.

Remove the garment promptly from the dryer to prevent unnecessary creases.

Between wearings, brush these suedes lightly to refresh the nap of the fabric.

To Press: Should you want to press a garment, work on the reverse side, using a presscloth and a low synthetic setting.

Dry Cleaning: If you dry-clean, use a professional cleaner.

Caution: These "suedes" burn easily. Even stray ashes from a cigarette can burn the fabric. Some burn marks can be removed by rubbing the spot with dry white scouring powder.

TIP

Note that on non-wovens, oily stains need pretreatment, as on any polyester.

SWEATERS

Despite the high-fashion sweaters with "Dry-clean Only" labels, most manufacturers are striving to give us easy-care sweaters. Machine-washable wools and cottons with dimensional stability, as well as synthetics, invite us to entrust sweaters to the washing machine. That option is increasingly available except in truly fragile knits. When in doubt, hand wash.

To Hand Wash: Squeeze suds through the sweater. Don't twist or wring. Rinse thoroughly.

Use lukewarm water for wool, letting the garment soak for a few minutes, then washing it gently and rinsing absolutely clean. Press out excess moisture with a towel, then dry the sweater on a flat surface away from direct heat, to help prevent both stretching and shrinkage.

If you hand wash and flat dry synthetics, use warm water and detergent with a cold-water rinse. Squeeze and roll the sweater in a towel to remove excess moisture. Don't stretch or hang it. Spread it on a smooth surface and bunch it into shape to dry. If synthetic sweaters stretch during wear or washing, wet thoroughly, squeeze and tumble dry to reshape.

To Machine-Wash: You should abide by care labels, but warm water with a gentle cycle and mild detergent is the general rule for all fibers. Thorough rinsing is important. Add a fabric softener with the final rinse water to keep the original hand and to control static in synthetics.

For some acrylic synthetics (Orlon, Civona, Wintuk and Sayelle), machine-washing is the method of choice. They should block automatically if they are machine-dried.

To Dry. Medium tumble drying is widely recommended for cottons and blends and synthetics, although air drying is always an option.

For faster air drying, whether you're working with hand-washed or machine-washed sweaters, spin out excess water with your washer. Take the sweaters dripping wet from the last rinse, set the washing machine control about halfway through the last spin or dry setting. Add a wet towel or so to balance the washer if necessary. Then block and dry flat.

To Block: One way to insure the shape and fit of a wool sweater, or in fact any stretchy knit, is to spread it on a brown paper bag before you wash it, and trace its shape to give you an accurate

TIP

Close zippers and hooks, and button buttons. Turn sweaters inside out to prevent fuzzing and damage to knit stitches. Put fragile knits in a mesh bag or pillowcase.

TIME SAVER

If you're a sweater collector you may want a mesh-screen sweater dryer to speed up flat air drying.

To repair runs: Use a crochet hook to pick up and recreate the stitches.

TIP

pattern for it. Arrange the wet washed sweater on the paper to dry, working it to fit the pattern during the drying process.

To Press: Sweaters rarely need ironing or pressing. Do not iron wool in any case. Steam press, if necessary.

To Remove Pills: Use a Dr. Scholl's Callus Remover. It is safer than a razor for wools and acrylics.

To Repair Snags: Pull the dangling yarn to the back with a Knit-Picker or Snag-Fix'r, available at notions counters.

To Store Wrinkle-Free: Lay sweater front-side-down and fold in half so bottom meets top; then cross each arm over the width.

To Reclaim Stretched-Out Shape: Wash the sweater (if washable) and dry it in the dryer at medium heat. It will shrink back to size but may stretch out again.

SYNTHETIC DETERGENTS

"Detergent," in this book, refers to synthetic cleansing agents, as they are distinguished from soap and soap products.

These synthetic detergents have largely replaced soap products in our kitchens and laundry rooms because they work well in both hard and soft water. They contain agents that prevent washed-out dirt from redepositing on clean laundry. Brighteners are common ingredients, so are bleach, enzymes, bluing and antibacterial agents. You can even buy combination laundry detergent products conveniently including detergent, fabric softener and antistatic in one package.

You will want to keep on hand both light-duty (nonalkaline) detergents, for hand washing, delicate cleaning, and for use on fine fabrics like silk, and heavy-duty (alkaline) detergents. The latter, which may be hard on the hands, can be used in dishwashers. They are also superior for tackling heavy dirt.

Follow package instructions: they can save you time and trouble, and guide you to buying the product that does the best job for you.

See also Laundry Mini Manual for instructions on use and Master Product List for examples.

TABLE LINENS   See Linens, Table.

TALC   This is an absorbent powder useful for removing stains. Available at drug stores.

TAMPING   This is a stain-removing technique of special help with tightly woven fabrics. Using a brush, tap on the back of the stained material with an up and down motion. Work on a glass pie pan (or similar hard surface). Don't use so much pressure that the bristles bend. Continue till the stain is removed. Never rub a stain. You may simply force the stain deeper into the fabric or damage the fabric surface.

TAPESTRIES   Valuable old tapestries should receive professional cleaning. Ordinary ones can often be washed with suds from mild soap flakes, applied to keep the hanging as dry as possible. Dry thoroughly and press with a steam iron.

Strong light is very damaging. So is moisture, which can cause colors to fade and fibers to deteriorate. Moths and mildew are major enemies of tapestries. See precautions and remedies under Mildew and Moths.

TAR STAINS   See Carpet Stain Removal Guide; Grout Stain Removal Guide; Vinyl Flooring Stain Removal Guide; Master Stain Removal Section.

TEA STAINS   See Carpet Stain Removal Guide; Grout Stain Removal Guide; Master Stain Removal Section.

TEFLON   See Cookware (Nonstick).

TELEPHONE   Telephones need to be cleaned very frequently. There is, in all probability, no other household item, with the exception of silverware, that comes in contact with both hand and mouth more often than the telephone.

Because the phone is used almost constantly by family, friends, neighbors, and even occasional strangers, it should be wiped clean daily. Use a sponge or cloth dampened with a liquid or spray disinfectant cleaner. (Do not spray or pour the cleaner directly onto the phone.) Wipe dry.

Once a month or so, lightly dampen a cotton swab with a liquid cleaner or detergent to clean in between and around push buttons.

During the flu season, or if there is illness in the home, wipe the mouth and handpiece with denatured alcohol.

TELEVISION SETS   See Video Equipment.

TERMITES   Call a licensed, qualified pest control operator if you believe you have termites. They can cause extensive damage in wood furniture and buildings. Only certified pest control operators may use the effective pesticides, a restriction established by the U. S. Environmental Protection Agency.

Termites swarm in spring and fall. This may be the first sign that a home is infested. Other signs: shelter tubes or runways on foundation walls.

TERRA COTTA   See Terrazzo, below.

TERRAZZO   Both Terra Cotta and Terrazzo are stone, responding to the same care that you usually give to marble or tile (ceramic, mosaic, quarry tile, and quarry natural). Correct treatment depends on whether they are glazed or unglazed. For further suggestions, see Marble, Tile, Tile Floors.

THERMOS (VACUUM) BOTTLES   Wash vacuum bottles inside with a bottle brush and hot sudsy water. To remove odors, soak overnight in a solution of baking soda and water.

TICKS   Ticks travel into the house in the fur of dogs or other pets on whom they feed. Having fed, they then drop off and hide under rugs and behind baseboards. They transmit viral diseases, and you should remove them. The methods are much like those for fleas.

First, do something about your pet. Get a pesticide labeled for tick control on dogs. You may want to have a veterinarian treat your pet. Spray or dust the dog's bed and wash (or discard) infested bedding. You can also buy aerosol bombs with pyrethrin to fog an infested room. If the infestation seems out of control, consult a pest-control professional.

TILE, CERAMIC   Ceramic tile is a durable, low-maintenance surface. Routine cleaning can be as minimal as a quick once-over with a damp mop. However, since tile is so popular in areas like bathrooms and kitchens, efforts at sanitation are in order.

Simple daily maintenance to prevent surface soil build-up should forever abolish any need for heavy-duty cleaning.

To prevent soap scum and hard-water residue buildup, quickly wipe counters and tub walls daily. The last family member to use the tub or shower should be in charge of the wipe-down.

To remove soap scum and hard-water residue, use a heavy-duty tile cleaner (Lime-A-Way, Tilex, dr. rust). A solution of white vinegar and water may also be used. (Test first—vinegar can etch some crystalline glazes.) Rinse and wipe dry. Use of steel wool pads may cause rust.

To disinfect, wash weekly with a liquid disinfectant cleaner. Let cleaners stand at least five minutes to reduce the need for scrubbing.

To protect, make future cleaning easier with a coat of silicone sealer (Star brite), or apply three coats of lemon oil polish; let stand one hour between coats.

To remove heavy soil, apply a thick solution of scouring powder and hot water. Allow it to set for at least ten minutes. Scrub with a stiff bristle brush and rinse thoroughly. Repeat the process if necessary. Treat remaining stains with chlorine bleach. Let stand for five minutes or more. Rinse and dry.

TILE FLOORS
(Ceramic Mosaic, Glazed Tile, Quarry Tile, Quarry Natural)

Cleaning

1. Sweep or vacuum daily to remove loose dust and dirt.

2. Use a damp mop to remove spills or heel marks.

3. For regular (weekly) cleaning, use a cleaner recommended and sold by your local tile supplier (e.g., Hillyard Super Shine-All). Apply cleaning solution to floor and scrub with a floor machine or mop. Scrub small areas at a time and rinse out mop or scrub brushes often.

4. For abrasive surfaces or joints, use a stiff scrub brush.

5. Do not allow cleaning solution to dry on floor.

For stubborn cleaning jobs or heavy-duty cleaning, double the strength of your regular cleaner in a solution of hot water. Or apply a scouring-powder paste (powder plus enough water to make it workable). Scrub area to be cleaned, and rinse well. Let floor dry, remove any remaining white spots with a damp mop.

Protecting

Ceramic, glazed, and quarry floors are not stainproof, but do not generally require sealing. However, you may want to seal the floor (1) to provide stain-resistant surfaces and grout joints, (2) to make cleaning easier, and (3) for a glossy wet look.

Unglazed Ceramics or Quarry: For a glossy finish, apply a clear, self-polishing acrylic (Hillyard Top Shape) to a clean, dry floor and let dry 1 hour. Apply a second coat. Let second application dry and apply a final coat. Thin film applications will get harder and resist wear better than thick coats. Follow regular cleaning procedures. Do not use cleaners containing ammonia. Ammonia will deteriorate sealer.

To restore sheen of sealer, mix 1 part acrylic sealer to 1½ parts water and spray-mist dull areas. Buff and let dry for 1 hour.

Boiled linseed oil can also be used to seal unglazed floors. Linseed oil actually stains the entire floor to a darker richer tone. It is functional for kitchen floors, where oil and grease staining may be a problem. (Test on an extra piece of tile or an inconspicuous spot before applying.) Linseed oil penetrates the pores of the quarry tile and forms a hard, clear filler keeping other stains out.

To apply:

1. Thin boiled linseed oil with 2 parts turpentine. (Do not attempt to boil linseed oil—it is flammable.)

2. Apply a generous coat of sealer to clean dry floor. Dispose of oily rags in bucket of water to prevent combustion.

3. Allow to dry for thirty minutes. Remove all excess sealer with clean, lint-free toweling.

4. Immediately clean with your regular cleaner.

5. On the following day repeat the procedure.

Repeat yearly.

Glazed Tile: Glazed tiles require no sealing because of their impervious surface. However, porous grout joints might be sealed to minimize staining. Use an acrylic sealer polish or silicone masonry-waterproofing liquid.

To apply:

1. Clean and dry joints thoroughly.

2. Mix protective coating according to manufacturer's directions.

3. Apply solution to grout joints with a paint brush.

4. Wait five minutes, then wipe off excess sealer from joints.

5. Wait one hour and apply a second coat of sealer.

6. Wipe excess with a cloth dampened with denatured alcohol.

Cleaners with ammonia will deteriorate acrylic-based sealers.

Stain Removal

Oil and Grease: Apply a solution of Spic and Span and very hot water to stained area. Scrub with a stiff brush, rinse, and dry. Repeat if necessary. Or mix a paste of cleanser and hot water. Apply to stain and let stand overnight. Wet paste and scrub with a stiff brush. Rinse and dry. Or steam out with iron set at highest steam setting. Apply iron over several layers of paper toweling placed over stain. Steam for about five minutes to blot up stain.

Paint: Scrape off dried paint with a single-edge razor blade. Then use a commercial paint remover on any residue. Scrub area with a solution of Spic and Span mixed with very hot water. Rinse and dry.

TIN   See Cookware (Tin).

TIN   Most of today's tinware is imported, with the exception of antique pieces such as candle molds and utensils. Even if worn and possibly corroded, it can still be cleaned and protected from future damage.

To Clean: Wash in hot, soapy water, rinse, and dry very thoroughly. Protect the finish with a coat of paste wax and buff to shine.

To Remove Rust: The Cooperative Extension Service of Northeastern States suggests the following formula:

1. Cut a raw potato and dip in whiting (available in hardware stores).

2. Rub the potato over the rusted areas.

3. Wash in hot, soapy water, rinse, and dry.

TOASTER-OVEN/ BROILER   This multi-function appliance offers space and energy savings as well as convenience.

Many of the new portables have continuous-clean oven walls. If you own one of these units, check the oven-cleaning section in its use-and-care manual.

Two Cautions for Toaster-Oven/Broiler Care: (1) Always turn all controls to the off position and unplug the unit before cleaning. (2) Some ovens have a heat/temperature sensor at the bottom of the oven cavity. Do not drip liquid on the sensor, or clean it. If necessary, crumbs can be brushed away with a soft pastry brush.

Routine cleaning saves work in the long run. Remove wire racks and soak in hot sudsy water. Stubborn spots respond to a soapy steel wool pad. Clean glass doors with hot, soapy water. Remove difficult food soils with a nylon or polyester scrubbing pad.

Oven pans and drip trays can be soaked in hot water and detergent or cleaned in the dishwasher. To clean stubborn stains, use a nylon scrub brush or pad. Avoid abrasive cleaners and metal scrub pads. These harsh cleaning products will scratch the shiny surface.

Wipe or brush away crumbs from the crumb tray often. Food spills should be removed with a nylon mesh pad dipped in hot soapy water.

The oven exterior may be cleaned (when cool) with warm water and soap or a mild liquid all-purpose or glass cleaner. Rinse with a damp cloth or paper towel and buff dry.

TOASTERS

Always disconnect the toaster before cleaning.

Item number one to watch is the crumb tray, because keeping it clean keeps the bright surface, better for toasting. To clean the tray, remove or open according to manufacturer's instructions. Empty crumbs into a waste can. Clean the corners with a soft brush. Wipe with a damp cloth. Remove burned-on spots with a nylon pad slightly dampened with sudsy water. Rinse with a damp cloth and dry.

Treat the outside surface of the toaster according to the finish. For chrome, clean with detergent and water, an all-purpose liquid cleaner or chrome cleaner. Rinse and wipe dry and polish with a soft cloth. Never use abrasives.

For painted, enameled, or anodized surfaces, clean with sudsy water or a mild all-purpose cleaner, rinse with a damp cloth and dry.

Never use metal (steel wool) scouring pads. Pieces of the metal may break off in the toaster and create an electrical hazard.

TOILET BOWLS

The finish on toilet bowls is usually vitreous china and may be cleaned the same way as porcelain enamel.

Once a day use a bowl brush to swish out the bowl and under the rim with detergent or a little liquid all-purpose cleaner. Flush.

Apply a spray cleaner to tank top and toilet seat, wipe with a damp sponge.

Once a week toilets need a thorough cleaning, not only to cleanse but to disinfect as well. If the toilet has had a light cleaning every day, or you have used a toilet-bowl deodorizer additive (Ty-D-Bol) on a regular basis, the job won't be a tough one. Another good method is a daily addition of $1/2$ cup of chlorine bleach to the water in the bowl.

Do not mix toilet bowl cleaners with chlorine bleach or cleansers that contain bleach.

To Clean and Disinfect: Use a commercial toilet-bowl cleaner (Vanish) and a toilet-bowl brush with stiff bristles in a shape that allows you to scrub all the way into the base of the bowl. The outer surface of the tank, base, seat, and rim should be sponged with a disinfectant cleaner (Pine Sol, Lysol), rinsed, and dried.

To Remove Stubborn Stains and Mineral Deposits: Pour one of the extra-thick toilet-bowl cleaners (Swish) into the bowl and let stand overnight.

Some mineral hard-water stains inside toilet bowls are very hard to deal with, especially if water has been standing in a bowl that has not been flushed over a long period of time. First, reduce the water level in the bowl (below the stain line), so you can try to attack the stain without the stain remover's being diluted by water. To do this, empty a full bucket of water directly into the toilet bowl. The toilet will automatically flush and the water will return to a level approximately three-quarters less than normal.

Make a paste from a thick liquid bowl cleaner (Lysol, Cling) or a stronger rust- and lime-remover product (Lime-A-Way) and cornmeal. Apply it directly to the stained area. Let the cleaner sit a few hours or overnight and scrub off. Flush, and the water will return to its normal level in the bowl.

To Deodorize: Add $1/4$ cup borax to the water in the toilet bowl and let stand for thirty minutes. Soak the bowl scrub brush as well.

TIP

Denture-cleaning tablets offer a handy way to clean the bowl. Just drop in a couple and brush the bowl and flush when they stop bubbling.

TIP

Add 1 cup of chlorine bleach to white or light-colored bowls before going away for the weekend or vacation. It will reduce water residue buildup and rings.

TIME SAVER

Add bowl cleaner before leaving the house or before bedtime. Swish out bowl when you arrive home or in the morning.

TOLE The surface of this distinctively painted tinware may craze, the colors fade, and the tin coating may even flake off. Unfortunately, there are no remedies for these problems. But if you spot rust in a piece of tole, you may arrest its spread by carefully cleaning and rubbing the rust spots with steel wool, then applying a thin coat of wax. Consult an expert if the rust is extensive, to determine if the piece can be repainted (and if it will lose value if it is redone).

TOMATO SAUCE STAINS See Master Stain Removal Section.

TRASH COMPACTORS To keep these work-savers odor free:

Once a week wipe down the enamel exterior and door or drawer edges with hot, sudsy water or a liquid disinfectant cleaner.

Once a month wash the compactor drawer inside and out with liquid disinfectant cleaner. Rinse and dry.

Periodically remove ram cover according to manufacturer's directions and wash with sudsy water. Rinse and dry.

To avoid the need for frequent cleaning, wrap soft food waste in a layer or two of newspaper before compacting.

Excessive odors can be avoided by not compacting such items as fish and melon rinds.

Troubleshooters

Continuous odor: Empty or clogged deodorant cans may cause it. Replace.

Trash not compacted: The trash container is less than one-third full.

Does not operate: Key-lock may be in off position.

TRIACETATE

Triacetate fiber is used in fabrics for pleated skirts and other pleated trim. It is shrink-resistant, wrinkle-resistant, resistant to fading, and easily washed. Look for it in crisp-finish fabrics like faille, sharkskin, and taffeta as well as flannel, jersey, textured knits, and tricot.

Most garments containing 100 percent triacetate can be machine-washed and dried, but hand wash pleated garments. Try using a fabric softener. Because of its low absorbency, triacetate produces garments that accumulate static cling.

If ironing is desired, you can use a high temperature setting; some triacetate fabrics are in fact glaze-resistant.

TRISODIUM PHOSPHATE (TSP)

This is a strong alkali, an ingredient in some major granular or powdered all-purpose cleaners. It is used on floors and walls, especially before repainting. It can be caustic, so avoid contact with skin and eyes.

TURNTABLES

See Audio.

TYPEWRITER RIBBON STAINS

See Master Stain Removal Section.

UPHOLSTERY

See Mini Manual on next page.

URINE

See Carpet Stain Removal Guide; Master Stain Removal Section.

Upholstery

A MINI MANUAL

Once a week, vacuum upholstery, using the upholstery brush and the crevice tool. This removes soil and dust and prevents imbedded dirt from causing abrasion and wear. It is the best maintenance you can give upholstered furniture.

Reverse or turn loose cushions to allow even distribution of wear.

Protect arms with "arm covers" or an extra piece of fabric.

Avoid direct sunlight and heat that may fade or discolor upholstery.

When upholstery needs a thorough cleaning, it may be professionally shampooed or you can rent or purchase a commercial upholstery cleaner and do it yourself.

UPHOLSTERY SHAMPOOS

Tips for the Do-It-Yourselfer

- There are many products on the market. Select one recommended for the fiber content of your upholstery.

- Use the cleaner sparingly.
- Do not over-wet the fabric.
- Do not remove zippered upholstery-cushion covers to clean. Keeping the covers on the cushions helps to preserve the fabric backing and prevent shrinkage of the covers themselves.

For Wool: The Wool Bureau suggests water and a mild detergent. (Smoke-damaged furniture has been cleaned this way with excellent results.) Never use ammonia, bleach, or other cleaners intended for use on hard surfaces. Select a cleaner recommended for wool.

Do not use dry-cleaning solvents on rubber foam; they make it sticky.

Professional Shampoo Services

These may be found in the Yellow Pages; many stores carrying home furnishings also offer professional cleaning. A professional job is recommended if you have any doubts about tackling the work yourself.

TECHNIQUES FOR SPOT AND STAIN REMOVAL

1. Check the label for manufacturer's suggestions. The industry has a new care code:

W	Use a water-base cleaner.
S	Use a solvent-base cleaner.
S–W	Use a water- or solvent-base cleaner.
X	Vacuum only. Do not clean with either water or solvent.

2. Pretest stain treatment in inconspicuous spot.

3. Work quickly.

4. Do not over-dampen the stained area with the cleaning agent.

5. Blot excess stain with a clean cloth.

6. Work from the outside of the stain toward the middle, to contain the spot as much as possible.

For more on stains, see Master Stain Removal Section.

LEATHER UPHOLSTERY

Leather upholstery should be dusted with a vacuum cleaner or untreated cloth. Never use furniture polish. If soiled, wash with saddle soap worked into a rich lather. Clean small areas at a time. Remove lather with a clean, dry cloth. Apply a second coat of saddle soap, let dry. Buff with a dry cloth. Or use a commercial leather cleaner according to manufacturer's directions.

A few drops of olive oil or lanolin applied with a soft cloth, then buffed, will help to restore softness to stiff, dry leather.

PLASTIC UPHOLSTERY

Plastic upholstery should be washed with a damp cloth and detergent. Rinse and dry. White vinegar added to the wash water will reduce static. Do not use abrasives, strong cleaners or chlorine bleach. (See Vinyl Fabrics.)

VACUUM, MINI (Hand-held)

Care is very simple: your only real concern is the filter bag. Empty the bag, located in the collector receptacle, after each two or three uses. Clean the bag by brushing or shaking it into a wastebasket.

Occasionally hand wash the polyester bag with a mild dishwashing detergent. Rinse well. Remove excess moisture with a few paper towels placed inside the bag; then squeeze tightly. Remove the towels and allow the bag to dry completely before replacing it.

Do not operate the appliance without the bag in place.

Replacement bags are available if the bag becomes worn or if you would rather not wash it.

Plastic parts should be cleaned with a cloth dampened with a mild soap and warm water. Avoid all detergents, cleaners and solvents.

If you own a cordless, rechargeable mini-vacuum, check the manufacturer's use-and-care booklet for battery care instructions.

The easy way to dust a drawerful of small collectibles is to vacuum the lot. Just put a nylon stocking over the hose.

VACUUM BOTTLE

See Thermos.

VACUUM CLEANERS

If you have been thumbing through this book, you probably realize that vacuuming is the method of choice in many housekeeping situations. Vacuums are invaluable, not only for general floor care, but also for dusting and precleaning.

Owning more than one would be ideal. An investment in a well-designed dual-purpose model would be the next best choice.

Choose a Vacuum to Suit Your Cleaning Needs

How and where will you use it? What surfaces do you plan to vacuum? Match the cleaner to the surface needing the most care.

There are four styles of vacuums, each designed to accomplish different tasks. If you find vacuuming tiresome, it may be that you are working with the wrong piece of equipment.

Upright Cleaners are designed primarily for carpet cleaning.

Canister Cleaners cope with hard-surface floors, draperies, upholstery, and stairs.

Combination Canisters offer power nozzles for carpets plus a suction cleaner for hard-surfaced upholstery.

Lightweight Vacuums (electric brooms) replace the broom and dustpan for quick spot-cleaning and last minute once-overs. Some work on suction; others come with a small beater bar.

Vacuum Cleaner Care

Warning on hard floors: Unless the cleaner is a convertible, don't use an upright style on hard floors. The beater bars so essential for carpet cleaning may scratch hard-surface flooring. Hard floors need the suction cleaning of a canister-type cleaner.

Vacuums work best if the air flow is strong. Make sure the dirt cup or dust bag is not extremely full. Empty or replace bags at $1/2$ or $3/4$ full. This also helps to reduce wear on the motor, especially in central vac systems.

Hard, sharp objects damage the cleaner. Make a quick visual check of the room before you start to vacuum. Pick up any small items, toys, clips, and so forth ahead of time.

Two Important Don'ts: (1) Don't use your vacuum to pick up cigarette butts. Aside from being hard on the vacuum, this is dangerous. One of the cigarettes could still be partially lit. (2) Don't yank the vacuum cord. Turn the cleaner off before unplugging.

VACUUMING

Dirt is a serious threat to the beauty and wear life of rugs and carpets. There are three kinds to cope with.

TIP

Moving the furniture as little as an inch or two when you vacuum will prevent those indentations furniture legs otherwise leave in your carpet.

1. Surface litter (lint, pet hair and carpet nap), unless removed, eventually makes a carpet mat, and appear worn.

2. Dust left on carpets settles just below the surface, absorbs moisture, and causes discoloration.

3. Grit damages the carpet backing and scratches hard-surface floors if it is not removed from carpets and floors. Grit most often comes in on the soles of shoes. Place doormats at entryways to reduce excess.

The right vacuum cleaner will cope with all three menaces, achieving this with a combination of sweeping, beating, and suction. An agitator or upright power nozzle type lifts the carpet off the floor, beats it to bring grit and deeply embedded dirt to the surface and then sweeps and suctions the dirt away.

The rule for light cleaning is three passes with the vacuum; for heavy cleaning, it's seven.

VAPONA Vapona, which goes by the name dichlorvos or the letters DDVP, is the active ingredient in the insecticidal No Pest strips. It is also formulated as a spray and as an aerosol.

VARNISH STAINS See Vinyl Flooring Stain Removal Guide.

VASE See China, Glassware.

VASELINE See Petroleum Jelly.

VASELINE STAINS See Master Stain Removal Section (Grease).

VEGETABLE STAINS   See Master Stain Removal Section.

VELOUR   Velour is a close, thick-bodied, evenly napped fabric with a soft hand and velvet appearance. See Pile Fabrics.

VELVET AND VELVETEEN   Modern velvet was developed in France, but the fabric goes back to 2000 B.C. at least. Once principally made from silk, it is now more often available in cotton or man-made fibers—acetate, rayon, nylon, polyester, and blends. Some of these are washable. Some velvets are also finished to be crush-resistant and water repellent.

Velveteen, often called "cotton velvet" is now not just 100 percent cotton, but comes in many blends and other fibers.

While there are significant differences between these two pile fabrics, they require the same sort of care.

Care

Between cleanings, remove lint and dust with a soft brush, brushing with the nap. Always hang on padded hangers. Don't use clamps or metal clips. Hang strapless gowns wrong side out from loops on the inside of the waistband. When you travel, pack velvets and velveteens with tissue paper between the layers. Don't fold for shelf storage.

Steaming: Frequent steaming enlivens the pile. Hang the garment over a bathtub of steaming water, taking a soft natural-bristle brush to it and brushing it once from the hem up. Then allow it to dry thoroughly before handling it further.

If the Pile Has Been Crushed: While the steam bath treatment above is the recognized method of "pressing" these pile fabrics, you may flatten the pile or crease it from sitting. One suggested remedy is to freshen and lift the pile by holding it above a steam iron or kettle and brushing while it is still damp, then letting the garment dry before wearing it again. Or try rubbing the area gently with another piece of the same fabric, or a soft brush, following this with a steam bath. You can also help some wrinkles by putting the article in a dryer on the fluff cycle for ten or fifteen minutes. Never rest an iron on velvets or velveteens. Never press nylon velvets: steam them.

Washing

Cotton velvets and most velveteens can be machine-washed. In fact, cottons tend to look richer the more they're laundered. Use warm water, mild detergent, and a delicate setting. Take your usual precautions and don't launder dark colors with light-colored clothing, because these pile fabrics may "bleed" in the first few washings.

Rinse and tumble dry. (Tumble drying is less likely than drip drying to leave wrinkles.)

Pile fabrics are lint-collectors, so turn items inside out before washing to prevent their picking up lint in the machine.

Dry Cleaning

Dry cleaning is recommended for many velvets, and some velveteens. You will preferably dry-clean the rayon and acetate/rayons widely used in evening and bridal wear, along with other precious velvets.

VENETIAN BLINDS   The easy way to avoid a big messy job is to dust blinds regularly.

Dust with a clean cloth, dusting mitt, or treated cloth; one of those special Venetian blind brushes that does several blades at once; or the dusting brush on your vacuum cleaner.

You'll find that if you tilt the horizontal louvers down, almost but not quite closed, you'll be able to reach the entire top surface.

Or turn the blades flat; dust first one side and then the other. Work from the top down.

To Wash

Protect your floor with toweling or a plastic dropcloth. Use two soft cloths, two sponges, or a pair of cotton work gloves. That's because you'll wash with one, rinse with the other. Use two pails, one holding sudsy water, the other your rinse water. Starting from the top, work one blind at a time, using a mild detergent and warm or cold (not hot) water. Wipe the slats dry after a thorough rinsing.

If you have wooden blinds, clean the slats as you would a piece of wood furniture. See Furniture Mini Manual.

You can clean fabric tapes with dry-cleaning fluid or scrub them with a stiff suds of soap or detergent, then rinse with a clean, damp cloth or sponge. When the tapes are too soiled to be scrubbed to your satisfaction, you can buy Venetian blind renewal kits complete with cord and tape.

Check out commercial products, including commercial glass cleaners.

It's also possible to wash a small Venetian blind in a sink or tub. (Do one end at a time.) Or to hose-wash blinds outdoors (hang them from the clothesline). (Do a thorough rinsing job, says Levolor, draining out the head rail and bottom rail, drying with a towel to avoid water marks, or by hanging the blind upside down to dry, separating and tilting the louvers to expose them to the air.

Professional Help

Commercial services will wash, retape, re-cord, and re-install Venetian blinds. See the Yellow Pages.

VICUNA   This soft, fine fiber from the wild llama of South America is used in wool-type textiles. It is in the same price category as fur. Dry-clean.

VIDEO EQUIPMENT   Television Set, VHS, and Beta Players

Clean with a soft cloth dampened with a mild household detergent. Do not use cleaning solvents; they can damage the cabinet.

If anything drops into the unit, check with your TV service facility.

Be sure the unit has good air circulation: don't block the ventilation slots.

Don't install near radiators, in a humid spot, or where it will be subjected to excessive dust or mechanical vibration.

Unplug the unit if it won't be used for several days.

Tips on VHS and Beta Players: Remove the video-cassettes after use. Avoid strong magnetic fields when you place your unit.

Movie Cameras (VHS and Beta)

Extremes of heat and cold, overexposure to direct sunlight or bright lights, high humidity, strong vibrations, dust, dirt, strong broadcast signals, or X-ray sources and strong magnetic fields all affect the performance of this equipment. *Special note:* Don't operate the camera if the temperature is over 104° F (40° C).

Also, don't store either movie tapes or camera at temperatures over 122° F (50° C). In other words, beware of attics or autos when doors and windows are closed.

Don't carry your camera by the lens or viewfinder.

VIDEO TAPES   The best way to insure long-lasting video tapes, according to the Electronic Industries Association, is to return them to their jackets after each use. Otherwise they collect dirt and dust, and when this accumulates between the tape and the record/playback heads you risk distortion or deterioration and possible head damage.

Video tapes are coated with oxide. When used for an extended period of time, they can shed some of the coating on the video cassette head assembly, damaging or clogging the head. To avoid this, discard the tape after approximately 200 reuse cycles.

TIP

Store in an upright position (like books).

VINEGAR This is a very mild acid. Use white vinegar to clean glassware, treat rust stains in sinks, and remove tarnish from brass and copper. It is useful in counteracting some alkalis.

Vinegar is safe for use on all fabrics, but may change the color of some dyes. When this happens, you may be able to restore the original color by rinsing out the vinegar with water and adding a few drops of ammonia to the area. Rinse again. *Caution:* Colored (cider) vinegar can leave a stain.

VINYL FABRICS These plastic fabrics are nonporous and generally a cinch to care for. In everyday use, you may do no more than simply wipe them off. While dry cleaning is recommended for some, it may cause other vinyl fabrics to stiffen and the layers to separate.

There are three basic types: the clear or cloudy plastics with no backing at all, the opaque vinyls laminated to a soft backing like a cotton knit, and the vinyl-coated fabrics, in which the vinyl is applied to the surface of a material like woven cotton or nylon.

In caring for vinyl-covered furniture, note that it can be punctured by sharp objects and is difficult to mend. While it generally resists staining, some polyvinyl chloride fabrics are color scavengers and pick up dye from colored objects rubbed across them. They may also be damaged by solvents in some household cleaners, shoe polish, and nailpolish remover. There are commercial cleaners for vinyl upholstery.

Some vinyl garments are machine-washable. Those that are take warm (not hot) water and should be hung to drip dry.

Vinyls generally don't require ironing and some cannot be ironed, since vinyl itself will melt or glaze under an iron. Some fabrics, however, can be pressed on the backing side with a warm, dry iron and presscloth. (No steam. It may remove the texture.)

Keep vinyl garments on padded hangers in a cool, dry place. If they're very heavy, fold them to prevent the weight of the garment from stretching or tearing the fabric.

VINYL FLOORING

There are two varieties of this resilient flooring: conventional vinyl and no-wax. The no-wax vinyls feature a protective top layer to preserve color and pattern. The no-wax finish can range from high gloss to no gloss.

Proper care and maintenance will not only keep a vinyl floor looking its best, according to Armstrong Industries but reduce the time and effort you spend on it.

Vacuum or dust mop the floor once a day. This removes loose dirt before it can scratch the surface of the vinyl and before it becomes ground in and a major cleaning problem.

Damp mop when floor looks slightly dirty. First vacuum, then go over it with a dampened sponge mop and warm water. Mop a small area at a time, rinse, and wring out the mop frequently. If the area is large, change water several times to prevent redepositing the dirt back onto the floor.

Use two buckets, one for mopping and one for rinsing the mop, and rinse frequently so you don't redistribute the dirt.

Washing the floor should be done once a week (less often in little-used areas). Vacuum thoroughly, then wash with a cleaning product designed for vinyl floors. A no-rinse product saves time and energy. Special cleaners for no-wax floors are also available. Change rinse water and use the two-bucket method again.

Waxing protects the pattern, surface, and color. No-wax vinyl floors do not require polishing, but standard vinyl flooring does. Use a water emulsion acrylic polish. It is easily removed by detergents and won't harm the flooring. Do not use a solvent-based polish or wax on any type of vinyl floor.

To remove wax, see Wax Removal.

Vinyl Flooring
Stain Removal Guide

Wipe up spills immediately with a clean, white cloth, using a pickup motion, moving toward the center of the stain.

Remove dried spills with a plastic spatula, then wash the area with a vinyl flooring cleaner, and rinse. If a stain remains, follow the removal techniques suggested below.

Ink: Dip a clean cloth in rubbing alcohol and wipe the stained area. Allow to stand for thirty minutes. If the stain remains, follow the same procedure using a liquid chlorine bleach. Rinse with water and let dry. Reapply floor finish if needed.

Lipstick: See Ink.

Mercurochrome: See Ink.

Nail Polish: Dip a clean white cloth in nailpolish remover and wipe over stained area. Allow to stand for thirty minutes. Rinse with clear water, dry and apply floor finish if needed.

Paint (Oil) and Varnish: Follow instructions for nail polish, but substitute turpentine for polish remover. (Turpentine is flammable—heed manufacturer's precautions.)

Rust: Apply a heavy-duty cleaner wax-remover (New Beginning Extra-Strength Cleaner by Armstrong) to the stained area and allow to stand for five to ten minutes. Scrub with a stiff bristle brush, wipe up, and dry. If stain remains, rub with a nylon pad dipped in an oxalic acid and water solution—one part oxalic acid to ten parts water. (Heed precautions on oxalic acid.)

Tar/Asphalt: Follow instructions for nail polish but substitute lighter fluid for polish remover. (Flammable—heed manufacturer's precautions.)

Vinyl Flooring Troubleshooters

All man-made floorings—vinyl (conventional and nonwax), asphalt tile, rubber tile, and linoleum share some problems. Here's a checklist, with solutions.

Slippery: Too much wax. Remove wax and apply a new thin coat.

Detergent not rinsed. Rinse floor again with clear water.

Wax applied over a wet floor. Remove wax, dry, rewax.

Poor polishing. Apply a thin coat of wax and buff.

Dull: Not enough wax. Apply a thin coat of wax evenly.

Wax applied to wet floor. Clean and rewax.

Floor dirty when waxed. Clean and rewax.

Streaked: Uneven wax application. Clean and apply wax evenly.

Wax buildup. Remove wax and apply a thin coat.

Different waxes applied one over the other. Clean and rewax.

Poor cleaning and rinsing. Clean and rewax.

Yellow/Gray: Wax buildup. Remove old wax; clean and rewax.

Scratched: Gritty type dirt. Clean and rewax. (Vacuum floor more often.)

TIP

Floors that are properly waxed and buffed are never slippery.

VINYL PLASTICS

Vinyl plastics can vary from resin to solid. Vinyl has a high chemical resistance. It is found in home flooring, countertops and fabrics. For cleaning instructions, see Plastics (Thermoplastic), Vinyl Flooring, Vinyl Fabrics.

VOMIT STAINS

See Carpet Stain Removal Guide; Master Stain Removal Section (Urine).

WAFFLE IRONS AND GRILLS

The exterior surface of waffle irons and grills should be cleaned after you unplug and cool the appliance. Use a sponge dampened with detergent and warm water, or an all-purpose cleaner. Rinse and dry.

Use the same procedure for a nonstick surface, but season with a thin coat of cooking oil before reusing.

For metal surfaces in general, remove the griddles or grid pans from the unit and soak in hot, sudsy water, then scrub with a nylon pad or brush. For excessive amounts of burned-on foods on metal grids, clean by placing a paper napkin soaked in ammonia between the grids and leave overnight. Finish cleaning with a soap-filled steel wool pad, rinse, and dry. For information on nonstick finishes, see Cookware (Nonstick).

WALL-COVERINGS

"Wall-covering" once meant paper or fabric. We now have vinyls, "wet look" vinyls, foils and mylars, flocked papers, grasscloth and cork, textile fabrics and burlaps, and new breeds of strippable wallcoverings, eminently smooth and durable.

Many of these wall-coverings, even flocks, are washable, and some can be scrubbed.

Washables generally respond to a sudsy solution of mild soap and lukewarm water, sponged-on, in overlapping circular strokes. Follow by thorough rinsing.

The National Decorating Products Association details the cleaning processes manufacturers suggest for their various kinds of wall-coverings.

Waterfast: Water alone can be used liberally to remove any surface soil. Don't use abrasive pressure, however.

Washable: More stubborn soil can be removed with a sponge and gentle pressure, using a mild detergent.

TIP

When washing a wall, start at the bottom and work upward, to prevent streaks that are difficult to remove.

Scrubbable: Reasonable pressure can be exerted, with a strong detergent. Don't rub abrasively, however.

Tedlar coatings are impervious to most stains and will withstand any reasonable amount of scrubbing.

If you don't have any manufacturer's clues about how to handle your wall, or the covering is so old it may no longer be washable, test first. Experiment in an area that won't be noticed. Start with just cold water. Then try water and mild soap, and rub a bit. Don't scrub unless it's necessary and the paper will withstand it.

If you want to make your own wallpaper cleaner, prepare dry detergent suds. For this you beat $1/4$ cup of light-duty liquid detergent and 1 cup of water with a rotary beater. When you have a stiff foam, use those dry suds, washing the paper lightly with a cloth or sponge.

Do-it-Yourself Stain-Resistant Coating

You can increase washability, stain-resistance and color-retention on both paper-surfaced coverings and some fabrics by applying a clear plastic coating, available from wall-covering dealers. Such a coating dries to a washable surface and won't usually alter the color of the paper. But test first to be sure the ink doesn't run, and don't apply to newly hung paper that hasn't fully dried, or you invite trouble with mildew.

Troubleshooters

Grease Spatters: Hot grease penetrates even vinyls. To lessen the damage from fresh grease spots, place a clean blotter on the spot, then press with a warm iron. Change the blotter often.

A paste of cleaning fluid and fuller's earth will draw grease from paper, and at least reduce the stain. Or use a gum eraser or the homemade dough cleaner described under Dough Cleaner.

Pile on Flocked Paper Going in Different Directions: Try brushing all the pile in the same direction with a soft brush, suede brush, or Styrofoam/mohair smoother. A light steaming with the aid of a tea kettle is a good preparatory measure.

Mildew: This is one of the worst problems, especially with nonporous coverings like vinyl. Once mildew spots show up it may be too late to do anything but remove the paper, wash wall (and paper, if it is reusable) with a Lysol solution; rinse, dry, resize the wall, and reapply paper. New paper should go on with an adhesive with a mildew-resistant additive. Also see Mildew.

Spot removers can change color or texture, so use on one spot may necessitate cleaning the entire wall.

WALLS AND CEILINGS

Excluding decorative surfaces, brick or ceramic, most walls are covered with a rigid covering like paneling, or a soft, flexible covering, such as vinyl or paint, and these are easy to care for.

When heavy dirt requires washing the entire wall, work from the bottom up. (Avoids clean-water streaks.) Use only enough pressure to loosen the soil. Rinse and wipe dry. Extra-stubborn dirt may require two washings.

For washable walls, remove everyday smudges with a solution of mild detergent and water. Rinse and wipe dry.

To remove cobwebs, lift them off the wall. Brushing them off can add greasy streaks to your cleaning problems.

For finger marks or tough spots, use a liquid or spray cleaner. Rinse well and dry.

Do not use abrasives or strong cleaning solutions or solvents.

For more information, see Paint, Wall-Coverings.

TIP

Dust from the top down so that loose soil falls to the bottom of the wall. Use the brush attachment of the vacuum cleaner or wrap a soft cloth over a broom or yardstick or use a long-handled nylon dust mop.

WASH AND WEAR

Today's wash and wear finishes to reduce the need for ironing are superior to those we knew before durable press was introduced. See Durable Press.

WASHING MACHINES   You want to protect the surface finish, so do not use stain removal or pretreatment products in, near, or on the machine. Wipe up spills immediately, rinse with clear water, and dry.

Every month or so, *wash* the exterior with liquid detergent and water, or use an all-purpose liquid or spray cleaner. Rinse with clear water and dry. Retard future soil buildup with a coat of appliance wax. When cleaning, don't forget about the control panel, buttons, and knobs. Use a cotton swab to reach small spaces.

Clean the lint filter regularly. If you don't, lint will redeposit itself on your wash load.

Don't use the washer as a hamper for soiled clothes.

Leave the lid open for a short time after each load of wash.

Take care not to overload the machine. This causes unnecessary strain on the motor and mechanical parts. Remove sharp objects from clothing to prevent scratching the interior finish.

Washing Machine Troubleshooters

Vibration in Spin: Rearrange the wash load for balance.

Level the machine with leveling screws on bottom of washer or wedge with a thin piece of wood.

Remove the shipping blocks located under the tub.

No Hot Water/Water Too Cold: Reset the wash cycle for hot water.

The household hot water supply is exhausted.

Temperature setting on the hot water heater is too low.

Hot- and cold-water fill hoses are reversed.

No Water: Water supply to washer is turned off.

Hose filter screens are clogged.

Noise: Small items (pins, nails) are caught in the spin basket holes.

Won't Run or Spin: Reset control to ON, pull knob fully out.

Cycle in normal pause position of cycle, wait two to three minutes.

Washer lid is not completely closed.

Won't Fill/Buzzes/Fills and Drains: Turn on both hot and cold faucets.

Set for correct wash time.

Clean the water inlet hose.

Clean the filter.

Unkink the drain hose, it should not be bent or jammed at pipe.

Clothes Too Wet: Washer turned itself off because of excessive vibration.

Rearrange wash load for better balance.

Cold-water rinse leaves clothes wetter.

Wrong spin cycle (delicate or heavy load).

Drain hose kinked or jammed.

Lid not completely closed.

WASHING SODA

This superb cleaner, sodium carbonate, differs from its cousin, baking soda, in that it is an effective water softener and grease-cutting agent.

It helps dissolve grease and dirt on kitchen cabinets, floors, walls, countertops, ovens, ranges, pots and pans (except for those of aluminum), range hoods, exhaust fans, dishes, glassware, plastics, toilets, sinks, tubs, blinds, grills, etc. It's effective also in treating some stubborn laundry problems found in washable cottons, linens, and man-made fabrics. (Just don't use it on fibers of animal origin like wool and silk.)

WATER, POLLUTED OR CONTAMINATED

If you worry that your water is unfit to drink, call your county health department. They may test it for you or send you to a laboratory.

If the water is found unsafe because of *bacterial* content, boil drinking or cooking water until the supply is treated.

If you are concerned about excessive iron content or other minerals, you may consider acquiring a water filtration unit. The Environmental Protection Agency says you should determine the quality of your water before you buy such equipment. Filters vary in their effectiveness and the attention they require. You hazard bacterial growth unless the carbon cartridge is changed regularly.

WATER HEATERS

Water heaters require little attention. However, all need to be partially drained to remove lime and sediment deposits that collect in the tank. Water should be drained until it runs clear. Do this every three to four months, or once a month if the water in your area is exceptionally hard.

When leaving home for vacations or long periods of time, turn off the water supply and lower the control to the lowest heat setting.

If your water heating unit is gas, keep pilot light area free of dust and dirt. Do not store combustibles near the heater or block the air circulation. To re-light the pilot, follow manufacturer's instructions printed on a metal plate located on the lower part of the tank, near the controls.

If there is no hot water, check for an extinguished pilot, closed gas-supply valve, or turned-off thermostat—if your heater is gas. If it is electric, check water-supply valve and circuit breaker or fuse. If there is not enough hot water or the water is too hot, check the thermostat setting. Also, the unit may not have enough capacity to meet your hot water needs. If you have an electric unit, the controls are located on the inside of the unit and you may have to call a service person to readjust them.

The American Gas Association warns that the faucets on old heaters that have not been drained on a regular basis may not close because of lime buildup and will drip after opening.

CAUTION

TIP

Check water temperature at kitchen and bathroom faucets with a candy or meat thermometer.

WATER MARKS

See Master Stain Removal Section.

WATER QUALITY
(Hard Water)

Eighty-five out of a hundred U.S. households struggle with hard water, which is loaded with the mineral salts that encourage dingy wash, spots on glassware, and rings around the bathtub.

Remedies

Use water softeners in your washer. Or attach mechanical conditioning units to your plumbing system for soft water throughout the house.

Nonprecipitating Water Softeners, like Calgon Spring Rain or Blue Raindrops, go into your wash and rinse water to inactivate the salts that cause hardness. They work well in all washers, and are useful when hardness measures more than seven grains per gallon. (Soap manufacturers base their recommendations on "moderate" water hardness of four to seven grains per gallon.)

Usually the water plant operator of your water company will know how hard your water is. You can also have your water tested by water-conditioning service companies, appliance dealers, or water treatment plants.

Here is a water hardness table to help you decide on an appropriate treatment for your water supply.

Hard water can be a big time-waster. An Ohio State University study showed that cleaning time can be cut almost in half by using softened water. Homemakers with hard water reported cutting the average time spent on cleaning to two hours and twenty-one minutes. It gave them a savings of over ten eight-hour weekdays per year!

Water Hardness Table

Water Types	Grains per Gallon
Soft	0.0–3.5
Moderately Hard	3.6–7.0
Hard	7.1–10.5
Very hard	10.6+

Precipitating Water Softeners, like washing soda or Borateem, work in wringer washers. They are not especially recommended for automatics.

Such softeners may solve your laundry problems, but they are expensive for use in large volumes of water. If you need to soften or treat all household water, consider the purchase or rental of water-softening equipment. You may save money by going this route.

Your plumbing system may be adapted to soften just the hot and cold water you use for cleaning with soap and detergent. (No need to treat *all* water.) Appliance and service dealers listed in the Yellow Pages carry many makes and models of water softeners, also filters for excessive iron content, or other minerals.

WATER-REPELLENT FINISHES

Many sports jackets, all-weather coats, etc., are treated by the manufacturer to be water-repellent, and fabrics not so treated can be given this finish by your dry cleaner or by home use of a water-repellent spray. These finishes may be durable, nondurable, or permanent.

Check the care label to see if your garment should be washed or dry-cleaned. If you do launder it, rinse thoroughly to remove detergent. To iron, use a press cloth with a dry iron at the appropriate temperature for the fabric, pressing on the wrong or uncoated side. Some heavily coated fabrics should not be pressed.

A spray like Scotchgard works on any new or freshly dry-cleaned or laundered fabric, with periodic reapplication suggested.

WATERBEDS

Waterbeds do not require extraordinary care. But use common-sense cautions: Be careful with pins, pens, needles, hairpins, and scissors around the waterbed. Don't lose rings, watches, earrings, or other jewelry in it, since they too can create punctures.

Don't spill hot drinks on the mattress. If hot enough they weaken or destroy the vinyl.

Water and electricity don't mix. Never use an electric blanket on your waterbed. Nor hair dryers and curling irons—the heat from them can also be damaging.

Always unplug the heater when filling or draining the mattress.

And never let the cat sit on your waterbed. (Dogs are not so dangerous, unless they chew mattresses, says the Waterbed Manufacturers Association.)

Care

- A mattress pad is a good idea, to reduce the chances of damage or puncture caused by pets. Bedding also helps retain heat and can cut your energy consumption.
- When you change the sheets, wipe any debris off the mattress, and occasionally clean the surface with a vinyl cleaner. Check for moisture and remove any objects that may have fallen between mattress and frame.
- Check the valve from time to time to be sure it's tightly sealed.
- "Burp" the mattress to remove noisy air bubbles.
- Treat the bed frame itself as you would any fine piece of furniture.

Once in a while, wipe the mattress clean with a mild soap, or disinfectant, and warm water on a sponge. There are also special-purpose waterbed vinyl cleansers. Vinyl conditioners can help maintain the life of the vinyl, but avoid oil-based conditioners.

If you see water on the floor, do not panic. The safety liner is designed to catch water: it will not start flowing out. Take off the bedding and find the leak. If the water is around the valve, it may not be a leak at all but spillage from the last time you filled the mattress. Or maybe the valve's screw-on top isn't tightly secured. Water on top of the mattress may indicate a puncture. You can locate it exactly if you lay a dry paper towel over the suspect

When you change linen on a water-bed, put your knee in one corner, says Jane Pyle, a Merry Maid cleaner in Miami, Florida. "It's easier to tuck in the sheets this way."

area. To remedy a puncture, you apply a patch (patch kits generally come with the mattress; you can also buy them).

If the puncture or tear is in the mattress seam, the mattress may have to be drained. Consult the dealer.

If you wipe up the water, and more appears, your safety liner also leaks or you are making the mistake of not using a liner at all. Repair the liner as you would the mattress.

Sweating on top may be due to defective vinyl and calls for a talk with your dealer.

To Store a Mattress: Drain it, let it dry completely, roll it loosely and gently (do not fold), and avoid hot or cold storage areas. The same procedure holds for the liner.

WATERPROOF / BREATHABLE COATINGS

More and more storm-proof outerwear features a microporous membrane that keeps out wind and water but lets perspiration vapor escape.

One of the most established, Gore-Tex, allows for machine-washing in cold water with powdered detergent. Rinse thoroughly. Do not dry-clean.

To treat stains on Gore-Tex fabric, saturate area with Spray 'n Wash or Shout, then wash as above. Repeat procedure if necessary for heavily stained garments.

Other coatings are urethane- or polyester-based. Some may be dry-cleaned, as well as washed.

WAX (Polishing and Self-polishing)

See Floors; Furniture Mini Manual; Tile (Ceramic); Tile Floors; Vinyl Flooring; Wood Flooring. See Master Product List for brand-name examples.

WAX REMOVAL (From Nonwood Floors)

You can purchase a commercial resilient-flooring wax-remover (Parson's) and follow label instructions, or make your own with

TIP

*Keep wax remover
solution in an empty
floor-cleaner squirt bottle.
You will have better control
of the removal solution and a
place to store leftover
cleaner. Be sure bottle is well
rinsed of previous cleaner before using.*

the following ingredients suggested by U.S. Department of Agriculture home economists:

¾ cup detergent (Spic and Span)
⅓ cup ammonia
1 gallon warm water

Spread the cleaning solution on a small area (3' × 4') of the
floor. Let stand for five minutes. Rub cleaner off with a rough-
textured cloth; use a scrub brush for tough spots. Rinse with clear
warm water. Go on to the next section and repeat the process.
Be sure to use lots of clean rags each time so that you don't spread
dirty wax scum onto cleaned areas.

Wash the entire floor with your usual floor-cleaning product.
Allow the floor to dry thoroughly and rewax if desired.

WAX STAINS   See Master Stain Removal Section (Candle Wax).

**WEATHER-PROOF
OUTERWEAR**

The outdoors grows more and more inviting with apparel that
offers protection against cold, wind, and water.
The offerings include:

- Water-repellent, water-resistant, and waterproof finishes,
  applied to fabric for outdoor wear.
- Plastic or plastic-coated fabrics like the vinyls—nonporous,
  so waterproof.
- Waterproof/breathable coatings
- Insulation for warmth provided by down, needlepunch, and
  a variety of fiberfill products, including newcomers like 3M's
  Thinsulate and Du Pont's Thermolite.
- And the variety of quilted, bonded, and laminated garments
  for more—or less—rugged weather.

There are ABC listings covering the care of all these.

WET SPOTTER

This is a stain-removal solution easily made at home. Mix 1 part of glycerine, 1 part liquid hand dishwashing detergent, and 8 parts water.

Do not use other kinds of detergents for stain removal. They sometimes contain alkalis that set some stains.

Shake the mixture well before each use. It can be stored in a plastic squeeze bottle with a small cap.

WHITE STREAKS ON FABRIC

See Laundry Troubleshooters; Master Stain Removal Section.

WHITE WINE STAINS

See Carpet Stain Removal Guide; Master Stain Removal Section (Wine).

WHITEWASH

This is an impermanent white finish used for walls. It is too water-soluble to be cleaned. When dirty, remove, and refinish the surface.

WHITING

This is a white powder (very pure form of calcium carbonate) that mixes with linseed oil to make putty, and with water and other ingredients to make whitewash. In this book we refer to it as a mild abrasive for polishing.

WICKER, BAMBOO, CANE, RATTAN

Contemporary furniture made from these woven reeds, stalks, or grasses can be finished with paint or traditional wood finishes. Clean by dusting with the brush attachment of your vacuum. Wash with a well-wrung-out cloth, using as little moisture as possible. A little ammonia can be added to the cleaning solution if a stronger cleaner is needed. Rinse with a damp cloth and dry thoroughly. Try using a tooth brush to reach intricate parts.

Note: If you have unfinished bamboo, cane, reed, wicker, or rattan furniture, do not oil or wax. Because such pieces may dry out, give them a bath with the garden hose or in the shower. Dry thoroughly.

Some antique furniture, dry with age, is susceptible to insect attacks. Check frequently for newly chewed holes and little heaps of powder. If woodworms are discovered, use an insecticide, spraying it directly into the holes.

WINDOWS

Before you wash, dust the window, wipe the sills, woodwork, and grids surrounding the window, taking care not to scratch the glass by rubbing the dry window surface too hard.

A commercial spray is most convenient. Squirt it on, then wipe it off with paper towels or lint-free absorbent cloths. Your hands stay clean and dry, you don't need a bucket, you can get by with only one cloth.

However, many experienced housekeepers and virtually all professionals swear by other methods.

Four common home formulas are:

- One-half cup ammonia, $1/2$ cup white vinegar, and 2 tablespoons cornstarch to a bucket of warm water.
- Four tablespoons of ammonia to 1 quart of warm water. (To remove heavy, greasy soil on glass surfaces inside the home.)
- One tablespoon kerosene to 2 quarts of warm water for light, greasy soil.
- Two tablespoons vinegar to 1 quart of warm water. Vinegar attacks rust or lime deposits on the outsides of windows.

Do one side of the window with horizontal strokes and the other side with vertical strokes. (If the window streaks, you'll know which side needs to be redone.) Take care not to drop cleaning solution on woodwork.

Using two buckets—one for the cleaning solution and one filled with clear water for rinsing—apply your solution with a cloth or sponge, rinse with clear water with another cloth, then rub dry with a paper towel, lint-free cloth, or chamois.

To make window-washing easier, avoid streaks. Don't use soap

To loosen stubborn window sashes, rub a candle along the grooves where the sash meets the frame.

or attempt to clean windows in direct sunlight. (Sunlight causes fast, uneven drying.)

If you must clean windows during very cold weather, add $1/2$ cup denatured alcohol to the cleaning solution to prevent freezing.

Professionals use a double-sided sponge and blade squeegee as a time-saver for large panes of glass, stroking downward with it and wiping the edge after each stroke.

See Mirrors, for the technique appropriate for them.

WINDOW SHADES

Frequent dusting will reduce the need for an all-out cleaning job. Use the dust brush attachment on your vacuum cleaner. When you need heavy cleaning, test the cleaning solution on an inconspicuous spot to see if it is safe to use. Not all shades can be cleaned at home; some require professional attention.

Washable shades are cleaned with warm, sudsy water. Spread the shade unrolled on a clean, flat surface. Scrub lightly with a soft brush or cloth. Try to use more suds than liquid. Wash the reverse side, rinse, dry, and reroll. For an even finish, work small areas at a time, overlapping cleaning strokes.

Nonwashable shades can be cleaned with an artgum eraser or a dough cleaner available in wall-covering and hardware stores. See do-it-yourself recipe under Dough Cleaner.

WINDOW SILLS

See Woodwork.

WINE STAINS

See Carpet Stain Removal Guide; Master Stain Removal Section.

WOOD FINISHES (On Furniture)

Lacquer

A form of lacquer is used as a protective finish on most quality, commercially finished furniture. It consists of a resin and/or a cellulose ester dissolved in solvent and produces a highly polished, lustrous surface.

To Clean: Use a solvent-based furniture cleaner. Working quickly, apply the solvent with a clean, lint-free cloth with one hand and wipe the solvent off with the other hand, using a different clean, lint-free cloth. Clean small areas at a time.

To Protect: Use a polish or wax suited to the degree of gloss. The National Paint and Coatings Association suggests the following: high gloss—liquid polish or paste wax; satin gloss—cleaning polish or silicone-free cream wax; low gloss—a liquid polish for low-luster finished wood or a cleaning wax to give protection without shine.

Oil

Often found on old or antique furniture and some high-quality contemporary furniture.

To Clean: Wipe the surface with a soft cloth dipped in a solution of a few drops of lemon juice added to soap and water.

To Protect: Re-oil once a year with boiled linseed oil. (Use it as purchased; do not boil it.) Do not use wax or furniture polish on oil-finished surfaces.

Paint

To Clean: Use a cloth dampened (and wrung almost dry) with a solution of mild detergent and water. Work small sections at a time. Rinse with a cloth dampened with clear water and dry. Do not use wax or linseed oil. These products may hinder repainting and linseed oil will darken the paint color.

Shellac/Varnish

Minerals dissolved in alcohol or a similar solvent produce these hard, transparent protective coatings.

To Clean: Use a mixture of I part turpentine to 3 parts boiled linseed oil. Moisten a clean, lint-free cloth with the cleaner and rub surface briskly, changing cloth surface often. Repeat if necessary. Purchase boiled linseed oil; do not attempt to boil it yourself.

To Protect: Apply a coating of liquid wax or cream polish suited to the gloss. (See Lacquer, above.)

Wood Protector

Scotchgard-finished wood protector is a clear component of thermoplastic, ultraviolet curable, synthetic resin producing a traditional lacquer look. According to 3M, it prevents water-ring marks and resists spots and marks from alcohol, water, or oil-based liquids. It resists heat marks as well as stains from household cleaners and solvent-based items like fingernail polish and remover, and permanent ink.

To Clean: Use a damp cloth or soap and water. Protection is not necessary, but an application of wax may be used if desired. *Note:* This is a finish available on manufactured furniture only and, as of this printing, is not available for home (do-it-yourself) application.

WOOD OR CORK FLOORS

Both wood and cork are absorbent, porous materials. They should be protected with a permanent coating or sealer such as varnish, shellac, lacquer, or polyurethane.

Do not use water, soap, detergent, or ammonia on wood or cork floors unless they are sealed. These liquids can otherwise damage, warp, stain, or raise the grain.

Regular Cleaning

Vacuum or dust mop to remove daily dirt and dust.

Clean and polish two to six times a year with a solvent-based

cleaner polish (check label) in either paste or liquid form. There
are cleaner waxes that need buffing after use, and some that don't.
The choice is yours, depending on the result you want. (Floor care
products are listed in the Master Products List.)

Distressed Wood: This is textured or "antiqued" in appearance. Because the uneven surface traps dirt, the Oak Flooring
Institute recommends sweeping with a stiff broom and then vacuuming to remove dirt and dust.

Wood Floor Troubleshooters

A waxed floor is a good stain-preventer.

Too Slippery: Repolish the floor using an electric polisher/
buffer.

Scratches on *Light to Medium-Colored Floors:* These can
often be concealed with a small amount of paste wax applied with
a very fine steel wool pad (#000), rubbing gently until the color
is blended. Wipe off excess wax and polish with a clean, dry cloth.

Scratches on Dark Floors: Mix a small amount of paste wax
and burnt sienna or raw umber (artist's oil pigment) to the desired
shade. Apply as directed above. If color is too dark, wipe with a
dry-cleaning fluid.

Dark Spots: Usually caused by alkaline (urine, cleaning solutions, ammonia). To remove these spots:

1. Remove the solvent base wax with mineral spirits (available at
hardware stores).

2. Apply white vinegar to the stain, let stand for three to four
minutes.

3. Wipe area clean with a dry cloth.

4. If stain remains, repeat the process.

5. If several attempts with the vinegar treatment do not remove
the stain, then apply a solution of 1 tablespoon oxalic acid crystals

in 1 cup water. Let stand until spots disappear (two to three minutes). Wipe with a damp cloth, reseal, and rewax.

Heel Marks: Rub with a fine steel wool pad dipped in floor cleaner. Wipe dry, polish.

Ink: See Dark Spots.

Urine: See Dark Spots. Old stains may not be removed, floor will have to be refinished.

Mold: Apply cleaning fluid.

Chewing Gum, Crayon, Wax: Harden with ice and carefully scrape off residue. Pour cleaning fluid around (not on) remaining stain, allow to soak under the stain to loosen.

Cigarette Burns: Rub with steel wool dipped in floor cleaner.

Alcohol: Rub with boiled linseed oil (caution: flammable) or paste wax. Rewax.

Oil/Grease: Saturate cotton with hydrogen peroxide and place over stain. Saturate a second piece of cotton with ammonia and layer over the first piece. Repeat until stain is absorbed.

Wax Buildup: Strip with mineral spirits or naphtha (caution: flammable). Use clean cloths, steel wool for difficult spots. Rewax.

WOOD FURNITURE See Furniture Mini Manual for cleaning instructions, Wood Finishes specifics on lacquer, oil, paint, shellac, and varnish finishes.

WOODEN WORK SURFACE See Butcher Block.

WOODWORK (Painted, Enameled, Varnished) Clean with an oil- and glycerine-based soap (Murphy). Add enough oil-based soap to very warm water to make a sudsy solution. Wash woodwork with a clean cloth or sponge dipped in cleaning solution. Rinse with a clean cloth dipped in clear water and wrung damp-dry. Buff dry.

Strategy: Start with the baseboard, washing, rinsing, and drying areas of approximately arm's length. Next clean the doors and the woodwork trim around the doors and windows. Use the same method as for the baseboard but wash from the bottom up to avoid "clean streaks."

A heavy piece of cardboard held next to wall or floor will give protection from drips and spills.

WOOL

Though we generally think of wool as derived from the fleece of sheep or lamb, other animal hair may be classified as wool, including that from camels, Angora and Cashmere goats, etc.

Wool is comfortable in almost any climate, depending on fabric construction. Its ability to absorb moisture keeps you from feeling cold and clammy. Lightweight tropical worsted fabrics breathe, letting heat out and air in to keep you dry and cool. It is water-repellent, static-resistant, soil-resistant, and fire-resistant. It also resists wrinkling, pilling, and snagging.

Finishing Processes: Today's finishes endow wool with other virtues. Many wool fabrics are preshrunk, mothproofed, given additional rain-proofing and spot-proofing.

Washing

Are woolens washable? The answer must be a qualified Yes, though you should consider dry-cleaning many fine wools. The old rules for washing pure wools suggest using cold water in gentle (non-alkaline) suds, carefully avoiding excessive handling. Do not use chlorine bleach. It may yellow or even dissolve wool.

Are they machine-washable? Yes. Pure wool products labeled "Machine Washable" or "Superwash" (a Wool Bureau tradename) are completely machine-washable and machine-dryable. They won't shrink, they won't fade.

Your usual procedure with a Superwash fabric:

- Turn the garment inside out.
- Machine-wash on the gentle cycle, using a mild detergent and the warm temperature setting.
- Rinse and spin at normal temperature.
- Tumble dry for fifteen to twenty minutes. (Don't overdry, as wool needs some moisture.)
- Again, do not use chlorine bleach.

Tips on some special items:

- Sweaters. Proceed as above, machine-drying until just dry, then removing promptly.
- Single-knit jersey. Standard procedure, but at the gentle setting. Machine-dry until just dry. Touch-up ironing is recommended.

Cleaning and Pressing

To reduce the need for frequent cleaning and pressing:

- Brush after every wearing.
- Use hangers that fit, and set the shoulders properly on the hanger.
- Empty pockets between wearings.
- Hang clothes so they can breathe (don't jam them into your closet).

TIP

Give wool clothes a twenty-four-hour rest, if you can, to allow them a chance to spring back into shape.

To Press: Use the wool setting, and work with steam or a press cloth. (A wool cloth is preferable.) Raise and lower the iron as you go, lift the press cloth frequently from the fabric surface to help raise the nap. Do not use the iron directly on the fabric, and do not press completely dry.

Periodically a professional cleaning and pressing will preserve the life and beauty of the fabric.

If a garment gets wet, dry it away from direct heat. Let mud dry before brushing it off.

Soaking at low temperature is a very effective way of dealing with protein-content stains, i.e., tea or coffee with milk, gravy, blood, etc.

Treat stains promptly. A reliable dry cleaner is your best bet. If you attempt stain removal yourself, spot test first.

Storage

Clean your wools before you put them away. If they are not mothproofed, see Moths.

WRINKLE (CREASE) RESISTANT FINISHES

Cotton, rayon, acetate, and linen—all fabrics of cellulosic fibers—are surely a joy to wear in sticky weather. If only they wouldn't wrinkle during wear and crumple in the laundry!

Today's many finishes ameliorate such wrinkling.

Correct laundering preserves such finishes.

WRINKLES IN DURABLE PRESS

See Laundry Troubleshooters.

WROUGHT IRON

Wrought iron may be washed with a soft brush dipped in a solution of mild liquid detergent and warm water. Rinse and dry thoroughly.

Decorative wrought iron used indoors as railings, furniture frames, lamp bases, and the like is, under most circumstances, not subject to rust.

If rusting does occur, scrape the rust and bubbled paint with a wire brush. Sand the area smooth with a coarse-grade sandpaper. Apply a coat of rust-resistant primer to the sanded area, and paint with a product made specifically for wrought iron. Primer, paint, and wire brush are available at paint and hardware stores.

YELLOW/GRAY BUILDUP

For this sort of wax buildup on resilient flooring, remove old wax, clean, and rewax. See Wax Removal.

YELLOWING

See Laundry Troubleshooters; Master Stain Removal Section.

YOGURT STAINS

See Master Stain Removal Section.

Your Personal Household Hint Collection

....

....

....

....

....

....

....

....

....

....

....

....

....

....

How Much Must You Yourself Actually Do?

How People Get Help for Free—from Spouses, Children, Etc.

Smart people know when to holler for help, and for most of us responsible for keeping a house in order, that can mean now—or if not now, yesterday.

We encourage you to holler!

To whom? Why, to the family, of course. After all, people who live together have a big stake together in how enjoyable their environment is kept, and it can be a splendid surprise for people to learn how charming the head housekeeper can be if the head housekeeper is not overworked.

There are two approaches to this holler: women have been using both, for years. One is revolt, the other is diplomacy.

While we encourage diplomacy, you should know about the revolutionary tactics. The overburdened housekeeper simply declares a moratorium on housework. She (these revolutionaries have mostly been women) quits for a week or two. Let the family find out where the coffee can lives, she says. Let them figure out how to put shorts in the washer and divine where Junior's running shoes ran when he last took them off.

Traumatic as this is for the families involved, one and all survive, and more often than not, one and all grow more cooperative.

A variation on this is the moratorium on just certain jobs. The outraged housekeeper will no longer pick up other people's belongings flung down around the house. She may in fact impound these possessions and exact fines from the people who come begging to have them back.

For the person too softhearted for this drastic approach, there is diplomacy. But hardhearted (or at least hardheaded) diplomacy is in order. Most people gathered for an after-dinner meeting about housework are there reluctantly. They are not too interested.

Think through some strategies before you schedule this gathering. Think how terrific it will be if you can outline the problem so clearly and compellingly that they will try to develop a grand plan to solve it. People like to dream up schemes and like to think that the household can run better because of their ideas, even if it involves them in some of the work.

If they resist the idea of shaping a plan, it may be necessary to outline a work schedule. Decide what work is necessary, with what jobs you can reasonably hope to get reliable help, and lay these jobs before them. Be sure everybody has a good mix of jobs—including some that *show.* Are there jobs that a child will love to share with a grown up, or with another child? Never make the mistake of unloading just the chores you hate most (they won't be thrilled with them, either), and give everybody some choices, if possible, or rotate jobs so no one ever gets stuck in a rut.

One of the most common arrangements is a posted schedule of some sort. It should indicate what must be done, when it will be done, and who will do each job.

One family uses assignment cards labeled Playroom, Downstairs Bath, Living Room, Dining Room, Kitchen, Bedrooms, Upstairs Bath, and Staircases. These are slipped into four card pockets tacked up in the kitchen, and each person is responsible for two areas a week.

Another family has a weekly drawing for chores, with the children allowed to swap with each other if they want to or can.

In another variation, the family gets together on Saturdays and holidays and makes a game out of chores by drawing lots. There is one slip of paper for every family member with a chore written on each—except for one, which says, "Relax!"

"I don't think children really like to work," says one of these parents, "but they can be amazingly responsible if they recognize the fairness of the situation and aren't faulted for not doing as thorough a job as an adult would do. I've made it a rule never to redo a cleaning job one of the girls has done. That's discouraging. I just leave it until I can catch up with it the following week."

She doesn't, however, abandon the system just because the work isn't perfect. Many children, experts agree, may do a sloppy job so they won't be asked to undertake it again. (Children? Add grownups who also see this as a good if sneaky way to get out of work.)

Of course it's discouraging if you give a child a task that's beyond his skills. But even very young children can set and clear the table, pick up things, help with dishes, and empty wastebaskets. A little helper can dust low, while somebody else takes the higher spots.

As children grow bigger, they can undertake heavier and more responsible jobs. They can help younger children make beds, assist with ironing and mopping and waxing floors. They can even help wash windows and carry heavy things, as well as straightening and cleaning a room.

Some parents pay their children for help with the household chores, but many feel that this responsibility should be part of growing up and sharing the life of the family.

They do, however, feel that children need lavish recognition. Says one mother, "One reason for the children's cooperation is that they find me nice to be around. Another is undoubtedly the fact that I praise—oh, do I praise—not only to their face but to other people."

And many parents reward their children for extra chores or chores well done with special privileges, like staying up late or being allowed to have a friend over for dinner or the night.

Finally, there is one approach to soliciting help that *never* works, and there's scarcely a one of us who hasn't used it at one time or another. That is saying, "Oh, it's easier to do the job myself than to try to teach somebody else."

Don't hesitate to ask for help.

You will very likely be a nicer person if you don't feel harried by housework. The children will learn something, too.

And if you use the Mini Manuals in this book, you will be teaching them to handle tasks the fastest and best way. And if it's useful to learn to do something, it's most useful to learn the correct way.

One more tip to getting the most possible help from your helpers: make their jobs easy for them. Give them good tools. Make sure they're handy: it costs no more to keep bathroom cleaning products in all bathrooms. Keep trash bags in your wastebaskets so there's no need to carry the baskets themselves from room to room. (There are more hints like this in "50 Ways to Simplify Work Around the House.")

And of course when you have the family pitching in to help you, you will almost surely have greater success with the house rules that cut down housework. Like:

Everybody puts away his own stuff.

Everybody cleans his own room.

Anybody who uses a glass or a dish sticks it in the dishwasher.

Whoever takes a shower or a tub, or uses the washbowl, wipes up before leaving the bathroom.

Whoever uses the last of the toilet tissue, soap, or towels replaces these necessities.

Of course, you make sure the supplies are on hand and that there are appropriate supplies throughout the house to make it easy for anyone to wipe up a spill.

We know of no one for whom these rules work 100 percent, but they are a blessing if you can count on 80 percent adherence.

Meanwhile, if you can count on well-motivated family members to take on practically complete responsibility for home maintenance, check out the Housekeeping Planner that wraps up this section, following the Help for Sale chapter.

When a child balks at putting away his toys, offer to do this chore in exchange for doing one of yours.

When children work in the yard, give them the same courtesy you would give someone hired to work: Take them iced drinks for an occasional break.

How to Use the Help That's for Sale

If you don't have potential help living with you, or don't want to impose work schedules on a spouse, a child, or other close-by helpers, don't just throw up your hands and conclude that you have to do everything. Your time is worth money: it's smart to buy help when you need it.

In today's world of "two-career households," there are many options.

WEEKLY HELP

Your best bet may be a housecleaning service, through which you hire houseworkers by the hour, by the day, by the job. Most people engage such services to supply regular weekly cleaning.

You pay a set fee, which includes wages, plus all Social Security or required deductions. Your contract is with the service, rather than the individual employee.

The cost varies according to where you live and the size of your house. It may run more if the service supplies tools and products for cleaning, or if it covers its workers by bonding them or with liability insurance.

These employees will do what you tell them to do, or they will follow a set routine prescribed by the service sending them out. Most are maid services. They dust, vacuum, mop, wax, wipe, sweep, make beds, change linens, etc. Their goal is to leave things "shiny clean," as the head of Maid in the Shade, a service in suburban New Jersey, puts it. First, no streaks on mirrors or glass. Second, a fresh smell in the house (lemon scents rank high). Third, "everything in order"—pillows are plumped.

Generally speaking, such cleaners will not wash windows, clean closets, move heavy furniture, shampoo rugs, wash walls, or tackle anything they can't reach.

Many of these services are franchises like Merry Maids, with 475 offices in 45 states. They typify the newest development in such homecleaning operations: team cleaning.

Merry Maids dispatches a two-person team, one to do "wet work" and the other, "dry work." Mini Maids, another large franchise, offers four-person teams, with a four-way split: the kitchen area, the bathrooms, the floor (vacuuming), the dusting.

The national average Mini Maid charge is forty-five dollars for the weekly cleaning of a three-bedroom, two-bath home.

Merry Maids charges are comparable. If a customer wants to skip a through-the-house cleaning every other week, a biweekly visit costs $52. Or Merry Maids will do "wet work" one week and "dry work" the next for $38 per visit. Other services we checked offer similar help at similar prices.

When you engage these services, it is essential that you ask what they do, and what they don't do. Some (who charge more) specialize in difficult cleaning problems. Also ask if their workers are bonded, covered by workers' compensation, and by general liability insurance.

HEAVY-DUTY CLEANING

Many weekly cleaning services have divisions to wash windows, shampoo rugs, wash walls, wax and shine floors, clean chandeliers, etc.

Charges vary. You may find it wise to pay by the job, rather than try to guess how many hours it will take at an hourly rate.

Or maybe you want

A CLEANING PERSON ALL YOUR OWN

If you want highly personal service—the dog fed, plants watered—you may need to search further for a personal employee, as well as assume various extra costs and additional responsibilities.

No matter how you locate a prospective employee, cover your needs in your interview to be sure the candidate is equipped and willing to undertake the job.

Check references with friends, neighbors, or previous employers.

Arrange for the payment of Social Security, and any other necessary taxes. Some cleaning people may suggest that you skip Social Security payments. Don't! This could be an expensive mistake for you. If your employee later decides to collect Social Security, *you* will be responsible for all the unpaid taxes, with penalties and interest to boot.

To start this process, get the employee's Social Security number and write to the Internal Revenue Service for a Federal Employer Identification Number for yourself as employer, plus the IRS's "Employer's Tax Guide."

You may also be required to withhold federal or state personal income tax, take care of state disability insurance, unemployment insurance, and workers' compensation coverage. This depends on how many employees you have and how many hours they work for you. You are also wise to see if your homeowner's insurance policy covers employees working in your home.

You may be entitled to federal income tax credit on the cost of household employees if a portion of their job is the responsibility for a child or disabled adult. Check the IRS or your tax accountant for information on qualifying.

HOW TO GET THE BEST SERVICE FROM HOUSEHOLD HELP

You waste good money if your housekeeper must move a lot of clutter just to get to the cleaning job. Your housecleaner also gets more done if you keep the necessary cleaning agents in each bathroom (and certainly on each floor), and if you keep all needed supplies on hand all the time.

We hope you know the cost/benefits of having a good, fully working vacuum cleaner for your own use; ditto other equipment. Your housekeeper will also do a better, faster job with good equipment.

Most cleaning persons aren't mind readers: Tell them what you want. Tell them what you like, don't like. Use the Around-the-Year House-keeping Planner (page 333) or the instructions in our Mini Manuals to guide them.

Treat them the way you would treat any employee. They deserve some paid vacation time, pay when they're occasionally sick, and periodic raises or bonuses as they continue to serve you well.

What You Can Learn from the Professionals

Professionals in the cleaning business survive on the principle that time is money.

They plan ahead. "Work with a check list," says Jacques Taylor of Tailor Maid in New York City. One of his tips is to tape a three-by-five card by the light switch in each room, with cleaning instructions for that room. He does this when opening or closing apartments. It's a good idea for a teenager's room, too.

They avoid waste motions. Leone Ackerley went out and cleaned houses herself in her community before she started Mini Maid Services Company, Inc., in Marietta, Georgia.

"Don't run back and forth," she says. "Take a plastic bag with you, with everything you need—dust cloths in your pockets, brushes and cleaning solutions in a bucket. Put an extra-long extension cord on your vacuum so you don't have to plug and unplug it in every room."

She perfected a special step-saving system for bedrooms: "Make a bed from left to right (never go around it). Dust the bed table while you're by the bed, then go on dusting, as you come to it, each picture, chest, chair, mirror, lamp, and section of baseboard."

Merry Maids advises its cleaning teams to start at the back of the house and work down and forward to the front. (Again, you never backtrack.)

They don't use a lot of equipment. Leone Ackerley says you need only three household cleaners: a glass cleaner, a grease-cutting liquid, and a mildly abrasive powder.

To clean glass, appliances, counter tops, and the new nonwaxable floor coverings, she recommends a mixture of three or four parts water to one of vinegar. For greasy floors and counters, she suggests a mixture of ammonia and water and uses undiluted household bleach to remove bathroom mildew.

She finds a soft paintbrush handy to dust both lamp shades and the grooves and crevices of ornate furniture and porcelains. ("Carry it with you in your bucket along with lighter fluid to get up scuff marks and crayon marks from tile and vinyl floors. Add a brown felt-tip marker to cover up scratches on dark furniture.")

And with many pet-loving clients to please, she discovered that a wet but well-wrung-out terry cloth will whisk animal hair off upholstered furniture.

Carol Begosh, who runs Maid in the Shade in Hillsdale, New Jersey, also has a favorite carry-along, a lint pick ("great for capturing threads and bits of fluff that may elude the vacuum cleaner"). She advocates picking up before you vacuum. "It's better for the cleaner and prevents loss of small items."

An Around-the-Year Housekeeping Planner

A weekly cleanup on top of quick daily rounds normally keeps the house in condition. Appliances purr along, and if house and furnishings accumulate dirt, it doesn't show all that much. This is today's way of life, and we enjoy—and endorse—it.

It's easy to forget that there are occasional touches that make house, furnishings, and appliances last longer, and a few periodic chores that absolutely must be done.

Appliances are the easiest to forget, so we start with those, then go on to other household appurtenances. The list may be a good reminder for yourself, or a rundown you would like to hand to a house sitter or other helper who needs to know how you like your house kept.

The *musts* are bold-faced on the chart. The others are those a professional housekeeper would at least put on a high priority checklist.

APPLIANCES	WEEKLY	MONTHLY	AS NECESSARY	SEASONAL/ANNUAL
AIR CONDITIONER				Change or clean filter (spring)
AUDIO EQUIP-MENT			Clean and demagnetize	
COFFEE MAKER		Flush mineral deposits	Wash	
DISHWASHER	Wipe exterior		Vinegar rinse; clean door edge, gasket	
DRYER		Clean exterior	**Clean lint filter** (after each use)	Clean out lint duct
FANS				Wash
FIRE EXTINGUISHER		**Dry chemical— shake**		**Recharge**
HUMIDIFIERS				**Clean reservoir**
INDOOR GRILLS			Wash rocks and basin	
MICROWAVE	Wash cavity, walls and floor			
RADIATORS		Dust		Clean

APPLIANCES	WEEKLY	MONTHLY	AS NECESSARY	SEASONAL/ANNUAL
RANGE	Wipe exhaust fan exterior	Wash exhaust fan	Change or clean exhaust fan filter	
REFRIGERATOR/ FREEZER	Clean out/wipe Wash exterior		Vacuum air condenser and static condenser	Defrost chests yearly Defrost uprights spring/fall
SEPTIC TANK				**Inspect yearly**
SEWING MACHINE			Clean. Remove lint. Oil.	
SMOKE AND HEAT DETECTORS				**Test.** Clean. **Change battery yearly.**
SPACE HEATERS				Vacuum and wash
TRASH COMPACTORS AND DISPOSERS	**Deodorize**	Clean and disinfect		
VACUUM CLEANERS			**Empty bag**	
WASHING MACHINE		Wash exterior		
WATER HEATER		Drain in hardwater areas		Drain

SURFACES	WEEKLY	MONTHLY	AS NECESSARY	SEASONAL/ANNUAL
CARPETING/RUGS	Thorough vacuum			Shampoo
Kitchen and Bath Carpet		Spray to deodorize and disinfect installed carpet	Shampoo	
FLOORS—WOOD	Vacuum			Wax and polish
Natural (brick, slate, etc.)	Vacuum	Wash/Scrub		
Vinyl	Vacuum Wash in heavy-traffic areas			
WALLS/CEILINGS		Dust from top down	Clean	
WINDOWS		Wash interior		Wash inside and out
WINDOW SHADES/ BLINDS	Dust			Wash if necessary
WOODWORK, including window sills, baseboards	Dust			Wash

ROOMS	WEEKLY	MONTHLY	AS NECESSARY	SEASONAL/ANNUAL
BEDROOMS	Dust and vacuum			
Bedding	Change Linens		Wash or clean, including covers, dust ruffles	
Mattress				Turn mattress and vacuum, including frame and springs
BATH				
All surfaces	**Clean and dis-infect**			
Hamper		Disinfect and deodorize		
Mirrors	Wash			
Drains		Deodorize		
Shower Curtains			Wash and rehang	
Medicine Chest				Clean. Discard old medications.
BABY NURSERY			**Wash and disinfect all furniture and bedding**	
KITCHEN				
All surfaces, inc. floors, counters, appliances	Clean and disin-fect		FOR FLOOR AND APPLI-ANCE CARE, SEE PAGES 334–36	

MISCELLANEOUS	WEEKLY	MONTHLY	AS NECESSARY	SEASONAL/ANNUAL
DRAPERIES/CURTAINS	Dust			Dry-clean or launder
FURNITURE				
Wood	Dust with treated cloth			Wax/polish
Wicker	Dust			Wash if necessary
Upholstery	Vacuum			Shampoo/change slip-covers if desired
LIGHTING FIXTURES	Dust		Wash	
Lamp shades	Dust		Dust and wipe	
Decorative Metals	Dust			Polish
Books				Dust one by one
Fireplace				Remove ashes, vacuum
Garbage Cans	Wash	Disinfect		
Telephone and	Wipe and disin-	Damp-clean		
Door Knobs	fect	thoroughly		
Closets				Clean; organize; moth-proof if necessary

YOUR MASTER LIST OF SPECIAL HOUSEHOLD CHORES AND SOURCES OF HELP

Phone Numbers
Repairmen & Services You Use

Possessions needing special attention:
Appliances, Collectibles, etc.

YOUR MASTER LIST OF SPECIAL HOUSEHOLD CHORES AND SOURCES OF HELP

Phone Numbers	Possessions needing special attention:
Repairmen & Services You Use	Appliances, Collectibles, etc.

SECTION FOUR

Master
Product List

Master Product List

From time to time throughout this book we have mentioned a brand name to assist you in identifying the kind of product appropriate to a task in hand, and not necessarily to endorse the product cited as superior to others.

In this list we are trying to give you a broader view of available home-care products, even though we cannot possibly record all you may find in the marketplace. Space precludes our doing that, so please do not read special approval into our listings or disapproval into our omissions.

Before purchasing any product, first check your supply closet. There are many multiuse cleaning products, and you may already have what you need to do the job.

Know what kind of soil you need to tackle and the type of surface you want to clean. *Read each product label carefully* to determine if the product will handle your cleaning task.

Keep in mind that many cleaning compounds are poisonous or flammable. Use them with caution, and store them away from children and heat sources. *Don't mix one cleaning product with another.*

Finally, to achieve the best and easiest results, read and heed the manufacturer's directions.

Detergent All-in-One Combinations

Fab 1 Shot, Tide Multi-Action Sheets

Heavy-Duty Detergents

Granular (with or without phosphates): Ajax, Cheer, Fab, Fresh Start, Tide. *Liquid:* All, Arm & Hammer, Dynamo, Era Plus, Liquid Bold, Liquid Cheer, Liquid Tide, Solo, Wisk.

Laundry Soaps

Granular: Ivory Snow. *Bars:* Ivory, Octagon.

Fabric Softeners

Dryer Added: Bounce, Cling Free, Free n'Soft, Purex Toss'n Soft, StaPuf.
Washer Added: Downy, Final Touch, Rain Barrel, StaPuf.

Bleaches

Liquid Chlorine: Clorox, Purex.
Liquid All-Fabric: Snowy, Vivid. *Powdered All-Fabric:* Clorox 2, Purex,
Biz, Snowy, Borateem.

Pretreatment Products

Enzyme Presoaks: Axion, Biz.
Pre-Wash: Clorox Pre-Wash, Faultless Spray Pre-Wash, Miracle White
Laundry Soil & Stain Remover, Shout, Spray'n Wash.

Water Conditioners

Arm & Hammer Washing Soda, Calgon, Spring Rain.

Scouring Cleansers

Powder: Ajax (with or without phosphates), Bab-O, Bon Ami, Borax Non-
Abrasive Powder, Comet (with or without phosphates), Old Dutch.
Liquids: Comet, Soft Scrub, Sierra.

General Household Cleaners

Ajax All-Purpose, Boraxo Bathroom, Carbona Tile & Bath, chlorine bleach
(especially for mold), Dow Bathroom, Easy-Off Mildew Stain Remover,
Fantastik, Lestoil, Lime-A-Way Bathroom/Kitchen, Lysol, Mr. Clean All-
Purpose, Scrub Free Bathroom, Tilex Mildew Stain Remover, Top Job All-
Purpose, Tough Act Bathroom, X-14 Mildew Stain Remover.

All-Purpose Liquid Cleaners

Ajax, Fantastik, Lysol, Mr. Clean, Murphy Oil Soap, Spic and Span Pine Liquid, Top Job.

Fiberglass Cleaners

Boraxo Fiberglass Cleaner, Comet, Dow Chemical Bathroom Cleaner, Mr. Clean Cleanser.

Toilet Bowl Cleaners

Lysol, Lysol Cling, Swish, Ty-D-Bol, Vanish.

Mildew/Stain Removers for Tile

Tilex, X-14.

Disinfectants

Cleaning Sprays: Lysol Basin/Tub & Tile Cleaner, Dow Disinfectant Bathroom Cleaner.

Cleaning Liquids: King Pine, Lysol, Lysol Pine Action, Pine Sol, Real-Pine, Spic and Span Pine, Roccal (available in janitorial and swimming pool supply outlets).

Cleaning Aids for Appliances and Plumbing

Drain and Disposal Cleansers: Drain-aid, Drano, Liquid-plumr, Mister Plumber.

Septic Tank Cleaners: Lysol RID-X, Septi-kleen.

Hard-Water Stains/Soap Scum/Rust Removal Products: mr. dust, Lime-A-Way.

Resilient Floor Products

Resilient Floor Cleaners: Spic and Span, Tackle.
  Resilient Floor Cleaner/Polish: Mop & Glo, Step Saver.
  No-Wax Floor Cleaners: Brite, Perk, Step Saver.

Wood Floor Products

Floor Liquid: Wood Preen
  Floor Paste: Butcher's Bowling Alley Paste Wax.

Cleaners/Polishes for Woodwork and Furniture

Woodwork Cleaners: Liquid Finishing Wax, Murphy's Oil Soap.
  Dust and Polish Sprays: Behold, Endust, Favor, Pledge.
  Wood Cleaner/Polish: Butcher's Bowling Alley Paste Wax, Weiman
Furniture Cream.
  Wood Polish: Guardsman Furniture, Lemon Oil, Old English Lemon Oil,
Scott's Liquid Gold.

Carpet Cleaners

Glamorene, 1 Hour Rug Cleaner, Resolve, ScotchGard, Woolite Rug Cleaner.

Upholstery Cleaners

Carbona Shampooer, Glamorene.

Glass and Mirror Cleaners

Glass Plus, Glass Works (with vinegar), Glass Wax, Windex (with ammonia
or lemon).

Laminated Plastic Cleaners

Beauti-Fi, Counter Top Magic, Glass Plus.

Rust Removers

For metal surfaces: Naval Jelly, Aluminum Jelly.
   For fabrics: Tintex Rust Remover, Rit Rust Remover.

Stain Removal Products

Spot Lifter: K2r.
   Dry-Cleaning Fluid: Carbona, Energine.

Master Stain Removal Section

Master Stain Removal
Section for
Washable Fabrics

Successfully treating spots and stains is one of the finer arts, as people like the museum specialists in restoration and first-class dry cleaners regularly demonstrate. They achieve many small miracles that we can't promise with the instructions here.

But there are now on the market many aids to help get the results we want at home. They include not just products intended for use with non-washable fabrics but those newer "pretreat" items that cause some spots to vanish in a twinkling.

This section emphasizes washable fabrics because these are the materials for which there are many remedies on home shelves. You should also make a special point, when you attempt spot removal on nonwashables, of paying close attention to the instructions for the dry-cleaning solvent you choose. It also pays to know as much as possible about the fabric. To that end, you may want to check into our ABCs to know more about silk and wool and other textiles with stains you would banish. In many instances we include special tips on handling stains.

Most of all, however, we encourage you to use a professional dry cleaner for any nonwashable item that you especially value.

There are also other stain removal sections in this book, in the ABCs. You will use other techniques to remove stains when you must deal simultaneously with several materials. The Carpet Care section is a prime example. And, of course, we also treat stains on wood and all sorts of flooring, grout, metals, etc. (Find all in the ABCs.)

We think you will be pleased and surprised many times by your success with the methods here. But the motto is "Try, try again" if you would succeed. And remember that some spots won't yield to even the professionals' professionals in the business.

Stain Aid Kit

Here's a list of handy products to have in laundry sorting areas.

1. Chlorine bleach
2. All-fabric bleach (oxygen)
3. Detergent presoak (enzyme)
4. Pretreat product
5. Spray spot lifter
6. Dry cleaning solvent
7. White vinegar
8. Lemon juice
9. White bar soap
10. Rubbing alcohol
11. Ammonia
12. Rust remover for fabrics
13. Paint thinner or turpentine
14. Liquid laundry detergent
15. Hydrogen peroxide
16. Acetone (nailpolish remover)
17. Dull knife
18. Color remover
19. Meat tenderizer (enzyme)
20. Paper towels

We give sample brand names for these in the Master Product List.

Stain Removal Treatments for Washable Fabrics

ACETATE FABRICS   Treat with dry-cleaning solvent.

ADHESIVE TAPE   Apply ice to residue to harden. Scrape with a dull knife. Sponge with dry-cleaning solvent. Rinse and launder in hottest water safe for fabric.

ALCOHOLIC BEVERAGES   Alcoholic beverage stains turn brown with age. Treat immediately with cold water.

    If rinsing alone does not remove stain, soak in $1/8$ cup all-fabric bleach to 1 gallon warm water for thirty minutes. Rub any remaining stain with detergent and launder in warm water.

    Older Stains: Soak in enzyme presoak and launder.

    Wool: Place towel under stained area. Rub gently toward center of spot with fizzed club soda.

TIP

Patience pays off. A treatment that fails the first time may succeed the second—or third.

ASPHALT   See Tar.

BABY FORMULA   See Dairy Products.

BEER   See Alcoholic Beverages.

BERRIES see Fruit/Juice.

BEVERAGES See Alcohol, Chocolate, Coffee, Dairy, Fruit, Tea, Wine.

BLOOD Soak in an enzyme presoak and cold water if the stain is fresh, warm water if stain is dry. Launder in hottest water safe for fabric.
OR Rinse immediately in cold water. Unless you are working on wool, which is a protein, treat with a paste of meat tenderizer and warm water. Allow to sit for thirty minutes. Launder with bleach safe for fabric.
OR Soak in cold water. Rub in liquid laundry detergent and wash in warm water and bleach safe for fabric.
OR Soak fifteen minutes in bleach safe for fabric. Use 2 tablespoons bleach to 1 quart cold water. Rinse and launder.
OR Rinse immediately in cold water. Mix hydrogen peroxide with a few drops of ammonia. Soak, rinse, and launder in hottest water safe for fabric. (Pretest for colorfastness.)
Silk (washable): Soak in cold water. Wash gently with detergent in cool water, or remove with a solution of equal parts ammonia and water.
100 Percent Wool: Blot stain with a paste made of dry laundry starch and rinse from back with mild soapy water.

Do not rub unless the stain is ground-in dirt or grime, or unless directed by the stain removal procedure. Rubbing may set or spread some stains.

CAUTION

BUTTER See also Grease.
100 Percent Wool: Sponge with dry-cleaning solvent.

CANDLE WAX Scrape surface with a dull knife to remove residue. Place stained article between white paper towels and press with a warm iron. Replace paper towels frequently to avoid transferring stain back into fabric. Sponge remaining stain with dry-cleaning solvent. Blot, air-dry, and launder.

A persistent stain may be removed by applying white vinegar or lemon juice and laundering as usual. Check for colorfastness.

CARBON PAPER   Remove with spot lifter or dry-cleaning solvent and launder.
OR   Rub liquid detergent into dampened stain and rinse. If stain remains, apply a few drops of ammonia to stain and repeat treatment. Rinse and launder.
OR   Sponge with denatured alcohol, rinse, and launder.

CATSUP   See Tomato Sauce.

CHEWING GUM   See also Adhesive Tape.
   100 Percent Wool: Scrape residue of stain with a dull knife. Sponge with dry-cleaning solvent.

CHOCOLATE   Rinse stain with cool water. Apply a paste of liquid detergent and all-fabric bleach to stain. Wait thirty minutes. Wash as usual. If greasy stain remains; (1) soak in an enzyme presoak overnight, or (2) sponge with a dry-cleaning solvent, rinse, and launder in hottest water safe for fabric.
OR   Rinse immediately in cool water. Mix hydrogen peroxide with a few drops of ammonia, soak, rinse, and launder.
   100 Percent Wool: Sponge with mild, soapy water.

Are you sure your fabric will wash?   **CAUTION**

COFFEE   Rinse with cool water. Soak thirty minutes with all-fabric bleach and warm water. Launder. If grease stain remains, apply an enzyme presoak for one minute and launder in detergent and warm water.
OR   Rinse immediately in cool water. Mix hydrogen peroxide with a few drops of ammonia, soak, and rinse. Launder.
OR   If chlorine bleach is safe for fabric, soak fifteen minutes in a

solution of 2 tablespoons chlorine bleach to 1 quart cold water for fifteen minutes; rinse and launder.

OR Spray with a pretreatment product, wait one minute, and launder.

100 Percent Wool: Sponge with glycerine. If none available, use warm water.

**COSMETICS
(Eye shadow, Lipstick,
Liquid Makeup,
Mascara, Powder,
Blush)**

Rub liquid detergent into dampened stain until outline of stain is gone. Launder in hottest water safe for fabric.

OR Apply pretreatment product to stain. Wait one minute and launder. Repeat if necessary.

See also Lipstick.

CRAYON

Scrape residue with a dull knife. Soak fabric in an enzyme presoak or concentrated liquid detergent and launder, using hottest water safe for fabric.

Be sure to pretest your procedure.

If an entire load of wash is stained by crayons, rewash the entire load using detergent and 2 cups of baking soda.

CREAM-BASED

See Dairy.

**DAIRY PRODUCTS
(Milk, Ice Cream,
Yogurt, Sour Cream,
Cream Soups, Baby
Formula, Eggs)**

Soak in an enzyme presoak overnight. Launder in hottest water and bleach safe for fabric.

OR Spray with pretreatment product, let sit one minute and launder.

DEODORANTS

Apply ammonia to fresh stains—white vinegar to old stains. Rinse. While fabric is damp, apply liquid laundry detergent to stain. Launder in hottest water and bleach safe for fabric.

OR Place stain face down on white paper towels and apply a paste of ammonia and all-fabric bleach. Let stand for thirty minutes. Rinse. If stain remains, apply denatured alcohol and allow to sit for two minutes, launder in an all-fabric bleach and hottest water safe for fabric.

Yellowing may be removed by sponging stain with hydrogen peroxide.

Silk: Rinse garment in cold water, then sponge with a solution of equal parts ammonia and water.

DYE TRANSFER

Treat white fabric with commercial color remover. Launder. If color remains, launder again with bleach safe for fabric.

Soak colored fabrics in all-fabric bleach and launder.

OR Soak overnight in an enzyme presoak and launder.

Dye transfer stains on polyester are generally permanent.

EGG

Rinse with cold water. Soak thirty minutes in an enzyme presoak and launder. (See Dairy Products.)

Do not use hot water. It will set stain.

100 Percent Wool: Scrape off residue and sponge with concentrated liquid detergent.

FABRIC SOFTENER

(greasy or bluish appearance)

Rub stain with laundry bar soap and launder as usual.

FECES

See Urine.

FOOD COLORING

See Fruit/Juice.

FORMULA (BABY)   See Dairy.

FRUIT/JUICE   Soak in cool water thirty minutes. Apply a paste of detergent and all-fabric bleach, rub, and launder.

OR   Place fabric face down over pan or mixing bowl and pour boiling water through stain. Work liquid laundry detergent into stain, rinse, and launder.

OR   Rinse immediately. Mix hydrogen peroxide with a few drops of ammonia. Soak, rinse, and launder. (Test for colorfastness.)

OR   Cover stained area with a paste of all-fabric bleach, a few drops of ammonia and a few drops of hot water. Let stand for thirty minutes, launder.

OR   If fabric allows, soak for fifteen minutes in a solution of chlorine bleach (2 tablespoons to 1 quart cold water). Rinse and launder.

OR   Spray with pretreatment product. Wait one minute and launder.

Do not use soap on fruit stains. It will set them.

To avoid spotting, treat the entire article when using bleach to remove stains. This will avoid an uneven color change.

TROUBLE SHOOTER

GLUE   *Wool:* Sponge with denatured alcohol.

GRASS STAINS   Soak in cold water and sponge with denatured alcohol. (Test for colorfastness.) Wash in bleach and hottest water safe for fabric.

OR   Rub with liquid laundry detergent and launder in bleach safe for fabric.

OR   Soak overnight in enzyme presoak. Launder in hot water and bleach safe for fabric.

GRAVY   Rinse stain in cold water. Soak thirty minutes in enzyme presoak and launder. Treat any remaining stain with dry-cleaning solvent and launder.

GREASE   Pretreat stain with liquid shampoo and wash in hottest water and bleach safe for fabric.

OR   Spray with pretreatment product, let sit one minute, and launder.

OR   Scrape or blot residue. Place stain face down on white paper towels. Sponge dry-cleaning solvent onto back of stain. When cleaning solvent dries pretreat stain with liquid laundry detergent. Launder, using an extra $1/2$ cup of detergent.

OR   Scrape or blot residue. Apply paste of liquid detergent and all-fabric bleach. Rub into stain. Wait thirty minutes. Launder in hottest water safe for fabric.

Silk (Spots): Use a spot lifter or sponge with dry-cleaning solvent.

Silk (Stains): Apply white tailor's chalk or white talcum powder. Put white blotting paper under and above stain. Iron stain through blotter.

100 Percent Wool: Sponge with dry-cleaning solvent.

> **TIP**
>
> *Laundry detergents hold soil in suspension and keep it from repositing itself on fabrics. So use extra amounts of detergent when treating and laundering stained fabrics.*

GUM   See Adhesive Tape.

ICE CREAM   See Dairy Products.

INK   Sponge around stain with denatured alcohol or dry-cleaning solvent, then apply directly to stain. Place stain face down on white paper towels and apply same remover to back of stain. Rinse. Rub in liquid laundry detergent and launder in hottest water safe for fabric.

OR   Spray stain with hair spray. Sponge stain until all bleeding stops. Let dry and repeat if necessary. Launder in hottest water, using bleach safe for fabric.

Felt Tip: Rub a liquid household cleaner into stain, rinse. Repeat

> **CAUTION**
>
> *Are you sure your fabric will wash? Always pretest.*

as many times as needed to remove the stain. Launder in hottest water safe for fabric.

Laundering may set some ink stains. Some inks may require a color remover, and some may be impossible to remove.

IODINE Apply a solution of sodium thiosulfate crystals (also known as photographer's hypo). Sponge stain. Rinse and launder. Both concentrated and dilute hypo solutions are available in camera stores.

Wool: Treat with cool water followed by denatured alcohol.

IRON See Rust.

KETCHUP See Tomato Sauce.

LACQUER Soak in turpentine, then treat with a spot lifter. Launder. (Test for colorfastness.)

LIPSTICK Apply spot lifter. Let stand for one minute. Rinse in warm water. If stain remains, soak one hour in an enzyme presoak and launder.

OR Sponge with dry-cleaning solvent and launder in bleach safe for fabric.

OR Apply a commercial rust remover for fabric. Rinse and launder. Do not spill rust remover on washer.

Silk: Place a piece of masking tape over the stain and quickly yank it off. Dab any remaining color with chalk or talcum powder.

100 Percent Wool: Try rubbing white bread over area with a firm, gentle motion.

See also Cosmetics.

Don't apply water to inks or lipstick stains. You may release their dyes and make the stains permanent.

MAKEUP See Cosmetics.

MEAT JUICE See Gravy.

MILDEW Untreated mildew stains can damage fabric beyond repair. Launder in chlorine bleach, if safe for fabric, and warm water. For other fabrics, soak thirty minutes in an all-fabric bleach and launder.

OR If safe for fabric, moisten with lemon juice and salt and allow to dry in the sun.

OR Sponge with hydrogen peroxide (may change the color of some dyes) and launder.

See Mildew in the ABCs for more on stains.

MILK See Dairy Products.

MUCUS See Urine.

MUD Brush off excess mud and apply a paste of liquid detergent and all-fabric bleach. Rub into stain and launder. For heavy stains, soak thirty minutes in a solution of detergent and all-fabric bleach. Drain soaking solution and launder as usual.

Red Clay: Apply a paste of table salt and white vinegar and rub into stain, wait thirty minutes, and launder.

Iron Clay: See Rust.

Wool: After mud dries, brush off excess and sponge stain from back with soapy water.

Are you sure your fabric will wash? Always pretest.

CAUTION

MUSTARD Dampen stain. Rub with liquid laundry detergent and wash in hottest water and bleach safe for fabric.

OR Pretreat with an enzyme presoak and launder with an all-fabric bleach.

OR Soak overnight in a solution of all-fabric bleach, detergent and water. Launder.

NAIL POLISH Blot excess with a white paper towel. Apply nailpolish remover (after testing on an inside seam) to back of the stain, blot, and repeat process until no nail polish is picked up by the blotter. Rinse with warm water.

If stain persists, blot with ammonia followed by white vinegar. Rinse and launder as usual. Or treat with spot lifter.

Do not use on acetate. If fabric is acetate, use a dab of turpentine and then a few drops of ammonia. Launder.

OIL See Grease.

PAINT, OIL-BASED Must treat before paint dries. Scrape residue, sponge with paint thinner or turpentine. Let sit for two minutes and blot.

Repeat until no stain appears on blotter.

Spray stain with spot lifter and launder.

PAINT, WATER-BASED Must treat before paint dries. Rinse with warm water. Treat with enzyme presoak. Rinse and launder.

PARAFFIN See Candle Wax.

PENCIL Use soft eraser.

PERFUME Sponge stain with cold water. Rub liquid laundry detergent into stain and wash in hottest water safe for fabric.

OR Apply spot lifter, rinse. Mix hydrogen peroxide with a few drops of ammonia. Rinse and launder. (Check for colorfastness.)

PERSPIRATION Dampen and sprinkle stain with enzyme presoak or meat tenderizer. Let stand thirty minutes to an hour. Rub detergent on stain and launder.

Also see Deodorant.

PINE RESIN/TREE SAP Sponge with dry-cleaning solvent or turpentine and dry. Soak in a solution of detergent and ammonia for thirty minutes, launder.

RUBBER CEMENT See Adhesive Tape.

RUST *Caution:* Test all procedures in an inconspicuous spot!

Apply a commercial rust remover for fabrics. Rinse in cool water and launder.

OR Apply a paste of lemon juice and salt. Allow fabric to dry in the sun. If stain remains use a commercial rust remover for fabrics.

OR Apply a paste of white vinegar and table salt. Rub paste into stain and let sit for half an hour. Rinse with cool water. Repeat process three times and launder.

Wool: Sponge with a weak solution of oxalic acid until stain disappears. Then sponge carefully with ammonia and rinse with water.

Also see Rust in the ABCs.

Chlorine will darken rust stains.

Do not use commercial rust remover for fabric in or near the washer. It will harm the appliance finish.

> **TIP**
>
> *Wash fabric normally as soon as possible after any stain removal treatment. This will remove stain remover as well as any residue of stain.*

SALAD DRESSING See Grease.

SCORCH Soak in all-fabric or chlorine bleach for half an hour. Launder. Some scorch marks may be impossible to remove because of permanent fabric damage.

SHOE POLISH (Liquid)	Dampen stain with water and rub with liquid detergent. Launder.
SHOE POLISH (Wax)	Scrape residue with a dull knife. Rub liquid laundry detergent into dampened stain. Launder in hottest water and bleach safe for fabric. If stain remains, sponge with denatured alcohol and launder.
SOFT DRINKS	See Beverages.
SUNTAN LOTION	See Grease.
TAR	Scrape off residue with a dull knife. Place stain face down on white paper towels and sponge with turpentine or paint thinner. Rinse. Apply pretreatment product and launder. *100 Percent Wool:* Sponge with dry-cleaning solvent.
TEA	Apply spot lifter, sponge off residue with a damp cloth. Rinse and apply hydrogen peroxide with a few drops of ammonia, soak, rinse, and launder. (Pretest for colorfastness.) **OR** If fabric allows, soak fifteen minutes in a chlorine bleach solution (2 tablespoons bleach to 1 quart water). Launder.
TOMATO SAUCE	Rinse in cool water. Soak thirty minutes in an all-fabric bleach or presoak. Launder. **OR** Spray with a pretreatment product, wait one minute, and launder.

TYPEWRITER RIBBON   Use a spot lifter or dry-cleaning solvent. May require several applications.

URINE   Acid stains can damage fabric. Blot excess. Soak half an hour in enzyme presoak and liquid detergent solution. Rinse in cold water. If stain remains, sponge with white vinegar, rinse, and launder.

VASELINE   See Grease.

VEGETABLE   Soak fifteen minutes in solution of 2 tablespoons bleach safe for fabric to 1 quart water. Rinse and launder.

VOMIT   See Urine.

WATER MARKS   They disappear with regular hand washing or dry cleaning.

WHITE STREAKS   These are caused by continued use of nonphosphate laundry products when washing in hard water. Remove by applying white vinegar to the streak; launder.

White chlorine bleach streaks are permanent.

WINE   Rinse immediately in cold water. Rub in liquid laundry detergent and rinse. If stain remains, soak thirty minutes in an all-fabric bleach and launder.

Red: Apply spot lifter, rinse. Mix hydrogen peroxide and a few drops of ammonia. Soak, rinse, and launder. (Test for colorfastness.)

Are you sure your fabric will wash? Always pretest.

CAUTION

If a fresh stain, pour table salt over the spot, rub it in gently; rinse with cool water. If a dried stain, pouring club soda through it may help.

White/Champagne: Rinse immediately, apply peroxide-ammonia solution mentioned above. Soak, rinse, and launder.

OR If fabric allows, soak fifteen minutes in chlorine bleach and water.

YELLOWING   Fill washer with hot water. Add 2 cups of detergent and 1 cup of all-fabric bleach. Agitate until dissolved. Add discolored fabrics and agitate for a few minutes. Let soak overnight. The next day agitate again for a few minutes and then drain off soaking solution. Wash in a full cycle with a cup of bleach but no detergent. Repeat until original appearance is restored. For more information, see Yellowing under Laundry Troubleshooters.

YOGURT   See Dairy.

The Three Stains

There are only three principal varieties of stains. Knowing the basic treatments for them can save you lots of time.

1. Greasy/Oily

(Butter, margarine, auto and cooking grease, oil and motor oil, salad dressing, lipstick, bacon, suntan lotion, crayon)

Apply a paste of liquid detergent and powdered all-fabric bleach (nonchlorine) to stain. Rub into stain and launder in hottest water safe for fabric.

OR

Place fabric facedown on white paper towels and sponge with a commercial dry-cleaning solvent. Replace towels frequently to prevent stain from redepositing itself back on the fabric.

OR

Place fabric facedown on white paper towels, apply a dry-cleaning solvent to back of stain and blot with a paper towel or a clean, white absorbent cloth. Apply a pre-treat laundry product, wait one minute. Wash in hottest water safe for fabric. If stain remains, treat and launder again.

OR

Mix a paste of 4 tablespoons washing soda and $1/4$ cup (2 ounces) warm water. Gently rub paste into dampened stain, then wash as usual. When using a liquid detergent, add an additional $1/2$ cup of washing soda to the wash cycle.

2. Nongreasy

(coffee, fruit, ink, mustard, tea, urine, beverages)

Soak half an hour in an all-fabric bleach and launder in hottest water safe for fabric.

OR

Soak in a laundry presoak product, with hottest water safe for fabric. Rinse and launder.

OR

Apply a paste of liquid detergent and all-fabric bleach to stain and launder.

3. Combination

(Baby formula, blood, catsup, chocolate, cream soups, egg, grass, gravy, milk)

Scrape off excess staining residue and rinse stain in cool water. Soak thirty minutes in an enzyme presoak product. Launder in all-fabric bleach and hottest water safe for fabric.

 Is your fabric washable? Check the label. And try your procedure on an inconspicuous area of the stained article. Let stand for five minutes.

NOTES

....

....

....

....

....

Treating
Unknown Stains

Try the following five-step procedure, on stains of unknown origin. If Step I does not work, go to Step II and so on. If the stain has not been removed by Step V, there is probably little hope of ever removing it.

STEP I

1. Soak stained fabric in cold water for twenty minutes.

2. Apply liquid detergent to the stain and allow to sit for thirty minutes.

3. Rinse stained area.

4. Launder in hottest water and bleach safe for fabric.

5. Air dry.

STEP II

1. Soak in an enzyme presoak product overnight.

2. Wash five minutes in the hottest water safe for fabric.

3. Air dry.

STEP III

1. Sponge stain with dry-cleaning fluid, let stand for twenty minutes.

2. Apply liquid laundry detergent to the stain.

3. Rinse.

4. Air dry.

STEP IV

1. Apply commercial rust- or color-remover for fabric according to manufacturer's instructions.

2. Air dry.

STEP V

1. Dip fabric in chlorine or all-fabric bleach solution (safe for fabric) of equal parts bleach and water.

2. Launder five minutes in hottest water safe for fabric.

3. Air dry.

Nine Good Techniques
to Know

Wick up a stain, without contacting the fabric at all, just touching it with the corner of a paper towel or absorbent cloth.

Absorb grease stains with powdered absorbents like talcum, French chalk, cornstarch, cornmeal, etc., then brush off the residue.

Soak (when fiber content permits this), taking into account the fact that an excessively long soak can cause color transfer even in colorfast items.

Flushing is pouring water through stained fabric, best done by laying the stained area over a bowl and then pouring from six inches or more above. It is a great way with fabrics that can stand this water treatment.

Sponge: Put the stain over an absorbent surface like white paper towels, white cloths, or white desk blotter, then apply solvent with a pad, rotating the absorbent so you don't return the stain to the fabric.

This sponging technique is the method you also use when testing a fabric's colorfastness or tolerance for your stain removing solvent. Find an inconspicuous place for the test, like an inside seam, inside hem, interfacing (if it's the same fabric as the garment), etc.

Freeze: Ice will harden sticky residues like gum, tar, etc., making them easier to scrape off.

Spooning (gently scraping staining material with the back of a stainless steel spoon) and **tamping** (knocking out the staining substance with a brush) are intended for sturdier fabrics and are covered in the ABCs.

To prevent rings: You usually work from the outside of a stain into the center, to restrict the affected area. However, when rings form, you do the opposite, working from the center of the stain toward the outer edge, "feathering" or sponging irregularly along the edges. Your sponging pad should be barely damp. Don't overdo with the stain remover, because you still want to keep the wet area as small as possible.

Also remove excess moisture before you air dry by placing the sponged area between two pieces of dry absorbent material.

SPECIAL TIPS

- Always work from the underside of a stain. You want to push the stain out, not in.
- A big no-no: do not press or machine-dry stained fabrics, or use hot water on an unknown stain. Heat sets stains!
- Air dry items you've spot-cleaned, then if the stain isn't gone, you can treat it again.
- Test your solvent (even if it's only water) on an inconspicuous spot (seam allowance or other inside area) to be sure it won't damage your fabric.
- Rinse thoroughly after treating a stain. You must remove not only all stain but all stain remover before you wash an item! Don't machine-wash or dry an article if you have not removed all dry-cleaner solvent.
- Soap sets fruit stains.
- Hot water sets egg stains.
- Do not use chlorine bleach on silk, wool, spandex, urethane, or poly-urethane foam.
- Never mix stain removal solvents—especially chlorine bleach and ammonia or vinegar.
- Don't try to treat leather, suede, or fur.
- Be patient. As noted in our Stain Removal Guide, if you don't succeed with your first try at stain removal, there are at the very least second, third, and fourth ways you may achieve success.

Also note that the techniques for treating stains on carpets, upholstery, tile, etc., differ from those recommended for textiles. See these various subjects, with their own removal sections, in the ABCs.

1-2-3 Strategies for Emergency Stain Treatment

1. Act fast. Set-in stains are harder to remove. Never, never wash or iron stained fabrics prior to treating them. Heat, hot water, and ironing set stains.

2. Blot excess stain from the fabric. Use an absorbent cloth or tissue to wick up as much as you can. You may want to blot both sides of the fabric, though the rule is: When blotting or flushing a stain, work from the back. You don't want to force the stain through the fabric in the course of removing it.

OR Scrape excess away. Just be sure you don't rub the stain in further, or abrade the fabrics.

3. Answer Question Number One: Does the fabric wash? (Check the label.)

If yes, sponge immediately, with cold water. This may do the trick, and it can help if you must wait till you can take more remedial action.

If you don't know, the safest procedure is to get to a dry cleaner immediately. If you can't, try one of the home dry-cleaning agents such as Energine, Carbona, or K2r on an inconspicuous spot, studiously following directions on the package.

If your procedure tests out, move on to the primary steps for the fabric you are handling.